Preparing Lawyers for Technology Transformation

The Exponential Age Mindset

DR CATHERINE MCGREGOR
LLOYD M. JOHNSON

Commissioning editor
Alex Davies

Managing director
Sian O'Neill

Preparing Lawyers for Technology Transformation: The Exponential Age Mindset
is published by

Globe Law and Business Ltd
3 Mylor Close
Horsell
Woking
Surrey GU21 4DD
United Kingdom
Tel: +44 20 3745 4770
www.globelawandbusiness.com

Preparing Lawyers for Technology Transformation: The Exponential Age Mindset

ISBN 978-1-83723-097-6
EPUB ISBN 978-1-83723-098-3
Adobe PDF ISBN 978-1-83723-099-0

Contents

Foreword ... xi
By Carlos M. Brown, president, Dominion Energy Services

Acknowledgments ... xv

About the authors ... xvii

Introduction ... xix

Chapter 1: What is the Exponential Age and why should legal professionals care about it? ... 1
The pace of change is unprecedented ... 3
Faster, faster – AI scaling ... 4
AI scaling in law ... 5
Interconnected systems amplify ripple effects ... 6
Shifting power dynamics ... 6
Societal and ethical uncertainty ... 7
Shorter feedback loops, higher stakes ... 8
The Exponential Age Mindset Attributes in practice ... 9
The ingredients – the Exponential Age Mindset Attributes ... 10
The tools to mix the cake ... 15
The Six Dimensions of Business Risk ... 16
The Six Dimensions of Business Opportunity ... 16
The Four Zones of Curiosity ... 18
The Can If Problem Solving Framework ... 19
An adventure for everyone ... 19

Chapter 2: Setting the stage – exponential change and human identity ... 21
The neuroscience of the Exponential Age ... 21
From the Industrial Revolution to the Age of AI ... 22
The neuroscience of AI use ... 23

Human value at risk – the legal profession as a case study 24
The identity of the lawyer 25
The lawyer as survival prediction machine 26
Training for the Exponential Age 28
Joy and creativity are necessary 28
Redefining value 29

Part One: The Mindset Attributes 31

Chapter 3: Zoom Master – taking strategic oversight and focusing on detail 31
The need for Zoom Mastery in the Exponential Age 32
Zoom Master combats cognitive bias 33
Lawyers struggle with the Zoom 34
What's so hard about the Zoom? 34
Cultivating your Zoom Master 34
Starting with why 36
Accessing your strategic mind 36
Why we are doing what we do 37
Asking the right questions 38
Lawyers and questions 39
Unlocking your Zoom Master with the Four Zones of Curiosity 39

Chapter 4: Joyful Tightrope – being comfortable with ambiguity and not knowing all the answers 45
Understand your own relationship to uncertainty 45
Embracing uncertainty – acknowledging the elephant in the room ... 47
Finding the joy in your Joyful Tightrope 48
Cognitive flexibility and adaptability 50
Why cognitive flexibility matters 51
How to develop cognitive flexibility 51
Decision-making under stress 53
How to improve decision-making under stress 54
Empathy and psychological safety 55
How to foster empathy and safety 57
Continuous learning and growth mindset 59
How to cultivate continuous learning 60

The Joyful Tightrope summary ... 62
What this means for you – as a lawyer and a leader ... 63
Joyful Tightrope mindset and behaviors ... 63

Chapter 5: Chaos Converter – understanding the opportunity in chaos and crisis ... 65
Opportunity in chaos #1: Development and growth ... 65
Opportunity in chaos #2: Innovation and creativity ... 65
Opportunity in chaos #3: Action and reflection ... 66
Reframing challenge and opportunity ... 66
A beautiful constraint ... 67
Constraint and creativity ... 68
The power of Chaos Converter ... 69
Cognitive reframing or shifting perspective ... 69
Post-traumatic growth theory ... 70
Neuroplasticity and learning from uncertainty ... 71
Complexity and chaos theory ... 72
Techniques to convert chaos ... 74
Chaos or opportunity? Embrace the moment ... 76
Navigating crisis and seeing the bigger picture ... 77
Toolkit for lawyers to convert chaos ... 78

Chapter 6: Agile Juggler – balancing consistency and ability ... 83
The Exponential Age requires both stability and speed ... 83
Ambidexterity – exploit vs explore ... 85
The neuroscience of adaptive thinking ... 86
Leaders – VUCA and strategic responsiveness ... 87
Practical implications for leaders ... 88
The Agile Juggler mindset in in-house legal teams ... 89
What this looks like in practice ... 91
Organizational ambidexterity in legal ... 93
Agile legal operating models ... 93
Cognitive readiness in legal leadership ... 94
Legal Agile Juggling tactics ... 95
Why the Agile Juggler Attribute matters ... 95

Chapter 7: Supreme Storyteller – the value of a good story ... 97
Why storytelling matters in the Exponential Age ... 98
Why do leaders need storytelling? ... 99

Not fluffy or frivolous 100
Managing vs leading 101
Storytelling and the general counsel 102
How Supreme Storytelling enhances business relationships 103
What do we mean when we talk about storytelling? 104
How to tell a good story 106
Who is your audience? 106
The purpose – why am I telling you this? 108
The rule of three 109
Alliteration 110
Metaphor 110
More than facts 111
Reinforce it with rhetoric 111
Brutus versus Mark Anthony 112
Storytelling and influencing 113
Change management – influencing and storytelling 113
Examples of storytelling in a GC's role 114
Key takeaways for GCs: 115

Chapter 8: Duality Master – looking outside of your area of expertise 117
Divergent thinking 118
Reframing the problem to release creativity 119
How does Duality Master apply to lawyers? 120
Going wide 120
Can If – harnessing the power of Duality Master 121
How legal departments can use Duality Master 122
The Duality Master in practice 123
Doing things differently 124

Chapter 9: Champion Chameleon – the empathic part of communication and influence 125
Champion Chameleon in action 125
Why we need the Champion Chameleon skill in the Exponential Age 126
Tailoring your communication to your audience 127
"Don't lawyer me an answer" 127
Champion Chameleon equals champion influencer 128
The hostage negotiation perspective 129

SAFE communication ... 131
Toolkit: Techniques for supercharging your Champion Chameleon ... 132
Practical ways to boost your Champion Chameleon ... 135
Implementing the training program ... 139

Chapter 10: Bias Jiu Jitsu – different ways of understanding ... 141
The Gentle Art ... 141
Understanding our own biases ... 142
Bias is the enemy of adaptability ... 142
Innovation requires cognitive diversity – bias blocks it ... 144
Exponential change triggers threat responses – bias intensifies under stress ... 145
AI and data reliance can amplify bias ... 145
Empathy and inclusion are strategic imperatives ... 146
Exponential change demands a learning mindset – bias fights it ... 148
Bias Jiu Jitsu tools ... 150

Chapter 11: Supreme Synthesizer – getting to the point ... 153
Synthesization in the Exponential Age ... 153
Cognitive overload – too much information ... 153
Accelerated decision cycles ... 155
Interdisciplinary collaboration ... 155
Building and sustaining trust ... 156
Adding AI to the mix ... 156
Strategic sensemaking ... 156
The conciseness conundrum for lawyers ... 157
The psychology of lawyers ... 157
Tell me more, tell me more ... 159
Why clarity and conciseness are essential for in-house lawyers in times of ambiguity ... 159
The distinct role of in-house lawyers ... 161
Clarity as a strategic asset ... 161
Summary: Core arguments ... 162

Part Two: Exponential Age Tools 165

Chapter 12: The Six Dimensions of Business Risk and The Six Dimensions of Business Opportunity 165

Integrating risk and opportunity thinking 165
The Six Dimensions of Business Risk 165
The Six Dimensions of Opportunity 167
The interconnectedness of risk and opportunity 168
Risk, opportunity, and resilience in the Exponential Age 169
The new risks 170
The Six Dimensions of Business Opportunity 171
The wheels 172
Linear versus associative thinking 173
How the six dimensions of business risk and opportunity work together in practice for legal teams 174
The new breed of general counsel – opportunity spotters 183
Risk and opportunity toolkit for legal leaders and legal teams 185
Mindset shift: From "What could go wrong?" to "What could we make possible?" 185
Practical strategies to integrate risk and opportunity thinking 186

Chapter 13: The Four Zones of Curiosity 189

Why the Four Zones of Curiosity are important in the Exponential Age 190
Life in the different zones 192
An example of the Zones in practice 194
The Four Zones of Curiosity in action 195
Using the Four Zones of Curiosity in legal department training 196
Paralegal process example 197
Four Zones of Curiosity and your career 197
Aligning the Four Zones of Curiosity with the Exponential Age Mindset Attributes 201
Asking the right strategic questions 202
The coaching opportunity with your CEO 203

Chapter 14: The Can If Framework – paths to opportunity 205

The department of no 205
The influence piece 206

A unique problem solver 207
Saying and thinking 208
Why Can If is so powerful 208
Applying Can If 209
How we apply it 210
The possible versus the impossible 210
Taking a diversion 211
How it works in practice with legal teams 212
Disrupting the triggers 216
The impact of Can If 217
Lawyers do need to use their "no" words 217

Part Three: Putting it into practice 219

Chapter 15: Lift Off – propelling legal leadership into the Exponential Age 219
Program philosophy – from legal or operations expert to enterprise leader 220
Kick-off experience – ignition in New York City 221
How this worked for legal operations 223
Coaching insights 224
Capstone presentations – applying strategic vision 225
Core competencies developed 225
Becoming sherpas for legal transformation 227

Chapter 16: Upskilling paraprofessionals for the Exponential Age – the Paraprofessional Leadership Development Academy (PLDA) 229
Program overview and impact 229
The genesis of the PLDA 231
Creating the Paraprofessional Leadership Development Academy 232
The Six Criteria for Success 234
The paraprofessional program 234
The bigger picture 237
The sessions 238
The presentations 242
The learning journey – from discomfort to mastery 243

Chapter 17: Beyond law – training leaders for the Exponential Age 245
Outcomes and impact 245
Program 1: Developing future-ready legal leaders 246
Program structure and progression 247
Impact and outcomes from the Next Generation Leadership Program 250
Changing mindset and impact – participant feedback 251
Program 2: Developing an entrepreneurial mindset 253
Core frameworks and competencies 254
The genesis of the Entrepreneurial Mindset and the Five Lenses 255
The five lenses – resources, people, capability, technology, and transformation 256
Bringing it all together 260
Impact on participants 260
Conclusion 261

Chapter 18: Leading humanly in the Exponential Age 263
From expertise to influence 263
Discomfort as the doorway to growth 263
Reframing risk and redefining value 264
The human advantage 264
From tools to transformation 265
A call to lead differently 265
The future is human 265

About Globe Law and Business 267

Foreword

By Carlos M. Brown

When I first encountered the phrase *Exponential Age*, I paused. It perfectly captures what so many of us in business are experiencing – a moment of breathtaking transformation where the pace of change is constant, technology is reshaping every dimension of business, and leadership itself is being redefined. Yet amid this acceleration, what remains most vital is not the technology, but our humanity.

That belief is why this book resonated so deeply with me. *The Exponential Age* is not simply a guide to innovation; it is a reminder that people – our capacity to connect, learn, and lead with purpose – are at the center of sustainable transformation. Catherine McGregor and Lloyd M. Johnson have built a framework that helps businesses and their lawyers and legal professionals strengthen the very qualities that make us distinctively human – curiosity, creativity, empathy, and courage. It echoes my own thinking: how do we provide a blueprint for leaders to lead authentically and effectively in a time of unprecedented change?

Leadership as a collective mindset

Across my career, leading legal and compliance teams and latterly a much broader range of business teams, one truth has remained constant – meaningful change begins with mindset. I've talked about that as "dreaming in color" and *The Exponential Age Mindset Attributes* that Catherine and Lloyd describe reflect this notion. This is the leadership shift the legal profession needs – from control to collaboration, from narrow legal analysis to broad enterprise perspective.

Concepts like *Zoom Master*, *Joyful Tightrope*, and *Agile Juggler* may sound poetic, but they capture the practical reality of what it means to lead today. I see this in my teams – when lawyers begin to think beyond legal risk and engage with business, community, and societal impact, everything changes. We move from asking, "Can we do this?" to "How can we make this work responsibly, inclusively, and with integrity?" We become not only better lawyers, but more influential business leaders and trusted partners.

Reclaiming the human advantage

One of the most powerful insights in this work is that our greatest competitive advantage in an age of AI is not speed or scale – it is humanity. The lawyers who will thrive are those who combine analytical rigor with empathy, narrative, and connection.

I share this conviction that deep listening – to colleagues, clients, and communities – builds the foundation of trust and influence. The frameworks in this book give structure to that belief. They remind us that compassion and creativity are not "soft skills" but essential capabilities that power resilience and innovation.

The integration of neuroscience is especially resonant. It validates what I have seen as a leader – joy and curiosity are not luxuries, they are catalysts. They create the mental agility needed to lead with clarity and courage amid uncertainty.

From risk managers to strategic enablers

This book addresses one of the central challenges facing modern in-house counsel – the evolution from gatekeeper to growth partner. The *Six Dimensions of Business Risk and Opportunity*, *Four Zones of Curiosity*, and *Can If* frameworks equip legal teams to reframe how they engage with their organizations.

These tools encourage lawyers to translate complexity into clarity, and fear into forward motion. They help us guide our teams to anticipate where the business – and the world – is heading, and to shape that future with integrity and imagination.

At Dominion Energy, I have seen that the most effective leaders are those that unite technical excellence with a shared sense of purpose and service. We need subject matter expertise aligned with mindsets that allow us to think differently and keep learning. This book builds that capacity from the inside out.

The work of being human

Transformation is not merely procedural – it is deeply personal. True leadership is the work of being human – holding our values steady while stretching into new frontiers.

The Exponential Age offers tools and language for that journey. It challenges us to lead with presence rather than certainty, to stand with confidence amid ambiguity, and to help others find their footing there too.

In my work leading the services division at Dominion Energy, I have witnessed how these ideas can energize teams – unlocking not only performance but also optimism, creativity, and belonging. In a time when automation and algorithmic thinking dominate headlines, the courage to lead with heart is more essential than ever.

A call to courageous, human-centered leadership

This book is a call to action for our profession. It challenges every general counsel, legal leader, and aspiring professional to redefine success – not by output alone, but by impact, inclusion, and humanity.

We cannot slow the pace of the Exponential Age, but we can choose how we meet it. If we lead with empathy, curiosity, and courage, we will not only keep pace with change – we will help shape a more just, creative, and connected future.

Carlos M. Brown
President, Dominion Energy Services, executive vice president,
chief administrative and projects officer and corporate secretary,
Dominion Energy, Inc.

Acknowledgments

This book is the result of many conversations, collaborations, and moments of insight along the way. While I cannot name everyone who has influenced this work, I want to acknowledge those whose contributions were fundamental to shaping the thinking behind it.

My co-author and creative partner, Lloyd M. Johnson, has been on this journey with me from the beginning. Bringing these ideas to life together – through countless coaching engagements, workshops, and experiments – has been both intellectually stretching and deeply rewarding. Our shared curiosity and commitment to impact sit at the heart of this book.

My husband, Andrew, unknowingly set this entire project in motion. After reviewing the Exponential Age Mindset Attributes, he remarked – entirely unprompted – that these ideas were strong and worth writing about. Sometimes the clearest signals come from those closest to us. I must also mention my son Matthew and the dog, Peter – both are less interested in what this book is about but provide valuable emotional support!

Carlos Brown at Dominion Energy continues to be a powerful source of inspiration. His innovative mindset and constant encouragement to "dream in color" have influenced not just this work, but how I think about possibility more broadly.

Tracey Sinclair is an exceptional copy editor and a treasured friend. Her ability to help me find clarity, coherence, and my own voice – especially when navigating complex ideas – has been invaluable.

Dominique Ashby of Neuro at Work played a critical role in sharpening my thinking on the connection between neuroscience and the Exponential Age Mindset Attributes. Beyond her intellectual contributions, Dominique has been an unwavering supporter and champion of this work.

Larry Stubbings generously shared his deep expertise in the craft of storytelling. Having taught Larry many years ago, it was a particular privilege to learn from him in return.

Kenny Robertson, head of innovation and technology, legal and regulatory affairs at NatWest Group, has been an invaluable sounding board on how innovation and creativity can genuinely take root within the legal profession. He exemplifies what it means to walk the walk, not just talk the talk.

Similarly, Kevin Van Tonder, director of consulting at Consilio, has been a consistent source of insight and inspiration in both the development and application of these ideas.

My fellow University of Huddersfield alum, Chris Fowler, chief operating officer legal, governance and corporate affairs, Rio Tinto has also been a steady source of encouragement and support.

Lesley Wan, founder of the Eagle Club, has always had my back. Her belief in this work – and her partnership in developing programs and training that further shaped my thinking – has meant more than she knows.

Somewhat fittingly, the concept of Bias Jiu Jitsu emerged just as I began my own Jiu Jitsu journey. Becoming a beginner again – embracing humility, discipline, and continuous learning – proved to be the perfect mindset while writing about technological change in a world where we are all learning in real time. My thanks to Sensei Anthony Billings and my fellow students at Tiger Schulmann's Martial Arts in Princeton, who remind me of the power of progress over perfection.

Above all, my deepest thanks go to the participants and clients in our coaching and training programs. They brought these ideas to life, stress-tested them in real-world contexts, and revealed possibilities for application far beyond what Lloyd and I initially imagined.

Finally, this book is dedicated to the memory of my dear friend Lawson Crawford, who left us far too soon. His support, curiosity, and thoughtful conversations consistently helped expand my thinking while keeping me grounded. He is deeply missed.

Dr Catherine McGregor
February 2026

About the authors

Catherine McGregor is an author, executive coach, and management consultant. She has worked for a range of legal publications and now coaches and consults for legal departments and law firms around the world. She is the author of the successful book focused on the business of law for legal departments, *Business Thinking in Practice for In-House Counsel: Taking Your Seat at The Table* (Globe Law & Business 2020). The book focuses on the application of human-centred business skills by legal departments and has received numerous accolades.

Catherine spends most of her time working with executive leadership and chief legal executives, where she leads professional and executive development and executive coaching efforts, working with many Global 100 and Fortune 500 legal departments. Much of her work in talent development is now focused on developing the skills that professionals will need to master opportunities in the Exponential Age in blending human work with AI and other technologies. Together with her colleague, Lloyd M Johnson Jr, she has developed the nine Exponential Age mindset attributes and uses these as the basis for her leadership development and training programs.

After running 60+ leadership workshops over the past six years, executive coach **Lloyd M. Johnson** has developed a 360-degree view on the specific leadership development challenges faced by top legal department leaders – and those who would aspire to such positions. These insights – as well as others built over a career publishing magazines and running leadership conferences for general counsel and other law department leaders – inform Lloyd's work with clients as he provides them with integrated talent development, leadership development, and succession strategies through both group and individual coaching. His goal: building trust and rapport that allows his clients to be more open throughout the process, giving the work they do together more impact – not only on the executives themselves, but throughout the organizations they serve.

Introduction

The meeting

Interior boardroom; daytime; a group of executives sit around a table. One of them looks uncomfortable. It is the general counsel – who is not meant to be the most anxious person in the room.

Yet here they are, seated at the executive table, listening carefully while the conversation accelerates around them. The CEO is enthusiastic. The chief technology officer is already several steps ahead, outlining how a new AI-enabled platform will transform decision-making, compress timelines, and unlock value across the business. The CFO wants to know when the benefits will show up on the balance sheet. Someone mentions a competitor who has already moved.

Then the room turns – subtly, but unmistakably – towards the general counsel, towards legal.

Can we do this?
What's the risk?
What do you think?

The general counsel takes a breath.

There is no clear precedent. Regulation is evolving. The technology is advancing faster than guidance can be issued. The data inputs are imperfect. The ethical implications are real but not yet fully mapped. The business wants speed. The board wants assurance.

This is no longer a question of legal correctness.

It is a question of judgment.

In that moment, the general counsel is not being asked for a memo or a footnote. They are being asked to help the organization decide who it wants to be in a world where technology is reshaping power, responsibility, and risk. They are being asked to balance innovation with trust, ambition with accountability, and progress with principle – without the comfort of certainty.

This moment is now becoming routine.

Across boardrooms and executive meetings, legal leaders are finding themselves in similar positions. Not because they lack expertise, but because the nature of decision-making itself has changed. The questions arriving at Legal are broader, faster, and more strategic than before. They demand synthesis, not just analysis. Perspective, not just precision.

Welcome to the Exponential Age.

The rules have changed

The legal profession is facing a quiet reckoning.

Not because the law is disappearing.
Not because lawyers are no longer needed.
But because the way value is created – and recognized – has fundamentally shifted.

Technology is no longer knocking at the door of legal departments. It is already inside, embedded in workflows, shaping decisions, accelerating timelines, and exposing gaps in how lawyers think about risk, judgment, and leadership. Artificial intelligence, data-driven systems, and automation are not future concerns. They are present realities – often adopted faster than legal teams are prepared to understand, govern, or lead them.

And yet, much of the conversation in law remains strangely misplaced.

We debate tools instead of mindsets.
We focus on efficiency instead of judgment.
We talk about risk controls while ignoring the deeper question: what is the lawyer's role when technology changes the nature of thinking itself?

The uncomfortable truth is this: technical excellence alone is no longer enough.

In the Exponential Age, the lawyers who thrive will not be those who know the most, but those who can think most effectively under conditions of speed, uncertainty, and ambiguity. The ones who can zoom out as easily as they zoom in. Who can influence without defaulting to "no". Who can balance innovation with ethics, and pace with trust. Who can lead when the answer is not obvious – and may not even yet exist.

This is not a skills gap.

It is a mindset gap.

Embracing the tension

The Exponential Age is defined by compounding change. Progress no longer moves in straight lines – it accelerates, amplifies, and cascades. Small decisions create large ripple effects. Systems are deeply interconnected. Feedback loops are shorter. The cost of hesitation is higher.

For lawyers, this creates a collision between how they were trained and how they are now expected to operate.

Legal training prizes certainty, precedent, and precision. The Exponential Age rewards adaptability, synthesis, and strategic judgment. The law evolves slowly; technology evolves at speed. Regulation lags innovation. Ethics are tested before frameworks are in place.

In this environment, waiting for clarity is not a neutral act – it is a strategic choice, and now it is often the wrong one.

General counsel and legal leaders know this instinctively. Many feel the pressure daily – faster decisions, broader stakeholder expectations, technology-led business strategies that raise questions the law has not yet answered. Teams are being asked to move quicker, think more commercially, and engage earlier – often without additional resources or guidance on how to do so.

At the same time, lawyers are rightly wary. Over-reliance on technology introduces new risks – hallucinations, bias, opacity, and ethical blind spots. The solution is not blind adoption – but nor is it resistance. The real work lies in learning how to stand confidently in the tension between progress and caution.

That tension is not a problem to be solved.

It is a capability to be developed.

This book is written for lawyers who sense that the ground beneath them is shifting – and who want to lead, not retreat. It is for those who recognize that influence now matters as much as expertise, and that human judgment is becoming more – not less – valuable as machines grow more capable.

The Exponential Age does not need lawyers who cling to certainty. It needs lawyers who can think expansively, decide wisely, and lead humanly in the face of accelerating change.

That requires a different mindset.

The chapters that follow introduce the Exponential Age Mindset Attributes and their related tools – practical, developable ways of thinking and behaving that enable legal professionals to operate credibly and confidently in this new reality. These have been tried and tested through training we have undertaken with a range of general counsel and their legal teams. These are not theoretical ideals. They are patterns we have seen repeatedly in legal leaders who succeed at the enterprise level.

In our work with legal departments across industries, we have seen that the most effective legal leaders share a common set of mental habits. They are comfortable toggling between detail and strategy. They can sit in ambiguity without freezing. They tell compelling stories about risk and opportunity. They adapt their communication to the room. They recognize bias – both their own and others. They synthesize complexity into clarity.

But these are not personality traits. They are developable capabilities. This book takes you through them.

This is not about becoming more technical.
It is about becoming more strategic.
More influential.
More human.

The rules have changed.
The opportunity is deciding how you will play.

Chapter 1:
What is the Exponential Age and why should legal professionals care about it?

Imagine living in 1440 when Gutenberg invented the printing press, and the potential that opened. Suddenly, knowledge and ideas were much more widely available. Accepted ideas could be challenged, more people could learn to read and write. The rate of change brought about by mass printing was much more gradual but the shift it brought about for humanity is not unlike what's happening with Generative AI – only now, it's much faster and even bigger.

Welcome to the Exponential Age. This is where we are now as change happens more rapidly. Rather than there being 100 years of progress in the 21st century, it will feel more like 20,000 years of progress. This period of change will be unlike anything we have ever experienced.

We can already see this happening. After its launch in 2023, ChatGPT reached over 100 million users in two months, the fastest on-ramp ever of a consumer tech platform. The prior incumbent, TikTok, took nine months to reach 100 million users. Instagram took two-and-a-half years. If we look at a program with a more "workplace" application, Google Translate took six-and-a-half-years from its 2006 launch to reach 100 million monthly active users.

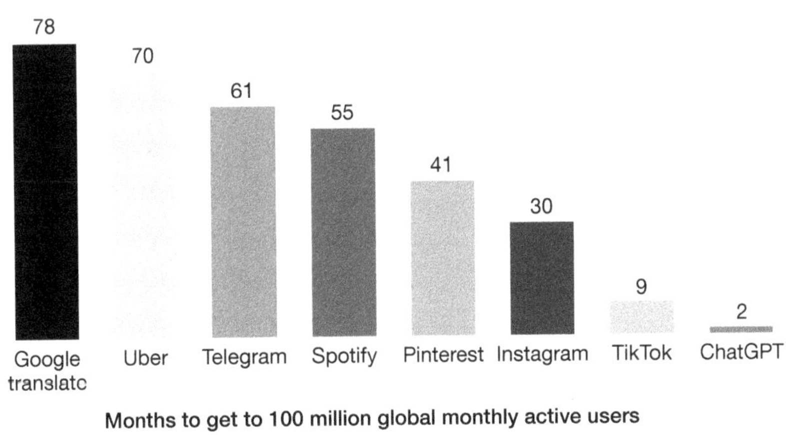

Figure 1: Time to reach 100m users. Adapted from data from UBS/Yahoo Finance.

This sounds intense but what will it mean for legal departments and the businesses they work in? There's a lot of buzz around how and where to use AI but there's little to no focus on what this is going to mean for professional development and career trajectories for in-house legal professionals. Where is the innovation in relation to legal department training? General counsel and CLOs – what are you doing differently to develop legal professionals, particularly at the mid-level? How are you helping them to be more strategic and more communicative with their business clients around change, the evolution of risk, ROI, and impact on profitability?

Leadership is going to change in the Exponential Age. It's imperative that all employees, not just those with formal leadership roles, are able to lead themselves and be more strategic.

To break that down:

- Mindsets around work will need to change.
- Focus will be on the highest value, most strategic work by legal professionals.
- What "being great at your job" means will change and shift as technology tools develop and are applied more quickly. An adaptable and continuous learning mindset will be essential, not just nice to have.
- Traditional academic qualifications will be less of a predictor of aptitude. Workplaces will need to adapt to what that means for recruitment and retention. This is going to be particularly interesting in law, where academic success at certain institutions has been the gateway of choice to the profession. Currently, we have a significant gap between the competencies taught in traditional legal education and the realities of working as a legal professional in a law firm – and even more so in-house. If legal education isn't adapting to this new world, then continuous learning and being able to flex in your role will be crucial.
- Success is going to be less about what you know and where you learnt it, but your mindset and *how* you learn.
- The core drivers for businesses and their legal teams will be "How can I do this better, more profitably and ultimately give more value to my end customer?".
- The more legal teams can focus beyond merely legal insights and look for business insights, the more they will be displaying the mindset needed in this Exponential Age. That's creative and connected, not linear and siloed.

- Generative AI will be central, not because it will replace humans, but because it will help humans be *more* creative in both ideating and realizing new and original solutions.
- The ability to embrace the possibility of this and adapt at scale and speed is what legal teams need to do now to be ready.

The pace of change is unprecedented

There's greater uncertainty in the Exponential Age because the pace of change is accelerating – driven primarily by rapid advances in technology, particularly AI, computing, biotech, and data.

Technology is improving at exponential rates. Take the example of Moore's Law – the idea that the power of computer chips roughly doubles every two years, while the cost stays about the same.

This was first observed by Gordon Moore, one of the founders of Intel, in 1965. He noticed that the number of transistors (the tiny switches that process information) on a chip was doubling every couple of years without the cost increasing.

What this means in simple terms is that computers keep getting faster, smaller, and cheaper, very quickly. For example, when personal computers became available in the 1980s, they were very much a luxury item. In the early 1980s, personal computers like the IBM PC were expensive, with a basic model costing around $2,880 (equivalent to about $8,352 now).

Similarly, a computer chip that contained 2,000 transistors and cost $1,000 in 1970, $500 in 1972, $250 in 1974, and $0.97 in 1990 now costs less than $0.02 to manufacture.

Imagine if the number of cases a lawyer could review in a day doubled every two years, without needing more staff or more hours in the day.

- In 2020, a lawyer can review 100 contracts per week.
- By 2022, that jumps to 200.
- By 2024, it's 400.
- By 2026, it's 800 – and so on.

It's not because the lawyer is working harder – it's because the tools they use (like AI review platforms or search algorithms) are getting exponentially more powerful, faster, and cheaper.

This matters for legal teams because technology is scaling legal capacity far beyond what traditional staffing by people can do. But the *law* itself doesn't evolve at the same pace – creating a growing gap between what's *tech-*

nically possible and what's *legally or ethically sound*. In-house teams must become fluent in tech's exponential curve, even as they operate in a world of slower-moving regulation. (We'll talk later about what the various Exponential Mindsets are and how they apply, but this is where what we call the Joyful Tightrope Attribute comes in.)

Faster, faster – AI scaling

Moore's Law – at least for computer chips – has physical limitations, which means it may cease to be true, likely this decade. We can put more components in a smaller and smaller chip, but we can't cool it (this is why many smartphones overheat and will not work until they cool down). But even if Moore's Law ends, technological advances continue. It's part of what makes the Exponential Age so unpredictable – progress isn't just steady, it's accelerating.

We only need to look at the adoption of technology, such as the pace of ChatGPT, outlined above. This is an example of once predictable progress disrupted by breakthroughs that shift the landscape almost overnight. Therefore, planning cycles and institutional adaptations struggle to keep up – despite the increased use of GenAI technology such as ChatGPT, many industries are still struggling with how to effectively implement it and understand its repercussions for the workforce, legally and ethically.

Both the power of AI and its use are increasing; the two are obviously interconnected. AI scaling refers to how AI systems become more powerful, capable, and useful as we give them more:

- Data;
- Computing power; and
- Model size (more parameters).

In simple terms, the more people use AI and the more information we feed AI, the smarter and more effective it gets – often in ways that are hard to predict. This progress follows an exponential curve – small changes in resources can lead to huge jumps in capability. Examples of this can be seen in Language Models (like ChatGPT). For example, early AI could complete a sentence. Now AI can draft business emails, write code, or even pass exams. That's a direct result of more data and bigger language learning models leading to surprising leaps in skill.

The same is true in image recognition. Early versions could spot a cat in a photo but might not recognize that it was a cat in certain situations. Now AI can detect cancer in scans more accurately than some doctors. Similarly, early voice assistants misunderstood basic commands, but now, with scaling, they can handle multi-step requests, learn preferences, and translate languages.

AI scaling in law

AI scaling has supercharged what is possible in law with the use of AI versus even a few years ago. In contract review, early legal AI could flag key clauses such as indemnity or termination. Some tools now summarize full contracts, detect unusual clauses, or benchmark terms against industry or organizational standards. Some platforms can even suggest redlines automatically.

In e-discovery, initial tools could keyword search; now, scaled AI can now detect patterns of misconduct, analyze sentiment, and predict relevance – often reducing manual review exponentially. For legal research, scaled AI can understand a legal question, scan thousands of cases, and synthesize reasoning – not just spit out results. With regulatory monitoring, the latest AI tools can now track global regulatory changes in real time, flagging what's relevant to your business and summarizing impact.

In a world where legal tasks can increasingly be handled by technology with only human checks and balances needed, the model of what lawyers need to focus on will change. For in-house lawyers, AI scaling means legal tech is no longer just about efficiency – it's becoming a thinking partner to lawyers. This moves the key work of lawyers into a much more strategic arena, where joining the dots between different ideas and more creative thinking will become table stakes, not just nice to have.

Lawyers will have to become more adept at operating in the areas where it's about strategic human interaction with technical legal skills. Often this means navigating the grey areas where the law is unclear or decisions that need to be made are not clear cut. This will grow in importance as technological advances outpace the development of law and regulations. This will also mean much more focus on not just what is legal but what is ethical. The best lawyers have always been able to do this – it's about being able to give their business clients the biscuit, not the recipe for the biscuit.

Lawyers in law firms will need a much stronger focus on understanding the strategic big picture of their clients' businesses and an ability to effectively modulate legal risk through the entire potential of business risk and opportunities. Being able to proactively spot trends and opportunities for clients and understanding how what has happened to one client could impact another will become the norm. Of course, the best external counsel do this already, but in the Exponential Age, this will be the new basic hygiene – not just technical legal excellence.

Lawyers – both in-house and in law firms – will need to be able to join the dots, see trends and make connections between them, as well as apply the human aspects of communication and stakeholder relations beyond mere technical legal skills. Many lawyers do this already, but many do not, or they still prioritize the legal details in a world where the bigger strategic uncertainties are becoming increasingly magnified.

But the scaling of AI also introduces new risks – hallucinations, over-reliance, and explainability issues. In a 2024 study,[1] Stanford University's Institute for Human Technology and Stanford's RegLab found that in between 69 and 88 percent of cases, large language models (LLMs) hallucinated answers in relation to specific legal queries, meaning that legal teams need to balance what AI *can* do with what it *should* do – and help business colleagues do the same. This is Joyful Tightrope in action – being comfortable with the progress that AI allows, while acknowledging the uncertainty of how that progress will unfold (and its limits).

Interconnected systems amplify ripple effects

Another massive uncertainty principle in the Exponential Age is the power and fragility of connected systems. Connected systems driven by the internet and the cloud do make everything more connected – which makes them interdependent. This is true of supply chains, financial systems, and information flows. But this means that a shock in one area (like a chip shortage or a regulatory shift) can cascade in unpredictable ways.

This connectivity causes complexity, which breeds volatility. What this means in practice is:

- Traditional models no longer predict well.
- Historical data is less useful in environments where past performance isn't indicative of future results.
- AI models can forecast short-term trends but often fail in "black swan" scenarios or novel contexts.
- This is a potentially fundamental issue in law, where so much of what is decided now is based on precedent.

Shifting power dynamics

An additional aspect of uncertainty is the fact that institutions such as governments, companies, and even the rule of law itself no longer have the same control or authority to steer events. There are many positive aspects to these shifting power dynamics, such as citizen journalists or the empowerment of individuals to be able to be ethical and informed consumers. But there are many downsides as well – "fake news", the questioning of truth and morality, and the devaluing of laws and regulations by both individuals and governments.

Another significant aspect of shifting power dynamics that is central to technological advancement is that innovation is decentralized – start-ups or lone researchers can now create world-changing tools, the best example being open-source AI.

These shifting sands around how power is held via heuristic models such as law create both significant new challenges and opportunities for in-house lawyers. If your executive is less convinced by the notion of the law, how can you ensure they do the right thing? Will your role as a lawyer be less significant than your ability as an individual to communicate and influence effectively? This is frankly already the case but is likely to be amplified further.

Societal and ethical uncertainty

We don't fully understand the implications of new tech on jobs, identity, geopolitics, or human agency. This creates moral and strategic ambiguity – what *should* we do, and who gets to decide? We're fond of using the ideas raised in the 2002 Tom Cruise film, *Minority Report* (an adaptation of a 1954 novella by Philip K. Dick, who also wrote the novel the film *Blade Runner* was based on). In *Minority Report*, technology allows the state to predict crimes before they have happened and therefore arrest "criminals" before they commit any crimes. Of course, these predictions turn out to be imperfect, with innocent people being wrongly accused due to false interpretations of data – raising questions of the ethics of over-reliance on technology, of letting computers carry out judgments that were once firmly in the human sphere.

There are more expert and more extensive writings on the topic of ethics in AI and new technology, but it is fair to say that this is raising issues that are beyond our current ethical and regulatory imaginings. A vital role for lawyers will be trying to manage this, which often may involve playing catch up in applying legal and ethical frameworks to technological advances. A degree of comfort with uncertainty – even extreme uncertainty – will be needed to navigate this.

At a practical, focused level, a significant Joyful Tightrope dilemma for many general counsel is how to effectively create a legal team that will work now and in five years' time. How do we manage our teams effectively when we don't even know if they will be in existence in five years? How can we plan for staffing when we don't know if the current roles will be needed in the future, and we do not yet know the new roles that will replace them? The answer is this is almost impossible. This is one of the reasons that the through line in most of the Exponential Age Mindset Attributes is agility.

Many paraprofessionals such as paralegals in legal departments may feel that their work will ultimately be replaced by technology. But is this really going to be the case? At least one legal department that we have designed a paralegal training program for feels that it is paralegals who will be central to the effective rollout and deployment of AI tools, which is why it is investing in our training. Will it be traditional lawyers who cannot adapt who will become obsolete faster?

What is certain is that a legal department in ten or 20 years will not be staffed solely by lawyers. Lawyers may even be in the minority. Operations, data scientists, and legal technologists will all play a much greater part than they do now.

Shorter feedback loops, higher stakes

Decisions made quickly can have immediate, large-scale effects (e.g., viral social media decisions, code pushed to millions instantly). The speed of iteration means less time to course correct. Lawyers also face increasing demand from many stakeholders for delivery of work with faster and faster timelines. This will affect in-house legal departments massively.

This is where the obvious requirement for AI and similar technology tools to meet this "need for speed" is going to be crucial. However, this is also where related competencies, such as the ability to make decisions quickly and with imperfect information – a central component of the Joyful Tightrope competency – will be key. In my coaching work, I have often found that this is something with which lawyers, trained for perfection, struggle.

When undertaking group coaching and training programs for in-house legal teams, we often use a role-play or scenario. It is common for participants to push back that they can't make a decision because they do not have all the information. Welcome to the Exponential Age, folks! The need to make decisions without all the information was a leadership skill required way before the Exponential Age. The difference now is that this cannot only be confined to leaders or even legal leaders but will need to be the norm throughout the team. Increasingly, we have seen general counsel wanting this aptitude to become a feature of how their broader teams operate, not just the general counsel and their direct reports.

In short, exponential progress introduces *non-linearity*, which means the future isn't just more of the past – it's qualitatively different. That makes prediction harder and strategic clarity more elusive.

The Exponential Age Mindset Attributes in practice

How do leaders, particularly in legal departments where the focus has often never been on leadership skills, equip themselves to lead in an Exponential Age defined by change, non-linearity, and uncertainty? We have taught leadership development for years and focused on six leadership competencies to develop legal leaders who are adaptable and able to excel as business leaders:

1. Self-awareness.
2. Strategic mindset.
3. Executive communication.
4. Influence.
5. Financial acumen.
6. Developing direct reports/leading others.

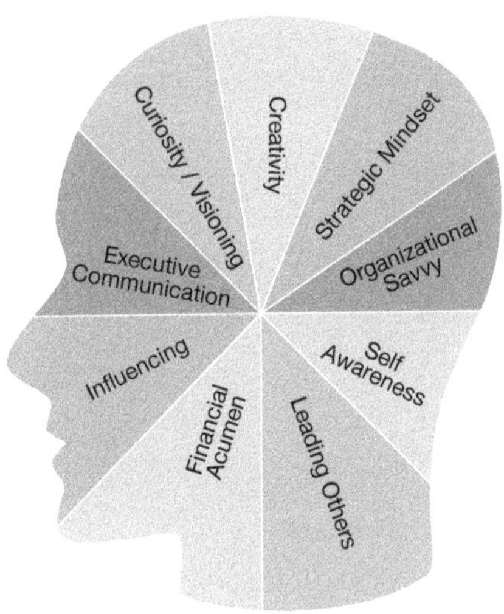

Figure 2: Leadership competencies to develop legal leaders. Source: Chief Legal Executive LLC.

In recent years, we have found that these have not been enough, given the pace of change in business due to technological developments. We also added in creativity and curiosity. Now we find that *creativity, curiosity, and influence* are the most important of the leadership attributes. This is because these allow individuals to cope with exponential change and continually search for the opportunities within it, but also bring others along with them on that change journey. This is fundamental to success in the Exponential Age. The Exponential Age competencies are like a cake – a wonderful blend of different ingredients. But what are these ingredients and how do you get them to work together to create your cake?

We need to understand the different ingredients and how we put them together.

The ingredients – the Exponential Age Mindset Attributes

In our work training legal departments and working as executive coaches, we have developed nine Exponential Age Mindset Attributes that we see as fundamental for leaders who wish to excel in these leadership competencies to succeed in the age of AI. By practicing these in their current roles, participants in our training can better get to grips with the Exponential Age leadership

Figure 3: The Exponential Age Mindset Attributes. Source: Chief Legal Executive LLC.

competencies and connect to bigger transformational changes happening in their department, their organization, and the wider world of work.

Zoom Master

The optimized ability to zoom in and zoom out. Knowing when to focus on the legal details and when to focus on the big picture. The significant aspect here is the movement between the two states and being able to know when to zoom out (strategic) and when to zoom in (detail and operational).

What this looks like in practice

An in-house lawyer wanted to get a more strategic viewpoint. He went to all the senior businesspeople he worked with directly and asked them what their top three strategic challenges will be over the next two years. He also asked if there was anything that his team was doing that they should do less of and anything they should do more of. He then asked how he and his team could help with the business's strategic aims and objectives. In this example, the in-house lawyer is moving between strategy and tangible outputs.

Joyful Tightrope

A heightened level of comfort with uncertainty. This is key when practicing law in business as the "legal" issue may not be obvious or may be more than just legal. Also, it's a significant attribute when organizations and departments are going through transformations and the accepted way of doing things is disrupted.

What this looks like in practice

A contract management team leader and her team were in flux, and she did not have certainty on what their new roles and structure would be. Usually, she would not say anything until she had clarity from her leadership. However, this time she leaned into her Joyful Tightrope competency. She shared this uncertainty with her team and, rather than being upset, the team rallied around and embarked on a spontaneous brainstorming session about how the team could pivot depending on what leadership decided.

Chaos Converter

Seeing the opportunity in chaos and calamity. This is where a really calibrated understanding of all the nuances of business risk becomes that legal professional's North Star. As does an understanding of the relationship between risk and reward, especially from the perspective of the broader business ROI. Understand the opportunities that lie in challenges.

What this looks like in practice
A GC was told that she needed to cut her budget by 30 percent. Initially horrified, she soon saw there was an opportunity to revamp how things were done. There had been too much reliance on outside counsel and little to no sharing of knowledge. She created an innovation challenge for the legal team, sharing that the aim was to make the 30 percent cost reduction via opportunity and efficiency, not via internal roles being axed. The team got behind this and created extensive savings with law firms as well as rationalizing internal spend via the introduction of a matter triage system.

Agile Juggler
The ability to balance consistency with agility. Law is a profession grounded in precedent, but the best legal professionals understand the need to be creative and not get locked into the status quo for the sake of it. This aptitude will be crucial as change becomes even more of a constant.

What this looks like in practice
An associate GC was moving into his first leadership role with a team of two lawyers and two paralegals reporting to him. The legal department was undergoing a process improvement exercise, so teams were reporting what they did and how they did it. There was an assumption that the status quo would change but no one was sure how. The new leader was uncertain what to do. His instincts told him to try and keep as much as possible consistent for the team without avoiding that the team needed to lean into change. He emphasized the key focus of their roles which remained the same but worked with the team on sharing the positive aspects of focusing on how work was done. He displayed consistency in his pastoral care as a leader during this time of change. He scheduled regular catch-ups with the team as a group and emphasized his availability for individual conversations. After the transformation, he felt his team was in better shape than that of another colleague who had not discussed the transformation with her team but had tried to continue with the status quo.

Supreme Storyteller
Storytelling is the most universal way that humans communicate and under-

stand information. It puts focus on how you say something as much as what you say. It's the ability to evoke an emotional reaction that will increase the probability of the adoption of a new idea. This is when legal professionals need to create change by understanding and using the basic human skill of telling a story.

What this looks like in practice

A director of legal operations wanted to get buy in from her head of legal operations and the GC to streamline outside counsel spend by introducing a law firm panel. Feeling nervous, she presented her ideas to a friend who was an actor. Her friend suggested that she needed to focus more on how she could make her listeners feel and not on what she was saying. With her friend's help, she made a deck that focused on the story and used the metaphor of a busy kitchen with staff working together to create amazing food. She used the analogy of the TV show, *The Bear*, creating a kitchen staff who could transform what they did with the right framework. She knew the GC was a fan of this show and her head of legal ops was a big foodie – illustrating that it's not just about creating a story, but one that your audience can relate to and understand.

Duality Master

This is the ability to take knowledge from one pursuit and apply it creatively to another. Knowing that some of the best ideas can be borrowed or stolen. Drawing on ideas from other areas stops your brain being constrained by "known" solutions.

What this looks like in practice

A chief legal officer had been asked to weigh in on an infrastructure deal that was of huge strategic importance to the power company he worked for. His CEO was always impressed by his creativity in the face of challenges. These projects were always approached via a structure of a Project Partnership Agreement (PPA), but this would not work in this instance as both sides were going round in circles over the question of liability for costs if the project ran over. The CLO had been involved in state government initiatives and proposed using a Public Private Partnership, bringing in private equity funding using an innovative structure not usually applied to these sorts of projects by his company. His mindset was focused on considering all the avenues to get to the best solution, and his thinking was not constrained by what was typical.

Champion Chameleon

This is a flexible and adaptable communication style that allows effective communication with all learning styles. Inextricably linked to storytelling, this is understanding how your audience will best receive information. Does your CEO have the attention span of a goldfish? Does your CFO only like charts? Make that work for you!

What this looks like in practice

A new GC received feedback from her chief of staff that her messaging was too formulaic and seemed geared to the US-based executive, never considering her own team and its cultural diversity. The GC decided she needed to make understanding her team and communicating across it her focus. She arranged visits to different geographies to get to know the teams. Even before these were completed, she was much more intentional about getting insights from her regional team leads on what issues were front of mind for their people. She then worked with her communications lead to craft messaging that emphasized what her global team shared as a team but also referenced the specific experiences and concerns of teams in particular regions.

Bias Jiu Jitsu

This is about being aware of cognitive biases and heuristics on decision making. Are there aspects you need to highlight for different audience – analogies or metaphors you need to evoke?

What this looks like in practice

A deputy GC was promoted to head up a function that included security and data professionals. He was uncertain about how to lead people who might be more expert in certain areas than he was. He realized it was less about being an expert, more about understanding how their expertise made them see the world, and how he might need to modify his communications with different groups to get the greatest effect.

Superlative Synthesizer

This is the ability to synthesize and simplify. Keeping it simple and keeping it relevant. Say no more...

What this looks like in practice

A new GC got feedback from the CEO that the board was questioning her executive presence. Her board presentations were too long-winded and detailed. The GC curbed her desire to go into the details and then reveal at the end why this was important. She worked with a coach to focus on synthesizing her message and leading with what was key and why the board should care. This changed the way she started to communicate to everyone, and how she asked her direct reports to communicate to her.

The tools to mix the cake

If these are our ingredients, how do we know which ones are needed in each instance? Just as a particular type of cake might need more of one ingredient than another to achieve the desired flavor, certain situations may require more utilization of one attribute over another. How do we decide?

We usually ask those we are working with – from business leaders down to executive assistants and paralegals – to choose two to three Exponential Age Mindset Attributes they feel they are uncomfortable with, but they need. We sometimes find it helpful to phrase this as "What's the work superpower that you need for the future?"

We then use several tools to apply these, the same way you might need different cooking utensils while baking – allowing participants to bring it all together and be intentional in applying the Exponential Mindset Attributes in their role.

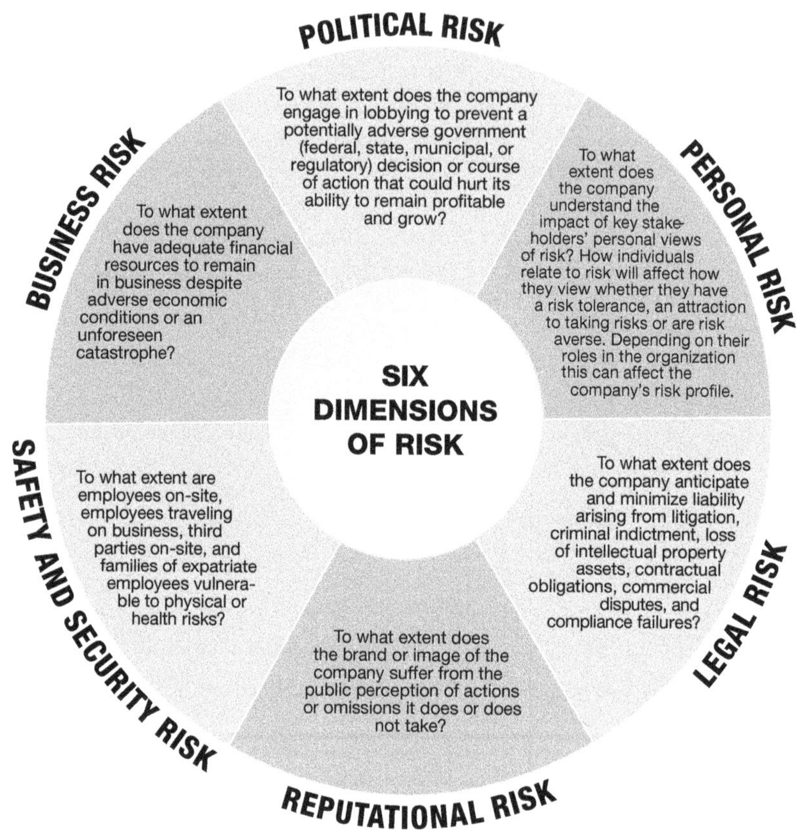

Figure 4: Six Dimensions of Business Risk. Source: Chief Legal Executive LLC.

The Six Dimensions of Business Risk

The Six Dimensions of Business Risk emphasize the interconnected aspects of risk in all situations and that risk is not necessarily a negative; it can be an opportunity. This is particularly helpful in aligning with the attributes of Zoom Master, Bias Jiu Jitsu, Champion Chameleon, and Duality Master to see beyond the day-to-day functions of a legal team.

The Six Dimensions of Business Opportunity

The Six Dimensions of Business Opportunity developed from our use of the Six Dimensions of Business Risk in training. The more we used this in training sessions, the more we felt that greater emphasis needed to be placed

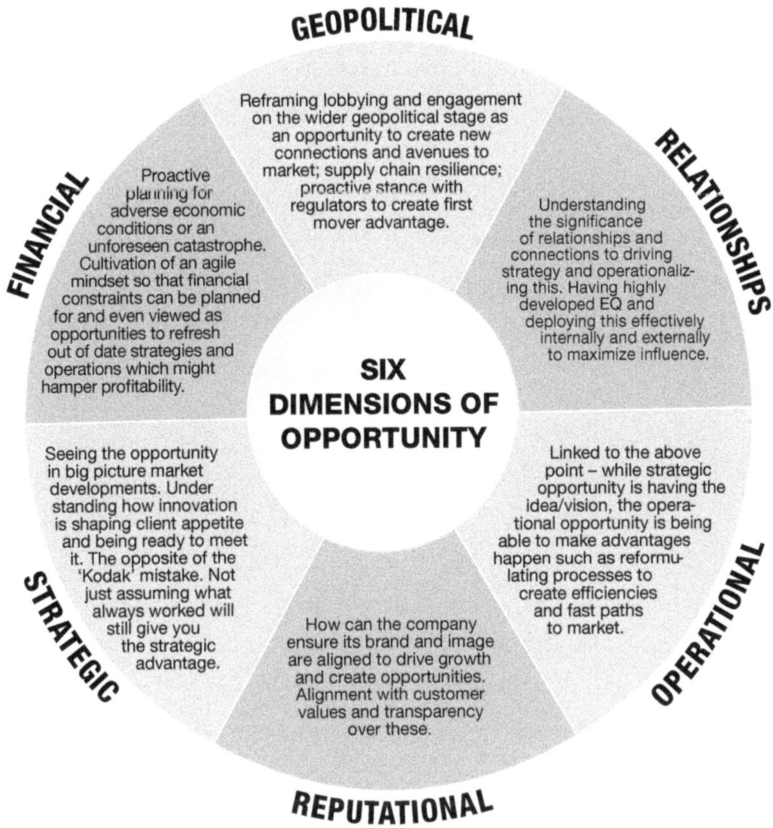

Figure 5: Six Dimensions of Business Opportunity. Source: Chief Legal Executive LLC.

on looking forward and creation, not just on where risk lay. The focus on risk when training lawyers in particular could lead to stasis, as so many lawyers have a fraught relationship with risk and want to be risk-avoidant.

This attitude is one that needs to be tempered as a leader. We found that showing more clearly the other side of risk via identifying key areas of business opportunities that correlated with the Six Dimensions of Risk was transformational in getting many of our participants to reframe their application of risk in our training and coaching.

The Four Zones of Curiosity

This allows participants to move from small picture operational solutions to developing a strategic view that makes connections and spots trends focused on business priorities.

Zone 1 **Known and met** *Focus is on my role and my team.* Known needs of GC/manager. Current projects. What I do now. Characterized by a siloed view. Reactive, detail-orientated mindset.	**Zone 2** **Known and unmet** *Focus is on my team and expanding what I do now within expected parameters that can help the entire legal team.* Known and unmet needs of GC/manager. Future projects in my sight. What I know I need to do. Peeking out of my silo to look at others around me in my legal team. Reactive but taking time to step back and look at the bigger picture.
Zone 3 **Unknown and unmet** *Focus on opportunities for the entire legal team and how they relate to the business.* Unknown and unmet needs of GC. Future projects I am not aware of. Connected view across the legal team and business stakeholders. View is looking at the legal team and how it relates to business then how my role connects to that. Strategic and operational.	**Zone 4** **Unknown and unmet** *Focus on the business and what I can do to provide strategic advances to the business.* Unknown and unmet needs of the business. Future strategies that I am not aware of. Focus on the business. View of what the business opportunities are and can be. Strategic and visionary.

Figure 6: The Four Zones of Curiosity. Source: Chief Legal Executive LLC.

The Can If Problem Solving Framework

This allows participants to explore different ways of looking at what is possible in every situation and enhancing their creative problem solving.

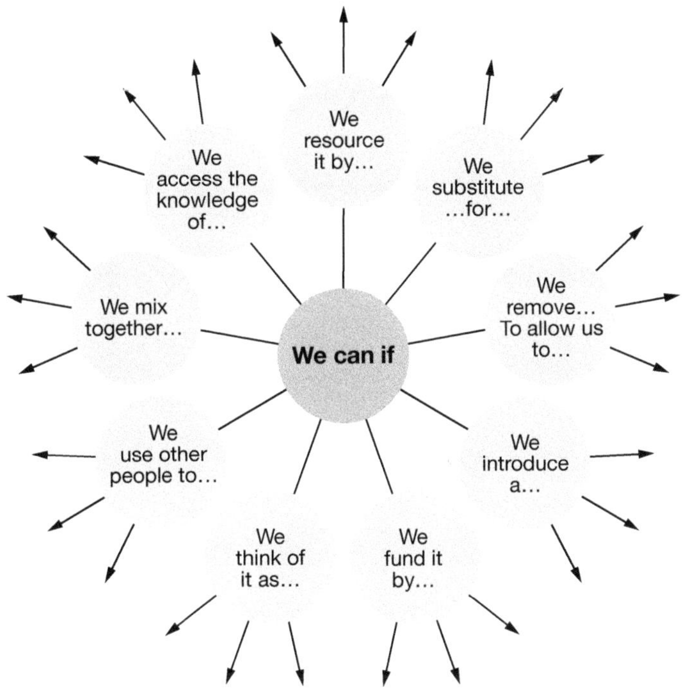

Figure 7: The Can If problem solving framework. Source: Chief Legal Executive LLC.

These are not new ideas, but we believe that the way we bring them together and the way we apply them in training all legal professionals in legal departments – not just senior lawyers – can help to make the uncertainty of the future an adventure, not a precipice.

An adventure for everyone

These attributes are not confined to those who are formally known as "leaders". We cannot rely on what has gone before to provide us with a roadmap. Those who followed leaders previously may now have as many answers as those leaders. This adaptability is at the heart of the Exponential Age Mindset Attributes and means that these should be a focus at *every* point of your career.

We use these competencies, attributes, and tools at every level of a legal department, from paralegals through mid-level legal professionals to legal operations to chief legal officers and general counsel. Changes in the world of work are going to be impossible to ignore. As you think about these potential changes, what's the Exponential Age Mindset Attribute that you need and how can you start to develop it?

References

1 Matthew Dahl, Varun Magesh, Mirac Suzgun, Daniel E Ho: "Large Legal Fictions: Profiling Legal Hallucinations in Large Language Models." *Journal of Legal Analysis*, January 2024: https://reglab.stanford.edu/publications/hlarge-legal-fictions-profiling-legal-hallucinations-in-large-language-models/

Chapter 2:
Setting the stage – exponential change and human identity

We are living in a moment where the rhythm of daily life often feels at odds with the speed of global change. On the one hand, family, community, and work routines can feel steady and even comforting. On the other, every headline brings reminders of political polarization, climate shocks, or technological upheaval. This disconnect creates cognitive dissonance – how can things feel so normal in our personal lives, while the wider world seems so unstable?

Artificial intelligence amplifies this paradox. Unlike previous industrial revolutions, AI is not a slow-moving, localized shift. It is exponential in pace and global in scope. For many, this transformation feels seismic and existential, forcing us to confront questions of identity and value. What does it mean to be human when machines can do so much of what we once considered our unique domain?

The neuroscience of the Exponential Age

Neuroscience is considering how the brain and nervous system interact to produce our thoughts and feelings and consciousness – our being human. This is at the heart of the changes and developments that Lloyd and I are exploring in our work and in this book.

How do we maximize human skills and potential and, as leaders, keep talent motivated and engaged when a lot of the messaging we hear plays on our subconscious fears that our very identity is under threat from the technological advances we ourselves created?

Uncertainty and fear have long been a staple of science fiction, including Philip K. Dick's seminal text *Do Androids Dream of Electric Sheep*, which was the inspiration for the *Blade Runner* films. This text is particularly apt for our work in preparing legal departments for the Exponential Age as it explores what it means to be human in a technologically advanced age via examining the nature of empathy. For those unfamiliar with the films or book, one of the tests that exposes "replicants" (non-humans) questions their empathic responses to certain situations. A failure in empathy is a failure in humanity.

What's crucial for legal departments, as with all business units, is to truly understand and be able to demonstrate the value of being human in the Exponential Age. This will take time, thought, and training way before we can enable technology to achieve its potential in the workplace. However, this thought and training of the human side is, we find, often not part of the equation. Our work is focused on this people part and how leaders can equip their people to thrive in the workplace in this new reality.

This chapter explores why understanding how we show up as human beings while technology continues to advance around us is so important. We have enlisted the expertise of neuroscientist Dominique Ashby,[1] who has a unique perspective on this, being a trained neuroscientist who has also practised law.

From the Industrial Revolution to the Age of AI

The most compelling point of reference we have for the Exponential Age is the Industrial Revolution. In the 18th and 19th century, the invention of more and better machines ushered in the birth of industry and mass production, creating a shift from a more agricultural-based economy to urbanized cities. This introduced ways of life that are still the norm today. This change was very linear. Progress was based on human expertise and human labor aided by machines; mass production was the way to maximize growth and therefore profits.

The Industrial Revolution transformed how many people lived and our expectations of what our lives would look like. But this is nothing compared to the shifts that the Exponential Age is bringing. According to Ashby:

> *"In the Industrial Revolution, we were starting from a different cognitive baseline in terms of what our work and personal lives demanded from our brains. While the pace of the last industrial revolution was quick for its time, today's industrial revolution is progressing at an accelerated, almost instantaneous, rate and covers a broader section of our home and work life. At work, our roles are being transformed or replaced. At home, our network of emotional connection is now increasingly including a feeling of connection with AI chat interfaces. To be perfectly honest, the pace at which it's going to impact what human value means and what our identity is, is scary, even for someone who is 100 percent looking into this and getting onto it and helping other people. It's seismic. It's existential."*[2]

Ashby helps companies with change, and her work is increasingly focused on AI – specifically, on our sense of identity as humans and what makes up that sense of identity at home and in the workplace against the backdrop of AI implementation in both. There are two phases to this work. She explains the emergence of AI versus the reality of AI arriving – fear of what might happen versus gradual implementation (i.e., what *is* happening). When implementation becomes wholescale, when the majority of things currently discussed come to fruition, there will be the question of human value itself. What does it mean, especially in a workplace?

Like us, Ashby spends a lot of time working with lawyers because she feels that they are at greater risk from the impact of the implementation of AI than many other professions and they have generally not come to terms with this in the ways required. This is also the starting point for our work – that the "people work" of AI implementation is being ignored, often to the detriment of the entire legal profession.

The neuroscience of AI use

Neuroscience offers a crucial lens for understanding how AI interacts with the human brain. There are two different paths we can take with AI. One is viewing it as a helper and a co-creator; the other is viewing it as doing the work for us. The latter makes us much more vulnerable to replacement than the former.

(There's potentially a third path, of course, of ignoring it completely and still expending time and effort on the routine tasks that AI can complete. But again, that's just another route to replacement – maybe it's even the fast track one!)

When we outsource thinking and doing to AI, we risk eroding key cognitive capacities – sustained attention, deep reading, and reflective problem-solving. Ashby summarizes the risk thus:

> *"The more we use AI to do the thinking, the less we use our own brain, and that's eroding our cognition. It's atrophying some of the ways that we're used to exercising our brains. Our sense of identity is rooted in our life experiences, including the opinions we form when we focus and analyze things, as well as the things we create and add to the world. The more we use AI to do the thinking, the less we feel a sense of ownership in the output – it doesn't feel like it's a part of us and a part of our identity. Pervasive use of AI as a way to delegate thinking can incrementally erode our sense of identity alongside our cognitive capabilities."*

At the same time, AI has the potential to *augment* cognition when used as a collaborative partner.

In Ashby's experience, this is where AI really adds value:

> *"Being on my own in business, I quite like a brainstorming partner – so I go to ChatGPT and ask it to challenge me. That co-creation is a positive impact on the brain, versus asking it to just summarize or write an essay for me."*

This illustrates how we can use AI as a springboard for co-creation rather than a replacement for creation. The exponential potential for most professions lies in this co-creation route – where we're using AI to optimize our human potential. This is when we have conversations with AI and use it as a co-creator or sparring partner, not a flawless font of all knowledge. Indeed, many of the well-publicized disasters of AI use in the legal field have come about because there was not enough human interrogation of the outputs and these were treated as wholly finalized, not a springboard for human interaction or finessing.

The current stage of the Exponential Age is one of much uncertainty. This is an important factor – neuroscience tells us that ambiguity activates the amygdala, the part of the brain responsible for fight-or-flight responses. Yet naming uncertainty reduces its power.

As Ashby explains:

> *"From the brain's point of view, sharing even a no-news update gives uncertainty a level of certainty. Leaders often think that saying 'I don't know' is weak, but it actually reduces stress and builds resilience."*

By confronting uncertainties about what work or the role of employees will look like in the Exponential Age, leaders are priming their teams' brains to cope in the most effective way. That is a large factor in why we are working in this space and why we have written this book. We saw a lot of legal teams not facing up to the reality of the "people" aspect of the Exponential Age and focusing merely on the technology. We believe that this is a massive mistake, and that the most forward-looking legal leaders will do both.

Human value at risk – the legal profession as a case study

Nowhere is the issue of human value conjured by the Exponential Age and the wholesale adoption of AI more visible than in the legal profession. For centuries, lawyers have anchored their worth in their mastery of knowledge, precedent, and precision. Their training reinforces the brain's most basic instinct – survival through prediction. To avoid harm, lawyers are taught to avoid risk, to rely on templates, and to fear being wrong.

As a lawyer and a neuroscientist, Ashby is uniquely placed to comment on this:

> *"Everything about legal training is reinforcing the brain's natural primary functioning of being a survival prediction and pattern recognition machine and avoiding anything that's new because it could be risky. Being wrong is drilled into you as a terrible thing."*

This mindset can make adaptation to AI particularly difficult. When machines begin to draft contracts or automate research, lawyers will experience this as a direct attack on their professional currency if they believe their only value is in their knowledge. Developments like AI are a threat because they're taking away that currency.

Interestingly, in our work, we often find that paralegals and legal operations professionals show greater openness to experimentation. Their identity is not as intertwined with their professional qualifications and knowledge as it is for lawyers. As their identity is not as threatened, they can see the pain points across processes, which can make them more open to creating innovation and improving effectiveness. This contrast underscores how identity and value are inseparable in shaping our response to AI.

The identity of the lawyer

A challenge for many lawyers dealing with the Exponential Age is this: if a machine can do fundamental parts of my job, what does that say about a core part of my identity – that of being a lawyer? One of the strengths of Lloyd and I working together as coaches in the legal sector is we bring different perspectives to this question, since Lloyd has been a lawyer and I have not.

It's this redefinition of what work will mean and who we are at work that is both the potential threat and opportunity of AI. It is also trying to process this that creates a struggle for our brains, according to Ashby. What AI conjures at a very fundamental level is the question of what it is to be human when something that is not starts to think and create almost like a human being and maybe – one day – will actually do so better.

The fundamental test for Artificial Intelligence is the Turing Test, named after computer pioneer Alan Turing. The Turing Test pits a machine against human competencies and qualities. It is not routinely being beaten by AI... yet. But that day will come.

When technology can produce the majority of a lawyer's work product better than a lawyer, what does that mean for that lawyer's identity and how they understand the world via their place and value in it? This creates fundamental questions around survivability and predictability.

When I wrote my PhD thesis many years ago on the work of the playwright Howard Barker, I noticed that most of Barker's characters were defined by the ability to reinvent themselves or not. This notion of self-reinvention, which was inspired by the work of the literary theorist Stephen Greenblatt and his study of the way Renaissance thinkers approached their identity in the world, is also very apt today in the world of work.[3] How we view ourselves and our relationship to the world is key to our adaptability and therefore our survival. One of the key challenges for lawyers in the Exponential Age is how to balance the uncertainty of reinvention with the desire for the certainty of the survival prediction mechanism.

The lawyer as survival prediction machine

Our primary function as humans is to be a survival prediction machine. This is how we did not become extinct thousands of years ago. Our brain, according to Ashby, is pretty much designed to fulfil this purpose and keep us from harm. But what has also been crucial to human development over the years is the balance between risk awareness and being able to seize opportunities.

Legal training is in complete alignment with risk awareness and aversion, but often less aligned with the ability and desire to seize opportunities. Understanding this has contributed to the design of many of the Exponential Age Mindset Attributes and our specific tools to address this – the Six Dimensions of Business Risk and Six Dimensions of Business Opportunity (see Chapter 12).

Ashby feels it is this perception of what constitutes a legal mindset developed by current legal education that means lawyers will be more at risk in the Exponential Age:

> *"Everything about legal training reinforces that primary objective. As a lawyer, we are taught to be risk averse through our legal training and*

rewarded for being risk averse in our practice. Everything is about using an existing template or way of working, because that's what has been proven to be a safe course of action before. And then you layer in on top of that the fact that being wrong as a lawyer could have serious consequences. Often it doesn't, but it could have, and it's drilled into lawyers that being wrong is therefore a terrible thing, in contrast to other professions such as engineering, where you can try and fail and test various things. Everything about legal training and practice is about reinforcing the brain's natural primary functioning of being a survival prediction machine. Anything that's new could be risky, and therefore don't do it."[4]

The creative aspect of designing solutions – failing and trying again – is fundamental to the mastery of new digital solutions like AI. Indeed, the most effective direction we have found for AI adoption is to play with it. This was the answer when we were children, and it doesn't change when we become adults. Similarly, in our training, Lloyd and I provide a playground for people to adopt and try out the Exponential Age Mindset Attributes and the aligned tools.

Being a risk-averse survival prediction machine only goes so far when you are in an age where change is going to happen with increasing speed and intensity. The awareness that we can't know or predict everything and must be able to make decisions with imperfect information will be needed to thrive. The best lawyers have always been able to role model these skills – what's going to change is that this ability will become a core skill for human lawyers, rather than just technical expertise and knowledge of a particular area of law.

Many of the mindsets and skillsets that we have identified as being aligned with leadership and effective development in the Exponential Age are those that can mitigate against the identity of the lawyer as survival prediction machine – being able to live with uncertainty (Joyful Tightrope); decision making under pressure with imperfect information (Joyful Tightrope, Agile Juggler, Chaos Converter); being able to pivot (Agile Juggler). Others also mitigate strongly against the identity of the lawyer as subject matter expert – taking ideas from different disciplines (Duality Master); being a generalist and seeing the big picture, not just the detail (Zoom Master).

Training for the Exponential Age

If AI is shifting identity and cognition, training must adapt accordingly. In our training, two approaches have proved particularly effective and, in discussion with Ashby, we have found an alignment in how we approach training and coaching with methods she uses and what is effective for our brains to adapt to change.

Opportunity versus challenge

This method invites participants to surface what they want to protect in their roles – their "anchors" – and what they wish to eliminate. Ashby defines this as headache versus happiness:

> *"Most of the things they want more of are things they don't have time to do because they're drowning in low-value, urgent tasks. That opens the opportunity: maybe AI could shift that balance."*

We often introduce this in our training and introduce the Exponential Age Mindset Attribute via our "Superpower you have and superpower you need for greater success".

We ask our participants in training to think about what their challenges are and what "superpowers" could help with these. This is the first step for us to build a bridge with new ways of looking at what people can do to be more effective in the Exponential Age. It falls into the framework of looking at exponential change via Ashby's "happiness versus headache" descriptor.

Exponential Age Attributes

Our framework uses nine attributes (as illustrated on p.10) designed to help people thrive in uncertainty. In a time of increased change and uncertainty, the "joy" comes from taking control and creating possibility – even if at times this is uncomfortable and challenging, it is also creative. The attributes focus on introducing the building blocks of control, creativity, and joy.

Joy and creativity are necessary

A final lesson is that joy and creativity are not optional extras – they are survival strategies. Joy is a neurological mechanism that offsets stress, builds resilience, and sustains long-term performance. Ashby notes:

> *"There's not a lot of joy being broadcast in the world right now. But creating the space and ability to switch into joy is what builds resilience."*

Equally, human creativity will be one of the greatest sources of value in an AI age. This creativity comes via diversity of thought in the broadest sense, including background and identity, but also of cognitive strengths and natural preferences.

When AI automates the generic, human uniqueness will become the ultimate differentiator. Says Ashby:

> *"You're not about to lose your job, but you do have to take an active, proactive stance of what it means for you. AI has access to, and can process, a volume of data that an individual human brain cannot. However, what AI doesn't have is the uniqueness baked into each individual human brain's "processing model" – every experience we have as an individual shapes what we think and what outputs we create. The way we make decisions, the way we innovate and come up with new ideas, is an aggregate of the specific individual experiences we have. It's how we leverage and grow our individual human diversity that is fundamental to our human value-add in a world of pervasive AI use."*[5]

This book and the training methods that it outlines are a way to ensure your legal team and legal function can embrace their human uniqueness and their ultimate differentiator.

Redefining value

AI is more than a technological shift – it is a redefinition of human value. For lawyers and other professionals, the challenge is not merely technical, but existential. Neuroscience shows us why fear and resistance are natural, yet also how resilience can be built – through naming uncertainty, reframing ambiguity, and strengthening cognitive flexibility.

Training programs like ours and Ashby's that help individuals protect what they value, let go of what drains them, and experiment with new attributes create the conditions to thrive. Above all, the future belongs to those who cultivate joy, creativity, and human super skills – the qualities machines cannot replicate.

References

1 For information on Dominique Ashby and her work see www.neuro@work.com
2 Dominique Ashby, in conversation with Catherine McGregor, 11 September 2025
3 Stephen Greenblatt, *Renaissance Self-Fashioning* (University of Chicago Press, 2005)
4 Dominique Ashby, in conversation with Catherine McGregor, 11 September 2025
5 Diversity in the workplace is a financial boost exactly because of this cognitive processing model diversity – more diverse groups of humans bring more innovative ideas.

Chapter 3:
Zoom Master – taking strategic oversight and focusing on detail

Changing your perspective is hard – but being able to do so may also be one of your greatest assets. Sometimes you need to look at the granular detail of a matter and sometimes you need to "zoom out" to see the bigger picture. This is the Zoom Master.

The power of perspective is something we have both learned more about as executive coaches. Too often, it is hard for clients to be able to see challenges from an alternative viewpoint or tell a story that differs from the narrative that is no longer serving them.

Most coaching clients we work with are leaders or aspiring leaders, who are also the focus of the work that we undertake as trainers or coaches. Increasingly, our work in this sphere has led us to realize that a significant shift in mindset and actions needs to take place to ensure that people are truly ready to both cope with the Exponential Age and also to maximize the potential of the digital and the human combined.

This is why the first Exponential Age Mindset we will focus on is that of Zoom Master. This attribute is all about perspective – about seeing the big picture but also knowing when you need to dive into specifics. What is most significant about Zoom Master is not the two different views of the world it gives, but the ability to move between the two – and to know when it is necessary or useful to switch. The secret of Zoom Master is in the movement between the perspectives.

Back in my performance days, I took part in a recreation of Hermann Nitsch's first Abreaction play.[1] Nitsch was a member of the Viennese Actionist school of art. He was influenced by both Ancient Greek drama and Catholic ritual in his art. This became increasingly extreme throughout his career, but his first Abreaction play was a little tamer.

Merriam-Webster defines abreaction as *"The expression and emotional discharge of unconscious material (such as a repressed idea or emotion) by verbalization"* and it is usually used in a therapeutic, rather than a dramatic, context.

The action as a performer involved periods of very highly controlled choreographed and conducted vocalization, which would then descend into abreaction – cathartic, uncontrolled physical movement and screaming. The longest episode of this was nine minutes. (This may not sound like a long time – but in the moment, it certainly *feels* like a long time!) The most interesting aspect of this experience was the move from abreaction back to the controlled performance. Something very interesting happened – emotionally – when you had to force your mind and body out of a lack of control into extreme control. The real talent for me as a performer lay not in either state, but in the ability to move between the two.

This is where the real skill in Zoom Master lies. The ability to know when to zoom in and zoom out is one that many lawyers we work with struggle to get to grips with. However, once they do, it can unlock many other leadership competencies for them and the ability to develop these in their teams. It is the movement *between* the two states and knowing when to bring each of them to the fore that is fundamental.

The need for Zoom Mastery in the Exponential Age

The ability to zoom fluidly between strategic ("zoom out") and detailed ("zoom in") perspectives is increasingly crucial in the Exponential Age.

Navigating exponential change requires both vision and agility. In a world defined by rapid and non-linear change, leaders must be able to envision future scenarios while continuously adapting their actions in real time. This dual capability ensures that long-term vision doesn't get lost in the immediacy of execution.

Institutions and their leaders must be capable of seeing the longterm vision (ten to 20 years ahead) and then also be able to pivot quickly into short-term actions (six-month initiatives), refining strategy through iterative learning.

But this is not easy. Humans are wired to think linearly, making it difficult to intuitively grasp exponential growth. This mismatch leads to under or over-estimation of technological progress and missed inflection points. A Zoom Master mindset helps counter these blind spots by enabling both broad framing and grounded, detail-oriented planning. Not being stuck in one viewpoint or the other but being able to shift as needed between the two.

Being aware of what we need to do and how we think is going to be even more significant as the use and capabilities of technologies such as AI increase. As technology automates routine cognitive tasks, essential human skills such as critical thinking, creative problem-solving, and independent judgment are at risk of decline (with measurable drops in ability over the past decades). The focus on mindsets and skillsets brought with the Exponential Age Mindset Attributes is a way of continually bringing self-awareness of *how* we process ideas as we process them.

You might notice in all the attributes there is a certain amount of recognition about how we are thinking and acting, which helps with mastery. Many of the attributes also have a strong sense of movement between different states. Metacognition – thinking about thinking – can significantly improve cognitive abilities. Which means, simply by thinking about thinking, we can become stronger thinkers. It's a bit like exercising and bringing awareness to that muscle to help focus effort. By consciously reflecting on your own thought processes, you can identify strengths and weaknesses, adjust strategies, and ultimately become a more effective learner and problem-solver.

Specifically, the practice of zooming – in both directions – helps maintain those cognitive muscles by alternating between broader, big-picture insight and detailed deep analysis.

Zoom Master combats cognitive bias

Zoom Mastery also helps counteract common cognitive biases by encouraging a regular shift in perspective. This back-and-forth allows individuals and teams to challenge assumptions, broaden their understanding, and recalibrate plans based on new information.

As technology increasingly automates routine tasks, there is a risk of cognitive skill decay. Engaging both high-level strategy and detail-oriented execution exercises critical thinking and preserves vital human judgment.

In the face of institutional rigidity, Zoom Mastery enables organizations to remain agile. It supports a balance between long-term strategic intent and short-term experimentation, fostering resilience and innovation in uncertain environments.

In an age where change happens at exponential speed, mastering the ability to zoom out for visionary strategy and zoom in for tactical execution is more than a useful cognitive tool – it's foundational. It enables leaders and teams to:

- Anticipate and shape the future rather than be overwhelmed by it.
- Continuously test and adapt plans in the short-term without losing sight of long term direction.
- Retain and grow cognitive and creative capabilities that technology alone cannot replicate.

Lawyers struggle with the Zoom

Most lawyers are taught to be completely detail orientated. Initial training focuses on skills such as drafting and much of a young lawyer's career is spent focusing on the detail and a view that is manifested via the lens of their specific legal practice area. This formative experience can be hard to shake off. It's less of an issue if lawyers stay in law firms, where the attention to detail and legal focus perspective are valued even as a lawyer advances up the ranks. In this aspect, law is one of the few professions where detailed technical expertise is often a substitute for other more expansive leadership skills.

However, when lawyers move in-house, the need to create a new perspective and the ability to move between the perspectives of detail and expansiveness is a necessity. Even for those lawyers who are subject matter experts in a large legal department, the ability to utilize Zoom Master will only enhance their efficacy with their business clients.

What's so hard about the Zoom?

For most in-house lawyers, it's about unlearning everything that went before. To quote leadership expert Marshall Goldsmith, "What got you here won't get you there".

Given that focus and detail are so highly thought of during training, this shift in perspective is almost like the red pill / blue pill moment in *The Matrix*, where a whole new reality is opened – one where everything you believe is turned on its head.

It's also the movement between the two. In-house lawyers, even general counsel, may be called upon at a moment's notice to think about specific legal details. Ensuring they do not get locked into this but can zoom out when needed is where success lies.

Cultivating your Zoom Master

This is where the competency of creativity and visioning come into play. Zoom Master is linked to the notion of purpose and being able to see how what we do day-to-day fits into the bigger picture of what your organization does and the purpose it serves. The father of modern management, Peter Drucker, stated that a company had to start with its purpose. Unless it has a purpose that is fulfilling a human need and has thought through that purpose, it can't succeed in the same way.

If employees of organizations have not thought through how they fit to the purpose of the company, they cannot succeed in the same way as if they had purpose. This is going to be even more true as the way in which companies do business, or how tasks are performed within that business, changes.

What does this mean in practice for lawyers? It means moving beyond the legal issues and understanding the broader business context. That might seem self-evident, but it is often astounding how many outside counsel approach a legal problem as if it existed in its own legal vacuum without the context of the client's operations and strategic objectives. When developing our senior associate and junior partner training program, Lloyd and I interviewed in-house counsel who instructed a substantial amount of law firms. The number one client service misstep they identified? Law firms not listening to and not understanding their clients.

This blinkered view is not confined to external lawyers, however. We have worked with in-house lawyers who are comfortable just focusing on the legal issues and not really exploring the broader context in which these legal issues sit. This siloed view can still work if you are a subject matter expert in a very large legal team, but increasingly that is also the role that is at greatest danger of being replaced by technology, especially AI.

This is where the attribute of Zoom Master is needed more than ever. The ability to master this movement between the big picture and the detail has always set lawyers apart, whether in-house or in private practice. However, as so many of the repetitive mundane aspects of lawyering get taken over by machines, being trapped in a silo of drafting legal documents won't cut it.

Kevin van Tonder has worked as a general counsel and now consults to a range of legal departments. He has a breadth of vision of what the in-house legal profession looks like, particularly in terms of its current adaptability to new ways of doing things including AI. For Kevin, the prerequisite to success – what we call Zoom Master – is being able to look out of the furrow you're ploughing to see the whole field.

Why will this be so fundamental? Mainly because AI tools will be ploughing the furrow better than you can but won't be able to shift between viewing the field and the furrow as well. They also won't be able to make sense of the interrelationship in a nuanced context. It is this agility of movement between these different ways of seeing issues where human brains still have a significant advantage over AI.

I don't want to set this up as a dichotomy between AI and human. The promise of the future is both working together, with AI as a tool to maximize the unique capacities of human perception and understanding. I am vehemently opposed to any discourse that positions the lawyer against AI. It is not a contest but a collaboration.

Starting with why

What is at the heart of Zoom Master is understanding the purpose of what you do. How your details fit into the big picture or your small cog makes the whole machine run. We have noticed that strategic mindset, which is the zoom out mode of Zoom Master, can feel inaccessible to some coaching and training clients. They believe that unless they are in the C-Suite they can't display strategic thinking. That is, of course, wrong. As with leadership, these are human competencies that we can display at any moment, in any role. In fact, the sooner we start, the easier it is when these become the main aspect of what we do. Sadly, too much of the corporate world still siloes these off as only the purview of the select few. Because of this lack of focus and training, even those who are the anointed and given the mantle of leadership are often woefully underprepared.

Simon Sinek's seminal business book *Start With Why*[2] was one of the first to explore how purpose can be a differentiator in marketing and engagement. His thesis was that those companies that have a fully formed sense of purpose as to their existence (their "why") will always be able to connect with their markets more effectively than those who just focus on what they do. This echoes Peter Drucker's thoughts nearly 50 years before. However, we believe that starting with why will take on even more resonance as we move into the Exponential Age of AI.

We have found that in our training and development an understanding of how what you do fits into the bigger picture (including the "why") is fundamental in connecting people to a more strategic mindset. This is the first stage in getting to grips with your Zoom Master capabilities. But how do you develop a strategic mindset?

Accessing your strategic mind

You may be closer than you think. The key is being open and curious as to how everything fits together. The blocker to a strategic mindset is working in a silo and only seeing what you do as a finite task in and of itself. To start, you need to be focused on the end point. What are we trying to achieve here?

In the broadest ongoing sense, this is the purpose of your organization and how it connects in its biggest way to what the company does and how it makes a difference in the world.

Sinek's famous definition of Apple's "why" was "Challenging the status quo, thinking differently, and creating beautifully designed products".[3] Think also about Patagonia's "We're in business to save our home planet".

A starting point is being curious about what your company does and asking questions to aid your understanding. There's a two-way perspective to the fundamental mindset change needed in the legal profession and in business that needs to be upheld by both lawyers and their internal clients to understand what they do as beyond just service delivery – beyond being reactive and incurious to being proactive and highly curious. It's that curiosity that is key here – asking questions and actively listening to the answers. Asking clients why they want to do something and what they want to achieve.

Why we are doing what we do

In training leaders, we often get asked the question, "How can I be more strategic?". The easiest answer to this is, how can you take every possible challenge, opportunity, and solution to not just fix the immediate issue at hand but consider the biggest perspective of the implications of this? Not just, "How will this help my team in the legal department?" but "How will it help the whole legal department? How will it help the business? How will it help the entire organization? How will it help the end user?" If lawyers start using AI tools in a legal department, what difference will that make to the individual? What difference will it make to their team? What difference will it make to the legal department? What difference will it make to the business? What difference will it make to the end consumer? Extrapolating in this way helps get you to a more strategic worldview and may give you a different perspective on the original issue. This is the power of Zoom Master in action.

When training a group of paraprofessionals, we used a well-known root cause analysis exercise called Five Whys and a Big So What. It's one that can be used in a training or team-building setting, but also one that you as an individual can use when faced with a challenge to give you a more strategic perspective.

To start, take the initial challenge or problem, state it as it is, and ask why. Continue with each piece of information, drilling down with whys. The traditional exercise has five iterations of asking why but these could be less or more depending on the problem.

- Contracts are taking too long to turn around.
  Why is that?

- Because the lawyers do not have all the information they need to complete the contracts.
  Why is that?
- The business does not communicate the information to the lawyers.
  Why is that?
- The business does not know the range of information needed all the time.
  Why is that?
- The legal department and the business clients are not communicating about some of the key fundamentals of the contracting process. *[This is the aha moment – you can stop asking why.]*
- *The big so what [i.e. what we'll do about it]*: Legal and the business unit could undertake a collaboration with the aim of developing a contract template intake form to make this process more efficient.
- *The result:* Faster turnaround time for contracts, sales realized faster, and profits realized quicker.

This process is explored further in the case study in chapter 16.

Asking the right questions

As AI develops, we need to be able to understand *why* we are asking it to do what we are asking it to do. The worst adoption of AI is when it's AI for AI's sake, with no clear determination of the reasons for it being used. The fundamental of "start with why" has not been adhered to. We will also need to be sure we are asking the right questions.

Hal Gregerson of MIT Sloan School of Management feels that the right questions are just as important, if not more so, than the right answers. Gregerson believes that the power and privilege of the C-suite can insulate leaders from internal trouble, external signals, and important insights. This "CEO bubble" means there is a disconnect for leaders, which can become dangerous when it prevents them from recognizing warning signals such as a crisis or when a change in direction is needed. It may even prevent them from taking advantage of a once-in-a-lifetime opportunity.[4]

This predicament prevents leaders from getting a true sense of corporate performance, innovation, culture, morale, outcomes, and other critically important issues. Gregerson's research showed that it's the questions that leaders didn't know to ask that often come back to haunt them. These unanticipated risks – or "unknown unknowns" – are business threats that can come out of nowhere.

Unknown threats can be uncovered by insightful questions. In the age of AI, asking the right question takes on an even more compelling edge as how we direct AI and how it learns depends on the questions we ask. There are numerous examples of leaders who found the answer to a serious challenge by reframing the questions they asked, and those who did not ask the right questions. When Steve Jobs returned to Apple in 1997, the company was near bankruptcy, with a bloated and unprofitable product line. Instead of asking, "How do we compete with Microsoft and other PC makers across all product categories?" Jobs reframed the question to, "What core products do we build best, and which ones should we eliminate?".[5]

This reframing led to a drastically simplified product matrix, focusing on four core computers – two desktops and two portables, divided into consumer and professional versions. This simplification eventually led Apple to create entirely new products, like the iPod, by reframing the problem of digital music from, "How do we sell more CDs?" to "How do people want to consume music in the digital age?"

In 2000, Netflix offered to sell itself to Blockbuster for $50 million, but the offer was laughed off by CEO John Antioco. Blockbuster was focusing on how to protect its established model, based on actual sites where customers went in to browse DVDs and rent the physical product. However, even under its earlier iteration of mail-order DVDs, Netflix was already asking, "How do we deliver movies to customers in the most convenient way possible?".

Lawyers and questions

Anyone who has watched lawyers on TV shows – where they are always on trial or conducting depositions (because that just makes for better TV than someone drafting a contract for the 20th time!) would assume that lawyers are great at asking questions.

However, we would argue that many lawyers are not good at asking a question in the spirit of curiosity and creativity, because too often a lawyer's question is predicated on already knowing the answer or wanting to lead the person being questioned to the answer you want.

Unlocking your Zoom Master with the Four Zones of Curiosity

This is a tool that we have used in training and coaching to take leaders through the various stages of an idea, rather than focusing purely on the detail or indeed just on the biggest picture view. It is, therefore, incredibly helpful in unlocking the movement aspect of Zoom Master and the balance between strategy and execution at its center.

Zone 1 **Known and met** *Focus is on my role and my team.* Known needs of GC/manager. Current projects. What I do now. Characterized by a siloed view. Reactive, detail-orientated mindset.	**Zone 2** **Known and unmet** *Focus is on my team and expanding what I do now within expected parameters that can help the entire legal team.* Known and unmet needs of GC/manager. Future projects in my sight. What I know I need to do. Peeking out of my silo to look at others around me in my legal team. Reactive but taking time to step back and look at the bigger picture.
Zone 3 **Unknown and unmet** *Focus on opportunities for the entire legal team and how they relate to the business.* Unknown and unmet needs of GC. Future projects I am not aware of. Connected view across the legal team and business stakeholders. View is looking at the legal team and how it relates to business then how my role connects to that. Strategic and operational.	**Zone 4** **Unknown and unmet** *Focus on the business and what I can do to provide strategic advances to the business.* Unknown and unmet needs of the business. Future strategies that I am not aware of. Focus on the business. View of what the business opportunities are and can be. Strategic and visionary.

Figure 8: The Four Zones of Curiosity. Source: Chief Legal Executive

- Zone 1 – today's projects.
- Zone 2 – tomorrow's projects that I am aware of, and my manager is aware of. These are tomorrow's achievements.
- Zone 3 – tomorrow's unknown projects. Uncommunicated and unmet are therefore tomorrow's challenges.
- Zone 4 – tomorrow's opportunities, currently unknown and unmet but offering the biggest strategic gains. Literally seeing around corners.

As technology, including AI, becomes more able to execute a greater range of routine tasks, the arena where humans will still have the biggest advantage is in thinking more strategically. It is also this sort of mindset that will allow humans to most effectively deploy AI and other such tools.

Typical in-house legal teams who do the basics of commercial contracting, litigation, and compliance rights, are fungible. This may seem harsh. They do good jobs, but if one leaves tomorrow, I can find another to slot in quite easily. GCs and legal teams who do the above well and can also slot this operational effectiveness into a strategic worldview focused on what adds value and creates a return for the business, are very rare.

This may seem counter-intuitive, but many of those who are suddenly jumping onto the Gen AI bandwagon are in this fungible category. They are not innovative. They have been at a loss as to how to drive the strategic value of their team in the business (as described above), so Gen AI has become the straw to cling to. It is a technology-first approach that can never end in real success.

When we coach clients through this transition, we find a significant part of the mindset shift in becoming an effective general counsel is the ability to understand how what their "work" looks like has changed. It is not merely performing the role of a lawyer with additional leadership functions – it is performing the role of a leader where there may be occasional legal, compliance, and governance questions. The challenge for many newly minted general counsel is not getting caught in a cycle of increasing reactivity and being unable to let go of the doing that will not allow them to even see beyond Zone 1 into Zone 2, let alone Zone 4.

It is the ability to move between the different zones from detail to big picture strategy (and to know when each is needed) that is fully at work in Zoom Master – not being stuck in one place or another. This is where the notion of why and how or purpose and execution and understanding the interplay between the two is vital. On a practical basis, what I see aiding coaching clients in this mastery is the ability to understand the issues but also to delegate effectively. Meaning you could execute something yourself, but you choose not to and also trust the different ideas and creativity that others can bring to the issues.

For more on the Four Zones of Curiosity, see chapter 13.

Amazon's rapid growth under Jeff Bezos demonstrates a powerful balance of long-term vision and operational detail, or the movement of Zoom Master in action. Bezos famously maintains a "Day 1" philosophy, emphasizing a focus on customers and constant innovation to avoid complacency.

The company's long-term vision was to create "the everything store" – an e-commerce platform that continually adds new services like Amazon Web Services (AWS) and the Kindle ecosystem. To achieve this vision, Bezos obsessed over the customer experience, monitoring reviews and relentlessly improving operational details such as logistics and delivery speed. He is known for diving into the weeds to solve specific customer issues and setting a company culture focused on measurable performance. That is: he nimbly zoomed out to the big picture (the purpose of becoming the "everything store") and zoomed into the details when looking to how to achieve this. This is the Zoom Master in action.

What this looks like for legal departments in the 21st century is legal leaders who understand the strategic breadth of their own and their teams' roles – not just legal but risk and ethics (zooming out to the big picture). However, these are also leaders who understand the importance of operational efficiency in achieving the breadth of this vision, and most crucially are empowering others to make this happen (zooming into the details).

It is this blend of vision and operationalization – and the ability to switch focus between the two – that I see at play in those legal leaders who are most committed to developing their people for success in the Exponential Age. It is about not seeing the human mindset and skillset as separate from technological and process advances, but rather knowing they are inextricably intertwined.

References

1 This anecdote should signal to you, the reader, that this is not going to be your typical law and business book. One of the key competencies needed in the Exponential Age is a creative mindset and the ability to apply knowledge from one area and apply it creatively to another. Expect examples from our diverse career paths, from sports to publishing to performance to executive coaching – even Beyoncé gets a mention! That ability to apply knowledge across areas is discussed

more in the chapter eight on Duality Master, but you will need to start using it a little bit now.

2 Simon Sinek, *Start with Why: How Great Leaders Inspire Everyone to Take Action*, 2009, Portfolio.

3 *Ibid.*, pp. 37-45.

4 MIT News: https://news.mit.edu/2019/hal-gregersen-says-questions-are-answer-0517, 17 May 2019

5 "The Amazing Story of How Steve Jobs took Apple from Near Bankruptcy To Billions in 13 years." *Business Insider*, 27 October 2010: www.businessinsider.com/how-steve-jobs-took-apple-from-near-bankruptcy-to-billions-in-13-years-2011-1

Chapter 4:
Joyful Tightrope – being comfortable with ambiguity and not knowing all the answers

This is the heightened level of comfort with uncertainty – maybe even allowing uncertainty to bring joy. Uncertainty is a defining feature of change, as we may think we know how change will work out, but can never be completely sure. As the Exponential Age is defined by increasing change, it follows that being okay with uncertainty will be a crucial skillset.

A "joyful tightrope walk" often refers to the iconic performance of French high-wire artist Philippe Petit, who walked between the Twin Towers in New York City in August 1974. While his feat was dangerous and illegal, it was also a celebratory, improvisational dance that captured the city's imagination. Petit spent 45 minutes walking, hopping, spinning, and lying down on a wire strung 1,350 feet in the air. He later described it as a "joyful adventure" and an "impossible" undertaking.[1] The memory of the walk is a powerful, joyful counterpoint to the 2001 tragedy that destroyed the Towers.

Beyond Petit, the phrase "joyful tightrope" can also refer to the psychological and philosophical idea of finding cheerfulness and balance in precarious situations. As philosopher Friedrich Nietzsche noted, life is often a tightrope walk where one must either stand or fall. Embracing that with a sense of joy is the underlying meaning of the phrase. The joy may not be obvious from the situation but it's up to our mindset and skillset changes to make it happen and take our own control over it.

My most "Joyful Tightrope" experience was taking up indoor rock climbing. As someone who does not like heights, this involved a mix of fear, uncertainty, elation, and joy. The juxtaposition of discomfort and achievement heightened the joy more than if it came from a place of comfort and ease.

So, what are the skills needed to lean into this age of uncertainty?

Understand your own relationship to uncertainty

Self-awareness is a necessary component for any leadership journey – whether you have an official leadership title or not. It's also a fundamental starting point for leaders who want to lean into the Joyful Tightrope. Do you cope well with uncertainty? Do you cope better with it in some situations over others? In his prior experience as the creator of *Chief Legal Executive* magazine 25 years ago, Lloyd had to simultaneously navigate three areas of high uncertainty – sourcing consistent articles, creating a need in the mind of general counsel, and convincing advertisers to pay. By balancing the vision of a "Harvard Business Review for GCs" with the ambiguity of an unproven market, he showed how to move from a need for guaranteed answers to embracing the venture to ensure the publication's success.

As humans, we generally do not like uncertainty. Our brains are hardwired to prefer routine over chaos. However, some people are less attuned to routine and prefer the realm of uncertainty, and there are varying degrees of comfort along the spectrum.

There is a relationship between how we feel about uncertainty and the specific event we are dealing with. This can be explained by the concept of the spheres of influence. There are three spheres of influence:

1. Control – what we can control and can do something about.
2. Influence – what we can't directly control but where we can influence directly.
3. Concern – where we have no direct control, and we may have minimal influence.

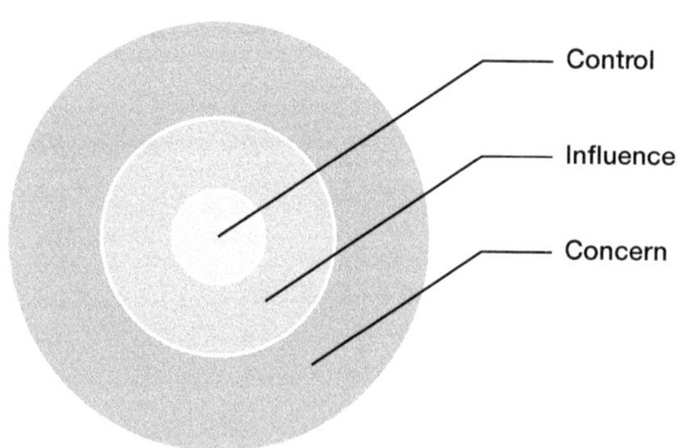

Figure 9: The three spheres of influence. Source: Chief Legal Executive.

As an example, let's take climate change. In the biggest picture sense, I may not be able to directly influence this because of historical actions of others and the attitudes of big business and governments. I can be concerned about this, but singlehandedly it's unlikely I could persuade a big oil company to stop drilling or a government to change its policies.

Influence: I can, however, write to my local representative who may take notice more than a national government might. I can try to influence those around me; maybe I can persuade my office to go paper-free.

Control: I can recycle more. Maybe I can buy an electric car or get rid of my car altogether. I can donate to climate change groups.

In our experiences as coaches, we find that the less awareness an individual has around their own relationship to uncertainty, the greater challenges they may have accepting what they cannot control and being okay with focusing their efforts on what they can.

In his coaching practice, Lloyd sees new general counsels of global departments struggle to simultaneously navigate a new Board, C-Suite, and diverse regional crises. By balancing the heavy scrutiny and infinitesimal margin for error with the reality that information is always incomplete, he shows them how to move from the paralysis of needing perfect answers to the confidence of making high-stakes decisions in the gray.

Embracing uncertainty – acknowledging the elephant in the room

In training and development, a core practice is taking something we have little or no certainty about and then practicing embracing this fact. This will inevitably involve failing at this, then gradually becoming more proficient before finally being comfortable with it.

In many of the leadership courses we run, we ask participants to pick three of the Exponential Age attributes to work on and apply more in their role. Generally, these will be the three attributes the participants feel the least competent at, and that they also see will have a specific benefit in helping them develop as a leader.

In a course we ran in 2024 with a group of leaders from a range of companies, one of the participants in my group was working on Joyful Tightrope.

This leader was managing a contracts team in a legal department whose very function and purpose was under debate – partly due to specific Exponential Age changes in how the legal team (and the wider company) was deploying technical tools.

Our leader freely admitted that she did not deal well with change or uncertainty. She did not like operating in a space where she did not have all the answers. If she did not have a definitive answer, she would rather not say anything.

Her instinct in this time of fundamental uncertainty for her team was to ignore the question until there was a definitive decision and pronouncement from leadership. Yet this was a massive "elephant in the room" for her and her team if she ignored it.

As a result of leaning into Joyful Tightrope as part of our course, she decided to do things differently. At the next team meeting, she led with the unsaid and raised the fact that the team's future was up for discussion. To her surprise, her team began to spontaneously brainstorm what different versions of the future would like and where they could most effectively pivot.

By confronting uncertainty, the leader and her team were able to exert some control and agency over it. She brought the different ideas that resulted from the brainstorming to her leaders, which was ultimately central in determining how the team was reconfigured.

Finding the joy in your Joyful Tightrope

Leading through uncertainty demands emotional resilience – the ability to stay calm and composed amid chaos. Emotional resilience is the process of managing one's emotional reactions, especially under stress or threat. As humans, our natural response where there is something different and potentially challenging is to activate the flight or fight mode. Yes, this might have originally been deployed because the large beast you were hunting for food was about to turn on you, but now it's more likely to be triggered by an email from the CEO! Now we could potentially add the freeze mode – the impulse to simply ignore the fact something is happening. Nevertheless, our brain responds in a similar way, whether the impetus is an attack from a predatory beast or an uncomfortable email.

Neuroscience shows that effective emotional regulation depends on the balance between the brain's amygdala and prefrontal cortex (PFC). The amygdala acts as an "alarm system", triggering fear and stress responses, while the prefrontal cortex is responsible for reasoning, self-control, and dampening excessive emotional reactions. In high-pressure situations, a well-regulated PFC can counteract impulsive fight-or-flight (or freeze) impulses from the amygdala, preventing an emotional hijack and enabling clear thinking. Leaders who master this skill project calm and confidence, helping their teams feel secure during turbulent times.

In uncertain environments, uncontrolled anxiety or anger in a leader can spread to the team, undermining morale and decision-making. Conversely, a leader who stays emotionally steady can think more clearly and instill confidence in others. Regulating stress also builds long-term resilience – the capacity to bounce back from setbacks – by reducing the harmful effects of chronic cortisol (the stress hormone) on the brain. Over time, practicing emotional regulation strengthens neural pathways that make you more resilient under future stress.

How to develop emotional regulation and reframe uncertainty:

- *Breathing techniques*. In moments of acute stress, controlled breathing (for instance, slow deep breaths, the golden thread breath, or box breathing) can rapidly engage the parasympathetic nervous system to calm the body. This lowers the heart rate and cortisol levels, giving your brain a chance to think. Taking even a 60-second breathing break before approaching a challenge rooted in uncertainty and is potentially stress-provoking can ensure your response is more well balanced.
- *Cognitive reappraisal*. This is the habit of reframing stressful situations in a more positive or neutral light. For example, instead of viewing a sudden change as a threat, see it as a learning opportunity. Neuroscience research supports reappraisal as an effective strategy that engages the brain's cognitive centers to reinterpret negative stimuli, thereby reducing emotional intensity. Leaders can practice by consciously challenging their initial interpretations and asking, "What else could this situation mean?" or "How can I grow from this?". This is a technique that Lloyd and I use frequently in coaching. When a client raises a challenge, we ask them to find the opportunity in it. What's another way of looking at this? If we take the example above of the contracts team in flux, a way of reframing that could be, "This is a great opportunity for the team to re-evaluate its role and pivot to new ways of working that will contribute to its effectiveness".
- *Affect labeling*. Simply naming your feelings can activate the brain's language centers and dampen the amygdala's response (e.g., "I am anxious about this deadline my CEO just imposed on the legal team"). This labeling of emotions creates psychological distance and helps the PFC regain control.
- *Use a framework*. Understanding your relationship to uncertainty through a framework of understanding such as the Exponential Age Attributes and Joyful Tightrope creates both objective distance from unregulated emotions and allows you to start reframing the experience. "This is not unbearable uncertainty but an opportunity for me to lean into my attribute of Joyful Tightrope."

By practicing these behaviors, leaders strengthen their emotional regulation. Over time, the brain becomes better at managing stress and recovering from adversity – a hallmark of resilient leadership. A leader who is centered and resilient can make thoughtful decisions in chaos and serve as an emotional anchor for their organization.

Cognitive flexibility and adaptability

In a fast-changing world – exactly the situation posed by the Exponential Age – cognitive flexibility is a critical leadership asset. This is the mental ability to switch between different ideas or approaches and to adapt one's strategy based on new information. It is the brain's agility that allows us to solve problems in novel situations. Neuroscience research shows that cognitive flexibility engages the prefrontal cortex and other neural circuits involved in learning and decision-making. High cognitive flexibility allows leaders to rapidly recognize when a plan isn't working and pivot to an alternative solution. This capability is crucial for navigating uncertainty, because it helps leaders learn under unpredictable conditions and negotiate complex problems.

Importantly, cognitive flexibility can be learned. Unlike raw IQ or working memory (which are more fixed), flexible thinking can be strengthened through deliberate practice. Entrepreneurs tend to have greater cognitive flexibility than other managers, helping them adapt and make decisions in risky, changing environments. In our experience working with lawyers across multiple companies and sectors, Lloyd and I have found that lawyers who are used to working in early-stage companies with an entrepreneurial mindset are much more likely to be able to tap into this mindset than those who work in very mature companies.

What accounts for this difference? Lawyers in less mature sectors often have to be able to work across a range of areas very flexibly as staffing is lean; they need to make decisions quickly; they need to work within the framework of constraints while able to think differently if the asks from the business are new or novel. This all means a set of circumstances that are more likely to place those in-house lawyers in a mindset to be able to deal with uncertainty.

The good news is that you do not have to immediately go and work for a start-up if you are not in one! Anyone can improve this skill by challenging the brain in new ways. Building cognitive flexibility also taps into the brain's capacity for neuroplasticity – the ability to form new neural connections throughout life. By pushing yourself to think outside habitual patterns, you essentially "rewire" your brain to be more adaptable. These are the same sorts of skills we need to apply to the aptitudes of Duality Master and Chaos Converter.

The Can If tool, which we discuss in chapter 14, is a significant help in building cognitive flexibility by focusing on what is possible in a situation, rather than what is impossible.

Exercises such as "Five whys and a so what" are also helpful in challenging our status quo and ensuring that our brains are more flexible in problem solving. This root cause analysis exercise identifies the root cause of a problem by repeatedly asking "Why?" with a "So What?" analysis that assesses the implications and impact of a situation or decision.

Why cognitive flexibility matters

When technology and market conditions evolve exponentially, leaders must continuously adjust strategies, learn new skills, and even unlearn outdated assumptions. A flexible mindset enables quicker adaptation to change and more creative problem-solving. Without it, leaders risk becoming mentally rigid – unable to escape old paradigms – which can be disastrous in a landscape where yesterday's playbook no longer works. As Barbara Jacquelyn Sahakian, professor of clinical neuropsychology at the University of Cambridge in England, noted, "The need to make good decisions under uncertainty is becoming exceedingly important" in modern business.[2] Cognitive flexibility underpins that ability by allowing leaders to update their thinking dynamically.

How to develop cognitive flexibility

- *Embrace lifelong learning.* Commit to regularly learning new skills or knowledge outside your comfort zone. Taking on a new domain (such as learning a language or mastering new software) challenges the brain to form fresh neural pathways. Research suggests that such "novel learning" activities can improve cognitive flexibility, as they force your brain to adapt to unfamiliar rules and patterns. Make it a habit to pursue a new micro-skill or topic each quarter – it will keep your brain in learning mode. It can also be a source of joy!
- *Diverse experiences.* Seek out diverse perspectives and experiences. Engaging with people from different backgrounds, rotating through different job roles, or simply changing your routine can all broaden your thinking. These "natural" methods of challenging your brain – like

exposing yourself to diverse social interactions – are thought to indirectly train cognitive flexibility. Encourage your team to do the same by cross-training in different functions or brainstorming with colleagues in other industries.

- *Brain-training games.* Some evidence indicates that adaptive brain training games or puzzles can help boost cognitive flexibility. For example, strategy games that force you to frequently change tactics might exercise the mental switching function. This could include the exercise to stimulate creativity suggested by neurologist Balder Onarheim, who suggests trying to think of as many different unconnected words as possible while performing a routine task such as brushing your teeth. While the research is ongoing, it doesn't hurt to occasionally challenge yourself with memory games, logic puzzles, or apps designed to stimulate quick thinking. Treat them as one tool among many – real-world learning and experience are even more effective.
- *Practice perspective shifting.* Deliberately challenge your own assumptions by viewing problems from multiple angles. This is exactly what the Can If framework and the Five Whys exercise do. A framework such as Can If trains cognitive agility by preventing tunnel vision. You can also roleplay scenarios – e.g., imagine how a scientist, an artist, or an engineer might approach your business problem differently. Such perspective shifts engage your frontal lobe in exploring alternative neural pathways, enhancing mental flexibility.
- *Adopt a growth mindset.* Cultivating a growth mindset – the belief that abilities can be developed – will support your cognitive flexibility. Neuroscience has shown that believing in the potential for improvement encourages the brain to rewire itself (greater neuroplasticity) when learning. This can be a challenge for lawyers when leading because of the focus on legal learning and the push towards specialist knowledge versus continuous learning.

By practicing these habits, leaders essentially "train the brain" to be more adaptable. Over time, you'll find it easier to adjust your thinking in the face of new data or setbacks. In an Exponential Age, mental agility is going to be as important as any technical skill. A leader with cognitive flexibility can pivot strategy quickly, innovate on the fly, and guide their team through change with agility and creativity. Hence the power of the Exponential Age Mindset Attributes.

Decision-making under stress

The Joyful Tightrope attribute is about comfort with uncertainty. Uncertainty often comes with high stress and time-pressured decisions. Whether it's a sudden market disruption or a critical operational failure, leaders must be able to make sound decisions under pressure. This is easier said than done – when we are stressed, our brains undergo physiological changes that can degrade decision quality. Neuroscience research shows that acute stress triggers the fight-or-flight response governed by the amygdala, flooding the body with adrenaline and cortisol. In this state, the prefrontal cortex's executive functions (problem-solving, memory, reasoning) often suffer, as energy is diverted to survival systems. In other words, stress can literally cloud our thinking, leading to rushed or poorly thought-out choices. Chronic high stress can even keep the brain in a state of hyper-vigilance that impairs strategic thinking.

Why it matters: In the Exponential Age, leaders frequently face critical decisions with incomplete information – this is something lawyers hate because it goes against the very rubric of their training. The added pressure can introduce cognitive biases or panic, causing leaders to overreact or freeze. A leader who hasn't developed strategies for decision-making under stress might fall prey to an "amygdala hijack", where emotional impulses override rational judgment. This can result in regrettable decisions – for example, reacting defensively to a sudden change rather than seeing an emerging opportunity. On the other hand, leaders who manage their stress response can maintain clarity of mind when it counts most. They make decisions based on analysis and creative thinking, not primal fear. Given that uncertainty is inevitable, the ability to think clearly under stress is a defining skill of effective leadership.

In our work together we have found that lawyers who are very focused on expertise in their subject matter whilst also being leaders will struggle more with this than those who have made the leap to a significant general counsel role. This is partly because the nature of the general counsel role has shifted so much away from a legal focus that those who adopt that narrow heuristic approach will rarely now be as successful as those who are more adaptable and able to find their own joy in Joyful Tightrope and make decisions in uncertainty. You must be willing to know when to let go of that narrow focus to truly succeed as a leader. This is even more crucial in the Exponential Age.

A lawyer may experience an "amygdala hijack" by reacting defensively to a suggestion and seeing it only through the lens of legal risk, rather than an emerging opportunity. The legal risk is the place of comfort and the learned response, rather than leaning into quick decision making and seeing opportunity. But this is not an either/or situation. The best legal leaders can use their legal knowledge as a grounding but also be able to respond in the moment and weigh the opportunity and the risk adequately.

How to improve decision-making under stress

The goal is twofold – manage the stress response in the moment and build capacity over time for handling pressure. Below are actionable techniques supported by neuroscience and behavioral research. The experience of uncertainty in action may be like a slow burning that flares up at times in your consciousness and induces feelings of panic, especially if you are someone who really values certainty and routine. Some of these techniques are also used in chapter 5 on Chaos Converter, which is linked to the skill of Joyful Tightrope.

- *Mindfulness and centering techniques.* Just as mindfulness aids emotional regulation, it also directly supports better decisions under stress. Taking a mindful pause – a few deep breaths, or a brief meditation – before deciding can prevent knee-jerk reactions. Physiologically, this reduces amygdala activity and cortisol levels, allowing the prefrontal cortex to regain control. Even in a crisis, a 30-second breathing exercise or a moment of silence can reset your brain. Train yourself to respond to stress with a calming ritual (like a slow inhale/exhale), which signals to your brain that you are safe to think.
- *Sleep and recovery.* Protect your decision-making capacity by prioritizing sleep and recovery time. Lack of sleep dramatically impairs the prefrontal cortex, akin to operating in a constant state of stress. In contrast, adequate sleep restores neural functioning and emotional balance. During intense periods, it's tempting to cut sleep for extra work hours, but that is a false economy – you risk making errors in judgment that could cost far more. Treat sleep as essential brain maintenance. Short naps or relaxation breaks during the day can also recharge your mental acuity when stress drains it. It will also help you be better with quick decisions when needed.
- *Planning.* One way to handle high-stakes decisions or uncertainty is to prepare for them. Conduct exercises with your team – imagine a project has failed and brainstorm reasons why. This strategy, recommended by psychologists, helps identify potential pitfalls and

countermeasures in a calm setting. Similarly, scenario planning forces you to consider various futures (good and bad) before they happen. By mentally rehearsing challenging scenarios, you reduce shock factor and engage your analytical brain ahead of time. In the "elephant in the room" section earlier, we looked at when the leader of a contracts team encouraged her team to consider a range of different futures in the face of uncertainty.

- *Decision frameworks and checklists.* Under stress, cognitive load increases and we may overlook important factors. Using structured decision frameworks (such as the Can If framework) or checklists can offload some mental burden. Pilots and emergency surgeons use checklists for this very reason.
- *Build a support network and delegate.* Don't shoulder big decisions alone when under extreme pressure. Neuroscience shows that social support can buffer stress responses – talking through a problem with a trusted colleague literally activates brain circuits that calm the stress reaction. Moreover, smart delegation prevents cognitive overload. Leaders who leverage their team (delegating tasks or seeking input) can lighten their mental load and gain perspective. This was clearly seen in action in the contracts team example where brainstorming the uncertainty with her team allowed the leader to get buy in and to access a range of ideas and possible futures she had not thought of.

By combining stress management techniques with good decision practices, leaders can significantly improve their judgment under fire. Remember that stress itself is not always bad – it can energize action – but it must be managed. Aim for an optimal zone where you feel alert but not panicked. Using these approaches, you train your brain to stay in "thinking mode" rather than survival mode when challenges arise. Over time, your neural networks adapt, and you become the leader who stays cool and makes wise choices, even in the toughest of times.

Empathy and psychological safety

Leading in uncertain times isn't just about one's own mental skills – it's also about supporting your people through change. This makes empathy and the creation of psychological safety indispensable leadership skills.

Empathy is the ability to understand and share the feelings of others, while psychological safety refers to an environment where people feel safe to express themselves and take risks without fear of blame. Neuroscience has shed light on the social aspects of leadership – when people feel trusted and safe, their brains produce oxytocin, a hormone that facilitates bonding and cooperation.

On the other hand, uncertainty and fear elevate cortisol, the stress hormone, which can shut down trust, impair decision-making, and hinder collaboration. Uncertainty will generally always cause stress and therefore impact a leader's ability to foster trust and psychological safety. How this uncertainty is handled can make the difference between a team that adapts and thrives, and one that fractures under stress.

We were involved in training and coaching a legal team where the broader organization had introduced a 'reorganization strategy' but where the details would not be announced for some time. This engendered a lot of uncertainty and fear throughout the team. It was noteworthy how the way this affected different teams in the organization was often down to the skill in which their individual team leader was able to lean into their Joyful Tightrope, show empathy, and create trust. Coaching a range of lawyers from across this large legal team, I saw clearly how much or how little their leader's ability to find the joy in the Joyful Tightrope would affect the way in which the team members coped with their own uncertainties.

Why it matters: Rapid change often brings anxiety among employees – fear of the unknown, fear of failure, or fear for job security. If these fears aren't addressed, they can erode team cohesion and innovation. People in low-trust, high-stress environments have measurably lower creativity and problem-solving ability. In contrast, high-trust teams handle uncertainty far better – they communicate openly, support one another, and are willing to experiment and learn (since they aren't paralyzed by fear of blame). High trust and support have been identified as the number one predictor of team performance in studies by Google.[3] If trust is there, it will create higher performing teams than if it isn't. It seems obvious but it still amazes me how many teams and organizations focus on the "head down, getting work done" approach, rather than on how a team can work together effectively.

For in-house lawyers, uncertainty and a lack of psychological safety may mean teams are more likely to over-index on risk. They may feel hampered in decision making or being able to give an opinion to stakeholders for fear of getting it wrong. This has led to legal teams being complicit in massive corporate failures – as much by being paralyzed by inaction as doing anything illegal or unethical. In the UK's Post Office scandal, for example, a frequently asked question was: Where were the internal lawyers and what were they doing?

For leaders, this means that soft skills such as listening and showing empathy are not "nice to have" – they are mission-critical in uncertain times. By keeping the team's stress in check and trust levels high, you create the conditions for agility and resilience. In essence, empathy from the leader counteracts the negative effects of uncertainty, replacing the brain's threat response with a sense of connection and shared purpose. Again, in our contracts team example, the leader leaned into her Joyful Tightrope in a time of uncertainty. This was against her normal instinct of saying nothing unless she had certainty – but it was absolutely the right thing to do for both her and her team.

How to foster empathy and safety

Cultivating these skills involves both personal mindset and specific behaviors that signal trustworthiness and care:

- *Active listening.* Make a practice of truly listening to your team members, especially when they express concerns or ideas. Active listening means giving someone your full attention, acknowledging their feelings, and responding thoughtfully. This can strengthen neural pathways associated with social bonding – when people feel heard, their brains release oxytocin, increasing trust. In team meetings, summarize what you heard and ask follow-up questions. This not only helps you understand people's perspectives (enhancing your own empathy) but also shows people their voice matters, which builds psychological safety.
- *Show empathy and validation.* Leaders should openly recognize and validate the emotions their team members are experiencing. If a big change has people worried, say, "I know this change is stressful, and it's normal to feel anxious. We're in this together." Acknowledging feelings does not make you weak; it makes you human and trustworthy. Studies indicate that when leaders demonstrate empathy, it boosts oxytocin levels in team members, which strengthens collaboration and engagement. Simple acts – like checking in on how someone is doing or recalling personal details they've shared – can go a long way in strengthening social bonds on the team.
- *Transparent communication.* Err on the side of transparency during

volatile times. Share what you know about the situation and admit what you don't know yet. Clearly communicate changes, decisions, and the reasons behind them. Even if the news is tough, people handle it better when they feel included and not blindsided. Research by the Society for Human Resource Management shows that 85 percent of employees believe open, honest communication from leaders builds trust and engagement.[4] A transparent leader calms the brain's fear centers by reducing ambiguity. Set clear expectations and update your team frequently – consistency between your words and actions will further reinforce trust.

- *Encourage input and risk-taking.* Create a climate where team members feel safe to speak up with ideas or concerns. Encourage smart risk-taking and treat failures as learning opportunities. Psychological safety is reinforced when people see that dissenting opinions or bad news are not punished. Deliberately solicit input – for example, ask quieter team members for their thoughts in meetings, and thank those who raise problems or alternate viewpoints. When mistakes happen, respond with curiosity instead of anger ("What can we learn?"). This kind of response pattern signals to everyone's brain that it's safe to take interpersonal risks. As a result, your team will share information faster, catch issues early, and innovate more – all crucial behaviors in times of uncertainty.
- *Lead by example with calm and compassion.* Teams look to leaders for cues on how to react. Model the empathetic, unruffled demeanor you want to see. If you remain calm, acknowledge challenges, and focus on solutions (rather than assign blame), you normalize that behavior. Showing a bit of vulnerability – for instance, saying, "I also find this challenging, but here's how I'm thinking it through" – can humanize you and invite others to contribute. It proves that admitting uncertainties or emotions is not taboo. Over time, this consistent, compassionate leadership builds a high-trust culture where oxytocin is abundant and cortisol is kept in check. In such an environment, teams can handle shocks more smoothly, because people trust that they will support each other.

When leaders lead with empathy and create psychological safety, the payoff is a more cohesive and adaptable team. In practical terms, an empathetic leader who communicates openly will find their team more willing to embrace change, speak up with ideas, and go the extra mile – all vital in navigating the rapids of the Exponential Age. This is exactly how the contracts team surprised their leader because she had the courage to lean into her Joyful Tightrope.

Continuous learning and growth mindset

The Exponential Age demands that leaders and their organizations be in a state of continuous learning. Technologies, market trends, and required skills are evolving so rapidly that what you mastered a few years ago may be obsolete tomorrow. A top leadership skill, therefore, is the ability to learn, adapt, and help others learn on an ongoing basis. This goes hand-in-hand with maintaining a growth mindset – a belief that talents and abilities can be developed through effort, good strategies, and input from others. Adopting a growth mindset has a neurobiological basis – it aligns with the concept of neuroplasticity, which is the brain's capacity to rewire and reorganize itself by forming new neural connections throughout life. In essence, if you believe you can learn, your brain is more likely to actually grow in response to challenges. Leaders with a learning mindset treat uncertainty as an opportunity to gain new knowledge rather than a threat to their ego. They can find joy in the achievement of navigating a challenge, rather than being paralyzed by it.

Why it matters: In periods of rapid change, the organizations that thrive are those that learn faster than their competition. A leader who models curiosity and adaptability sets the tone for a "learning organization". Conversely, a fixed mindset leader who sticks rigidly to old expertise can hold the company back. Embracing continuous learning also mitigates fear of the unknown – if you see yourself and your team as capable learners, you're less afraid of new tools or novel situations. Neuroscience underscores that brain plasticity is lifelong, meaning even senior leaders can develop new mental maps and habits. By leveraging this, leaders can continuously upgrade their skills (like updating software in the brain) to meet emerging challenges. Moreover, a learning-oriented leader encourages experimentation and resilience in the team – setbacks are seen as part of the learning curve, not permanent failures.

When undertaking a training program for 25 paraprofessionals in the legal department at a major company, Lloyd and I were initially met with mixed reactions. We could sense a lot of trepidation in the room. One of our proudest moments as coaches and facilitators was at the end of our first full-day session, where we were focusing on adapting for change and applying the Exponential Age mindsets. A legal assistant who was in her early sixties approached us at the end of the class and said, "Thank you. I was afraid of all the change coming around here but now I'm not."

We have sometimes encountered resistance when training lawyers, depending on their personality, their seniority, and how they view themselves. We have found that some lawyers want to sit firmly in the role of expert and do not want to learn anything. Their attitude is often skeptical. This is not going to work for anyone in the Exponential Age.

How to cultivate continuous learning

Here are some concrete ways leaders can develop a growth mindset for themselves and instill a learning culture in their teams. For legal leaders, it can be helpful to acknowledge the supreme effort of learning that many of their team have made to be the experts they are now but also to introduce them to the notion – as espoused by expert coach and leadership guru Marshal Goldsmith – that what got you here won't get you there.[5]

It's also important that legal leaders firmly role-model this themselves. In my experience, the best leaders are always learning, but it's certainly harder for a mid-level in-house lawyer to push back on continuous development if the general counsel or their leadership is also part of the training and themselves role-model continuous development!

- *Schedule learning time.* Treat learning as a priority task, not a luxury. Block out regular time on your calendar for learning activities – whether it's reading industry research, taking an online course, or attending workshops. By doing so, you signal its importance to yourself and others. This also keeps your brain engaged and adaptable. MRI studies have shown that learning new information stimulates neural growth, and even learning small bits regularly can sharpen cognitive function. Encourage your team to have "learning hours" or "lunch and learn" sessions to normalize continuous development.
- *Reflect and update.* Develop the habit of reflection. After major projects or events (successful or not), take time to debrief. What worked? What didn't? What can we learn? This practice cements lessons in the brain – reflection helps convert experiences into wisdom by reinforcing neural pathways associated with the new insights. It also combats the autopilot mode that can stifle growth. Leaders who are reflective learners continually update their mental models, which is crucial in a fast-changing environment.
- *Encourage experimentation.* Create an environment where experiments

are encouraged. Small pilot projects or A/B tests (a data-driven method for comparing two versions and showing each version to different, randomly assigned, groups of users to determine which performs better against a specific goal) are great ways to learn with low stakes. When proposing an initiative, frame it as an experiment to see what you can learn, rather than a sure bet. This removes fear of failure and promotes a growth mindset in the team. When experiments succeed, celebrate the new knowledge gained. When they fail, treat it as valuable data.

- Brain plasticity thrives on active experience, especially when we're allowed to try, fail, and try again – it's literally how neural connections are refined. Design thinking is a great example of this, but the prototyping stage of piloting something should not be overlooked. In deploying new technologies like Gen AI, failure will be inevitable and needs to be learned from. However, in a smaller way in individual or group coaching programs, an important part of the learning is experimenting with new ideas and behaviors and trying these out in role. This is something that forms the hallmark for most chief legal executive programs and in our use of the Exponential Age Mindset Attributes. The key is repeated application in role.
- *Stay curious and ask questions*. Leaders should role-model curiosity. Ask lots of questions – to your customers, your employees, mentors, even competitors if possible. Showing genuine curiosity signals to your team that it's good to admit what you don't know and seek answers. It also keeps you learning continuously. Neuroscience links curiosity to dopamine release, which enhances memory and learning. So being curious not only uncovers new information, it also primes your brain to remember and integrate that information effectively. Make "Why?" "What if...?" "How might we...?" and of course "We can if..." part of your daily vocabulary.
- *Provide learning resources and support*. Equip your team with resources to learn. This could mean budgeting for training programs, providing access to e-learning libraries, or simply sharing interesting articles and books. Pair less experienced employees with mentors (which benefits both parties' brains – teaching others reinforces the mentor's knowledge). Recognize and reward learning efforts, not just performance outcomes. For example, praise someone who has acquired a new certification or skill, even if they are still junior. This reinforces a culture where continuous improvement is valued. Leaders

who do this effectively transform their organization into a learning community that can dynamically adapt to new challenges.

By committing to continuous learning, you keep your own skills sharp and send a powerful message to your organization: we must keep evolving. In neurological terms, you are keeping your brain's "plasticity switch" turned on, so it remains flexible and ready for the next challenge. Rapid developments mean we will constantly have to learn new skills as new opportunities emerge. The leaders who excel will be those who learn eagerly – indeed, joyfully! – and foster that same spirit in others. In the Exponential Age, the ability to keep learning might just be the most important skill of all.

The Joyful Tightrope summary

The Joyful Tightrope recognizes and helps you navigate the following challenges.

1. The pace of change outruns the law
   - Technology is evolving faster than legal frameworks can respond.
   - You're being asked to advise on issues – like AI, data ethics, or platform regulation – where the law is unclear or still emerging.
   - "Wait for the legislation" is no longer an option – your business partners need real-time, principle-based judgment.

2. Complexity creates cascading risks
   - Legal issues don't sit neatly in one box anymore. A privacy decision today might impact your ESG profile, your market reputation, and your AI deployment tomorrow.
   - Interconnected risks require cross-functional thinking – and legal needs to be part of broader strategic conversations, not just clean-up.

3. Precedent has less power
   - Traditional legal reasoning based on precedent or historical patterns is becoming less reliable.
   - In-house teams must get comfortable operating in gray zones – where there's no case law, but plenty of potential fallout.

4. Business models are fluid
   - Many companies are evolving in real time – pivoting products, markets, and revenue models rapidly.

- Legal can't just guard the perimeter. You need to be embedded in the business to help shape compliant and resilient innovation.

5. New tech = new ethics
   - With tools like AI and big data, what's *legal* isn't always what's *right*.
   - Legal teams are increasingly asked to weigh in on values, reputation, and long-term trust – not just technical compliance.

6. Decision-making windows are shrinking
   - Legal input is often needed faster than ever – but with less certainty.
   - That creates a shift from purely risk-averse roles to ones where legal needs to enable confident decision-making under ambiguity.

What this means for you – as a lawyer and a leader

The Joyful Tightrope helps you pivot:

- From rule interpreter to strategic advisor. You're not just answering "Can we?", you're helping shape "Should we?"
- From reactive to proactive. Legal teams must build foresight and collaborate early in product and strategy discussions.
- From certainty-seekers to ambiguity navigators. The Exponential Age requires judgment, not just knowledge.

Joyful Tightrope mindset and behaviors

- Breathe to gain perspective in the moment.
- Don't shoulder big decisions alone – utilize the views of your team and others.
- Take perspective – you may not get this right but at this stage there may be no right answers.
- Stay curious about new developments as they are expanding your role and influence. Reframing a challenging issue as an opportunity, not a problem, can have positive effects on how you approach it.
- Demonstrate transparency as much as possible when making decisions in an atmosphere of uncertainty.
- Be focused on building connectivity and key relationships as early as possible in your role to ensure you and your team are part of the decision-making as early as possible.
- Ensure you look after yourself via SHED (Sleep, hydration, exercise, and diet) and your team does as well, so that decision-making can be as optimal as possible.

- Role-model continuous learning to your team and give them opportunities to do this.
- Become intentional about seeking outside opinions and using cross-functional collaboration.
- Use problem solving frameworks such as Can If to gain perspective and creativity.
- Take advantage of risk and opportunity frameworks such as the Six Dimensions of Business Risk and the Six Dimensions of Business Opportunity.

References

1 Inside Edition, Philippe Petit Commemorates Tightrope Walk Between New York City's Twin Towers 50 Years Later, 9 August 2024: www.insideedition.com/philippe-petit-commemorates-tightrope-walk-between-new-york-citys-twin-towers-50-years-later-88569

2 Barbara Jacquelyn Sahakian and Georgios Christopoulos, "Cognitive Flexibility: The Science of How to be Successful in Business and at Work." *The Conversation*, 13 April 2023, https://theconversation.com/cognitive-flexibility-the-science-of-how-to-be-successful-in-business-and-at-work-202981

3 Google's Project Aristotle, 26 March 2024: https://psychsafety.com/googles-project-aristotle/

4 Building a Connected Workforce: Key Insights on Employee Engagement: www.shrm.org/labs/resources/building-a-connected-workforce-key-insights-on-employee-engagement.

5 Marshal Goldsmith, *What Got You Here Won't Get You There.* Profile Books (2008).

Chapter 5:
Chaos Converter – understanding the opportunity in chaos and crisis

The Chaos Converter attribute is the ability to find opportunity in chaos. It is not necessarily about transforming chaos into order, although that can be an outcome. It's about being able to welcome the opportunities that chaos gives us, our teams and organizations – opportunities to test ourselves and open up the potential to view challenges differently. How we define "chaos" in this book can encompass several different components – constraints and limits, disruption, crisis, even innovation. It is something that forces us out of the status quo or business as usual mindset. The Chaos Converter attribute encourages us to see opportunities where others might only see challenges.

Opportunity in chaos #1: Development and growth

Experiencing chaos and getting through it builds many skills. By overcoming challenges, we build resilience and perseverance, allowing us to bounce back from setbacks and adapt to change. Challenges push individuals outside their comfort zones, prompting the development of new skills, knowledge, and capabilities. In the training and development that we deliver, we frequently start with the idea that growth is uncomfortable. If participants are not comfortable with being uncomfortable, they will likely not get the full benefits of the training.

Opportunity in chaos #2: Innovation and creativity

The more complex the challenge, the more addressing it requires critical thinking, analysis, and the development of creative solutions, thus enhancing problem-solving skills.

The much-hackneyed phrase "thinking outside the box" still resonates for a reason. Such thinking is vital during chaos. Challenges often necessitate unconventional approaches, leading to innovative solutions and breakthroughs that might not have occurred otherwise. In our Lift Off Program, we focus some of our analysis on the operational innovations carried out by BT Legal, which were an early example of operational creativity in a legal department. However, this was completely borne of chaos – the BT legal team had to change or potentially face a crisis that could have annihilated it due to a profits warning in the business.

BT's adaptability was created from chaos. Navigating challenges often requires flexibility and the ability to adapt strategies, leading to new and more effective solutions. Sometimes, opening our minds and leaning into chaos is the only way forward.

Opportunity in chaos #3: Action and reflection

Transforming challenges into opportunities requires a proactive stance, involving analyzing the root causes of obstacles and taking effective action. This is foundational for legal teams and will become increasingly the case as so many of the reactive functions of legal professionals can be taken over by technological solutions. However, the act of transforming those reactive challenges into opportunities is where human creativity will thrive. Finding ways to make proactive thinking and action a priority for everyone in your team is now a key responsibility of any general counsel who wants to win in the Exponential Age.

But proactively doing things differently will come with a cost. New ideas often fail before they succeed. This is where resilience and the ability to learn from setbacks are necessary. Viewing failure as feedback, rather than a final setback, allows individuals to learn from mistakes and refine their approach for future success. It is key to the development of legal teams during the age of AI that the search for perfection does not set back innovation and experimentation.

Building in time to reflect on experiences and outcomes helps to identify key learnings and insights for future growth. This be a key part of legal leaders' strategy for the Exponential Age.

In the kickboxing and Jiu Jitsu studio where I train, there's a motto painted on the wall: "Strive for progress not perfection". This is at the heart of successfully harnessing the Chaos Converter attribute.

Reframing challenge and opportunity

The word "challenge" tends to be used exclusively to mean a problem, yet a challenge is also something that tests us and pushes us to change and grow. In coaching, a useful tool is asking the client to reframe a challenge as an opportunity. This powerful shift in perspective is the starting point in Chaos Converter – viewing chaos, crisis, and constraint as an opportunity. This is not always easy to do and may only be available to us retrospectively when we reflect on an experience. The secret to the Chaos Converter attribute is developing a mindset that allows us to view it as such in the moment, not only in hindsight. What happens if, instead of viewing current challenges negatively, you can explore them as possibilities for learning, innovation, and improvement?

What is central to this is adopting a growth mindset – the belief that abilities can be developed. This encourages viewing challenges as steppingstones toward personal and professional development. For example, a consistent challenge in the in-house legal department is doing more with less. It's very easy to see this as a constraint – even chaos – that we have to manage day-to-day. The job just becomes about keeping your head above water. But what if this can be reframed?

In Ed Catmull's book *Creativity Inc* about his time leading Pixar (which he co-founded), he reflects that the company was often most creative when undergoing the most chaos.[1] Unlimited time and resources often stymied creativity. Once the company realized this, it tried to find ways to impose constraints on projects to stimulate greater creativity.

A beautiful constraint

A book that is fundamental to the idea of Chaos Converter is Adam Morgan and Mark Bardem's *A Beautiful Constraint*.[2] Its core thesis is that companies that can view constraint and challenge as opportunities, rather than blockers, will be better placed to innovate and succeed than those unable to do this.

This is crucial for most in-house legal departments. There may be a few exceptions where budget and resources are not constrained, such as legal teams in large private equity houses, but even here there is still a need to prove your worth against the bottom line and potential GP and LP profits.

As the Exponential Age becomes the new reality, in-house legal departments are operating against a backdrop of increased demand and decreased resources. This ever-growing need to do more with less means that technology tools such as generative AI will soon be a necessity, if they aren't already. But the adoption of these requires a shift in mindset from both leaders and teams.

A fundamental shift is needed to reframe the common constraints of in-house legal teams as opportunities. This is important because it empowers teams and encourages curiosity and creativity around new ways of working and the tools that will make this happen.

Those legal departments that bury their heads in the sand may face obsolescence via outsourcing. This may take different forms, but it leads to the same conclusion – change that is forced upon you as opposed to change that is experienced with an element of empowerment and agency. Of course, we are not naïve enough to suggest that adopting this mindset alone will save your job. It may be that your function is ripe for automation or that you were simply the wrong number through the door. However, what the Exponential Age Mindset Attributes such as Chaos Converter do is give you agility in how to approach what you can do to embody the mindset and behaviors of continuous learning, which will be essential to success in these volatile times.

Constraint and creativity

When I used to teach drama in university, and also put on my own one-woman shows, the byword was doing more with less – arguably on a much bigger conceptual scale than any faced in a legal department. For example, when directing *Euripides Medea* with students, the play calls for a Deus Ex Machina ending[3] (literally "the god in the machine") where Helios, the sun god and Medea's father, appears in a glowing chariot and carries Medea away to his kingdom. The students and I ended up recreating this with a bit of cardboard and some gold foil! In the end, rather than create laughably subpar effects that would alienate the audience or make them laugh at the exact wrong moment, we abandoned that idea. Instead, we used the performers' own bodies to create the chariot effect, feeling that was more interesting than trying to create an object. Instead of failing at the challenge of trying to deliver the expected on an impossible budget, we saw an opportunity to do something new and different that was both unexpected and effective.

My start in the creative arts imbued me with a need to approach constraint and challenge as an opportunity to be creative. Literally "We Can If..." in action versus "We can't because...".

It may seem like a stretch to draw parallels between low-budget theatre with being a lawyer. How is this relevant to in-house legal teams? But this opportunity-seeking mindset is central to being able to be truly creative. Lawyers often shy away from creativity – an idea I actively challenge in my last book, *Business Thinking in Practice for In-House Counsel.*[4] Humans are all creative, whether we define ourselves this way or not. We start as highly creative when we are children but lose this ability as we get older and move into the world of work. It does not help that when it comes to the practice of law, being "creative" can have negative connotations, equated with obfuscation or untruth. We have been taught to dampen our natural impulses. Certainly, that was the truth of the Industrial Age mindset.

In the Exponential Age, creativity is truly the human superpower. It's this quality that AI cannot replicate in anything approaching the way humanity can. AI can replicate the result of human creative ideas but cannot yet replicate the process by which those ideas are generated – the very act of creation. But in the act of creation, there is a fundamental link between constraints and generation of creative ideas.

In *A Beautiful Constraint*, the authors outline how the most innovative companies will not just embrace constraints but may actively apply them to stimulate creativity. In *Creativity Inc*, Ed Catmull explains that one of Pixar's best films, *Toy Story 2*, was also the one produced under the greatest constraints. Catmull focuses on the power of limits and identifies several different ways in which they inspire us. "Limits force us to rethink how we are working and push us to new heights of creativity."[5]

The power of Chaos Converter

There is a strong foundation of research and theory from psychology, neuroscience, business, and leadership studies that supports the benefits of reframing chaos and challenge as opportunity. There are several ways to think about this and a variety of theories that showcase these different perspectives. Below, I summarize some of the main ones and suggest what these might look like in action in a legal team.

Cognitive reframing or shifting perspective

Cognitive reframing is the process of shifting perspective on a situation to change its emotional impact. To quote Beyoncé (or, at least, Beyoncé's grandmother, via Beyoncé) on her 2016 album *Lemonade*: "Life gave me lemons, and I made lemonade". Life gave her an (allegedly!) cheating husband and professional disrespect from a racist media and music industry that minimized her achievements and regularly sidelined her from major awards. She transformed that into a genre-redefining smash hit album that reframed those events – or, at least, her empowered response to them – as triumphal.

It's a core idea in Cognitive Behavioral Therapy (CBT), which shows that how we *interpret* events is more important than the events themselves. This is also a technique used in coaching, where it is often described as shifting perspective. In 1976, Beck's research showed that reframing distorted thinking reduces anxiety and improves problem-solving.[6] In 2003, Gross and John found that cognitive reappraisal (a form of reframing) is linked to greater psychological resilience and wellbeing.[7] We can see both theories at play in Chaos Converter and the linked tool of the Can If problem solving framework.

In CBT, cognitive reframing is undertaken by taking the idea and then interrogating this via evidence to expose it as a mindset or perspective (i.e., not an objective, immutable truth). The next step from that – which is used in coaching – is reframing the original perspective. Whilst this is an important skill in life generally and certainly in personal development to unlock mindsets that may have negative impacts, it's also crucial in business in the Exponential Age. Leaders who can reframe uncertainty as a chance for innovation foster cultures of growth, not fear.

Many teams face the challenge of operating with a decreased or frozen budget, or hiring restraints, budgetary or otherwise. Strategic plans may need to be reevaluated, and it might seem like doing nothing is the only course of action. If you can't build the golden chariot to sweep down and collect Medea, is it even worth staging the play?

Initial thoughts might therefore be something like: "Our budget has been frozen – this is a disaster. We will have to freeze hiring and cut back on external counsel spend."

A reframe would be to consider this set of events not as a catastrophe, but instead an opportunity.

> *"As we can't make a new hire, can we look at how we are currently using resource? Can we find a way to share the work the new hire might have undertaken across a range of legal professionals and match this to professional development goals the team has?"*

> *"We can't increase our outside counsel spend, but can we work with existing providers on new forms of service delivery?"*

> *"Can we use new providers who may be more cost effective for some services? If we were really focused on this, might we even create savings from what we spent last year?"*

Post-traumatic growth theory

The central tenet of this theory is, as Kelly Clarkson would say, "What doesn't kill you makes you stronger". (Admittedly, as with the Beyoncé example, this isn't exactly original to the singer, but Clarkson presents another useful illustration of how someone has subverted expectations and overcome setbacks to reinvent herself and emerge stronger.)

Adversity can lead to significant psychological development, including new perspectives, stronger relationships, and greater personal strength. Individuals and teams who endure crisis often report positive outcomes, such as a renewed sense of purpose and innovation. This was seen in many businesses in the way they needed to adapt quickly during the COVID-19 era. For example, the fact that many restaurants and bars were forced to introduce outdoor seating to accommodate social distancing led to many places changing long-term licensing policies to allow more alfresco dining, recognizing the potential to revitalize the hospitality sector.

One general counsel we have worked with who is skilled at building teams states that her driving idea behind hiring is putting together the team that she would need in a crisis. In many instances, the legal team comes to the fore during a crisis. But for legal leaders, a crisis can also be an insight into hidden skills and strengths in their reports.

Organizations that reflect after crises often emerge stronger, more agile, and more values-driven. From a legal leader's perspective, one positive aspect of a major crisis is that it can serve as a complete reset for an organization – especially when leadership or business practices are creating legal, compliance, or ethical issues, or even all three. For example, Rio Tinto was forced into a wholescale examination of its culture and practices after the Jukkan Gorge scandal.[8] The sheer scope and scale of that scandal caused a re-examination and a re-think of not just the actions and circumstances around that particular crisis but a wholesale culture re-evaluation.

Neuroplasticity and learning from uncertainty

In a very real sense, the Chaos Converter attribute reflects the way we are built. The brain is wired to adapt to new challenges. Exposure to uncertainty can stimulate the brain's learning centers – especially the prefrontal cortex (PFC). American neuroscientist Andrew Huberman and others have shown that mild to moderate stress can activate dopaminergic pathways, enhancing focus and adaptability – if perceived as a challenge, not a threat. Leaders who model adaptive responses train teams to view ambiguity as a learning signal, not a panic trigger.[9]

This can be difficult for many lawyers, mainly because of the way in which legal training is grounded in certainty and precedent. It may be that some practice areas are more adept in coping with this than others – litigation versus corporate, for example. However, for most lawyers who move in-house, this is a skillset that is required to some degree, whether dealing with an actual crisis or chaos situation or just dealing with business as usual.

This will also flex considerably depending on the industry, the size of the legal team, and the growth stage of the company. A large legal team in an established company in a highly regulated industry such as financial services may have less neuroplasticity amongst its rank-and-file lawyers than a fintech start-up with two lawyers. The comfort with neuroplasticity demonstrated by those lawyers may also be a factor in them being where they are. Increasingly, the more senior in-house lawyers are, the more they will need neuroplasticity. For example, in a Fortune 100 company, the GC or CLO role will these days likely encompass a spectrum of functions that may only have a tenuous relation to legal. The GC or CLO will personally need to be highly comfortable with ambiguity and with agility. If they are not, they are unlikely to ascend to these roles or will not succeed in them. When training and coaching emerging leaders and potential succession candidates in legal teams, this is often a mindset and practice that we focus on.

Leadership role-modeling is fundamental to how teams can develop more neuroplasticity in the face of ambiguity or challenge. Linked to this are leaders who model that it is acceptable to not have all the answers, and that failure is both acceptable and needed to aid development.

One legal department I worked with encouraged sharing of failures, which were then discussed without blame to facilitate learning. Examples were also shared and modelled from industries where learning from failure is an accepted process and where – generally – the failures are more high stakes than in corporate legal departments, such as aviation and medicine.

In contrast, it was much more challenging delivering leadership training to a legal department that was emerging from a historical culture of blame. This meant participants were much more cautious about admitting vulnerabilities and exploring how these could become development opportunities.

Complexity and chaos theory

In complex systems, order arises from apparent chaos. The "edge of chaos" is where innovation and transformation are most likely to occur. These ideas help executives realize chaos is not the enemy, but often the birthplace of creativity.

Key frameworks include:

- *Stacey Matrix*. The Stacey Matrix is a conceptual framework that helps organizations make strategic decisions. It was developed by Ralph Stacey, a professor and management theorist, who was interested in the complexity and uncertainty inherent in managing an organization. It encourages leaders to shift from command-and-control in simple contexts to facilitation and experimentation in complex, uncertain ones.

- *Cynefin framework (Snowden).* This guides leaders to respond differently depending on whether the situation is clear, complicated, complex, or chaotic. The Cynefin framework is a decision-making tool that categorizes situations into five domains to help leaders choose appropriate responses. These domains are: Simple (Clear), Complicated, Complex, Chaotic, and Disorder. The framework emphasizes understanding the context of a situation before acting, rather than assuming a one-size-fits-all approach. The idea behind this is like the driver behind our Six Dimensions of Business Risk. Looking at an issue via all the applicable risk lenses (not just legal) gives you a much more holistic view.
- *Growth mindset.* The growth mindset, as defined by American psychologist Carol Dweck, is the belief that abilities can be developed through effort, learning, and persistence rather than being fixed traits. Research by Dweck[10] shows that individuals with a growth mindset are more resilient and more likely to learn from setbacks, adapting their approach rather than becoming discouraged. For in-house lawyers, this might mean treating a failed contract negotiation or an adverse regulatory outcome not as a defeat but as a rich source of insight – examining what went wrong, adjusting the playbook, and applying those lessons to future matters. It could also mean embracing new technologies, like AI-assisted contract review, not with fear of obsolescence but as a skill to be mastered and leveraged to deliver greater value to the business.
- *VUCA leadership model.* Complementing this is the VUCA leadership model – a framework designed for environments marked by volatility, uncertainty, complexity, and ambiguity. Under VUCA conditions, effective leadership shifts from seeking to control outcomes to making sense of shifting realities, and from rigid prediction to rapid adaptation. In practice, this means using vision and clarity to counter volatility – for example, articulating the legal department's role in enabling a high-risk market entry so the team understands its priorities. It involves

cultivating curiosity in the face of uncertainty – such as exploring unfamiliar regulatory regimes in new jurisdictions rather than resisting expansion. Navigating complexity requires agility and experimentation – an in-house lawyer might pilot a new compliance reporting tool in one region before rolling it out globally. Finally, managing ambiguity calls for adaptability and openness – for instance, staying flexible in the interpretation of evolving ESG disclosure requirements while the company's sustainability strategy is still forming.

Applied together, a growth mindset and VUCA leadership equip in-house lawyers to thrive in turbulent environments, turning legal challenges into strategic opportunities and ensuring their teams remain proactive, adaptable, and value-driven partners to the business.

Techniques to convert chaos

While a lot of these techniques are mentioned in other Mindset Attributes chapters, they are effective enough to be worth repeating.

- *Mindfulness meditation.* Regular mindfulness exercises (such as meditation or focused breathing) train your brain to observe emotions without impulsively reacting. These practices strengthen the connection between the prefrontal cortex (PFC) and amygdala, literally rewiring the brain for greater emotional control. This can be as simple as taking a few deep breaths and shifting your focus away from a challenging situation.
- *Cognitive reappraisal.* This is the habit of reframing stressful situations in a more positive or neutral light. For example, instead of viewing a sudden change as a threat, see it as a learning opportunity. Neuroscience research supports reappraisal as an effective strategy that engages the brain's cognitive centers to reinterpret negative stimuli, thereby reducing emotional intensity. Leaders can practice by consciously challenging their initial interpretations and asking, "What else could this situation mean?" or "How can I grow from this?". This is a technique used frequently in coaching. When a client raises a challenge, as coaches we ask them to find the opportunity in it. What's another way of looking at this? If we take an earlier example of a contracts team in flux, one way of reframing that could be: "This is a great opportunity for the team to re-evaluate its role and pivot to new ways of working that will contribute to the effectiveness of the team".

- *Effect labeling*. Simply naming your feelings can activate the brain's language centers and dampen the amygdala's response. This can be as straightforward as admitting, "I am anxious about this deadline my CEO just imposed on the legal team". This labeling of emotions creates psychological distance and helps the PFC regain control. Again, we both often use it in coaching – naming the problem. Even when we work with teams using the Exponential Age Mindset Attributes, there can be power in naming the attributes that participants feel most uncomfortable with and exploring where that discomfort comes from. Similarly, we have used a very powerful exercise with groups that have a high stakes presentation – maybe to a GC or the Board, particularly where there is lack of experience in such presentations. We invite everyone to name the fear. What's the worst that can happen? We will talk through it, but many participants report that even the act of just saying it out loud defuses a surprising number of tensions for them. Fear always thrives more in the dark than in the light!
- *Using a framework*. Understand your relationship to uncertainty through a framework such as the Exponential Age Mindset Attributes, Chaos Converter, or a problem-solving framework such as Can if (explained in more detail in chapter 14). This creates both objective distance from unregulated emotions and allows you to start reframing the experience. "This is not an unbearable crisis but an opportunity for me to lean into my attribute of Chaos Converter. What can I learn from this experience? How might this be a development opportunity for me or my team?" In applying these frameworks with legal and business teams, we have both heard time and time again how participants start to think differently about challenges and therefore approach them differently.
- *Physical wellbeing*. Maintain healthy sleep, exercise, and nutrition habits. Adequate sleep restores the PFC's capacity for self-control, while aerobic exercise reduces stress hormones and releases mood-boosting neurotransmitters. Research indicates that regular exercise and rest create a healthier stress response, preventing burnout and emotional flooding. Leaders should treat sleep and fitness as non-negotiable productivity tools. Don't just say this – walk the talk for your team. "We have all been working long and hard. Everyone needs to go home and rest. We can resume tomorrow when we're fresher and we have a better perspective on this case."

- *Breathing techniques.* In moments of acute stress, controlled breathing (for instance, slow deep breaths, the golden thread breath, or box breathing) can rapidly engage the parasympathetic nervous system to calm the body. This lowers heart rate and cortisol levels, giving your brain a chance to think. Taking even a 60-second breathing break before responding to a crisis can prevent rash reactions and improve your poise. The same can be true in situations that are not "crisis" but feel like a crisis for you! Imagine you're presenting to the Board and you get interrupted by a question you were not expecting. Your mind goes blank. Breathe. The pause will not be as long to others as it seems to you. The 60-second breathing break will ensure your response converts the chaos in your brain to something more meaningful.

When I worked as a journalist, an interviewee would often say, "That's an interesting question". I'm not sure my questions were necessarily super interesting – or maybe some were! – but that phrase gave the interviewee some time and a pause to think. Use that to convert a public speaking crisis from chaos to control!

Chaos or opportunity? Embrace the moment

The Exponential Age holds the promise of increased chaos. The pace of change means it's unlikely that chaos and crisis will go away or slow down. This presents a challenge for lawyers – but also an opportunity. In-house lawyers are valuable in a crisis due to their combination of legal expertise, business understanding, crisis management experience, and ability to collaborate across the organization. Their role is crucial in mitigating risk, managing the company's legal position, and supporting leadership in navigating turbulent situations. How can you ensure you and your legal team use this as a pivotal moment to demonstrate the highest value?

You and your team's deep knowledge of the company will be the foundational skill in any crisis. In-house lawyers have an intimate understanding of the company's operations, culture, and strategic goals. This enables you to quickly assess risks, understand the implications of a crisis, and tailor responses that align with the company's values and long-term objectives. It's that cultural piece that will bring more than even the most experienced outside counsel or consultants can. You and your team live that culture every day and it has meaning for you.

Proactive risk management rather than just responsiveness is the name of the game in the Exponential Age. The best legal teams are already firmly in this space. The increasing use of technology in reactive, repetitive tasks will make this even more the place where in-house lawyers need to be.

Many in-house lawyers are already skilled at anticipating legal risks and proactively implementing mitigation strategies. This foresight prepares them for handling crises when they arise, allowing them to respond more swiftly and effectively. Making this a consistent theme for your team and finding ways outside of crisis situations to flex these skills is going to be what the best general counsel needs to do to successfully convert chaos.

For most legal teams, knowledge of the company and its culture comes from cross-functional collaboration. In-house lawyers will work closely with various departments – such as finance, operations, HR, and marketing – making them adept at coordinating a multidisciplinary response during a crisis. The ability to navigate and influence across these departments ensures a unified and effective crisis management effort.

As mentioned in the chapter on Zoom Master, ensuring your teams do not stay in the comfort of a legal or subject matter expertise silo is absolutely vital. This is essential for all levels but especially for legal leaders in the Exponential Age. We have seen increasing examples of legal teams that are proactively rotating their leaders through opportunities and taking them out of their initial areas of expertise to cultivate this mindset. This can provoke a crisis in some new legal leaders when they are no longer the expert and are leading teams who are more expert than they are. However, as we remind coaching clients who go through this, the skills now needed in leadership are not subject matter expertise. Such moves provide useful opportunity to lean into Exponential Age Mindset Attributes like Chaos Converter, Zoom Master, and Duality Master.

Navigating crisis and seeing the bigger picture

The ability to see the bigger picture and context is a defining factor of several of the Exponential Age Mindset Attributes, like the three mentioned above. While managing the immediate crisis, in-house lawyers help the company maintain a long-term perspective. Their ability to think beyond short-term fixes ensures that crisis management strategies are aligned with the company's future goals and strategic direction. This also helps in-house lawyers to make sound decisions under pressure. During a crisis, they balance legal, ethical, and business considerations, helping to steer the company toward the best possible outcome while minimizing potential harm. This is further balanced by expertise in the legal and regulatory frameworks governing their industry, making legal teams invaluable during crises involving legal liabilities, government investigations, or compliance issues. This knowledge helps ensure that the company avoids additional legal complications while navigating the crisis.

Crisis situations often involve conflict, whether internal (e.g., between departments or executives) or external (e.g., with regulators or customers). In-house lawyers are skilled in conflict resolution and negotiation, helping to resolve disputes and prevent further escalation.

If a crisis leads to litigation, in-house lawyers can manage or oversee the legal proceedings, perhaps with the assistance of outside counsel. They are equipped to evaluate whether litigation is necessary, explore settlement options, and protect the company's interests in court or through alternative dispute resolution.

This also means that there is a significant need for in-house legal teams in crafting crisis communications, both internally and externally. This will help ensure that messaging is clear, legally sound, and aligned with company policy. Lawyers can also work to minimize reputational damage by managing public relations and regulatory responses.

These various areas of expertise mean that many in-house legal teams are increasingly responsible for preparing crisis management protocols. This experience allows them to act swiftly when crises occur, executing well-established plans that ensure a swift and coordinated response. If your team is not currently involved in doing this, perhaps this is the time to lean into some of the communication-focused attributes, such as Supreme Storyteller, to rectify that.

Toolkit for lawyers to convert chaos

1. Conducting regular crisis simulations and war games
    - *Why it helps:* These simulations stress-test assumptions, uncover blind spots, and prompt creative thinking.
    - *Example:* A pharmaceutical company staged a mock global supply chain breakdown to challenge teams to find alternative manufacturing or delivery methods. The result – a more flexible and resilient logistics model that becomes a competitive advantage. This helped them develop speedy responses to increased tariffs from the US government.

- *What are the blind spots or strategic issues your team can simulate to lean into a proactive mindset?* External law firms and/or PR agencies can be helpful with the logistics to help make one of these happen.

2. **Enabling cross-functional "chaos squads"**
   - *Why it helps:* Breaking down silos under pressure invites diverse perspectives and non-linear solutions.
   - *Example:* During COVID-19, many retail firms formed rapid-response teams across legal, tech, customer service, and ops to reinvent how they served customers digitally. This led to long-term digital transformations, not just short-term fixes.

3. **Reframing chaos as "permission to experiment"**
   - *Why it helps:* Crisis often relaxes rigid protocols. Leaders can use this as a sandbox for innovation.
   - *Example:* A utility firm facing climate-related disruptions invited teams including legal to prototype decentralized energy solutions. Some ideas that started as "emergency" experiments became new business lines. It also helped a range of teams, including legal, see the direct effect their ideas during crisis or chaos could have on strategy, creating a virtuous cycle of empowerment.

4. **Real-time customer co-creation**
   - *Why it helps:* Customers in chaos have immediate pain points. Partnering with them reveals unmet needs.
   - *Example:* A technology company legal team under a new general counsel and with a new head of legal operations prioritized rapidly deploying customer feedback loops with business stakeholders. This started as a pilot with one part of the legal team and one area of the business but worked so well in identifying opportunities and improving collaboration that it was extended throughout the entire legal department.

5. **Leadership transparency and adaptive learning culture**
   - *Why it helps:* Teams that see chaos as shared and navigable are more cohesive and braver.
   - *Example:* A consumer goods general counsel conducted livestreams and weekly updates during a company-wide restructure, which

affected many departments, including legal. Her communication stance of regular touchpoints and being available to answer difficult questions while inviting employee suggestions and recognizing resilience made chaos seem less challenging. Despite job losses, trust and staff engagement increased with those legal professionals that remained.

6. Embedding chaos in scenario planning

- *Why it helps:* Rather than planning *despite* uncertainty, organizations plan *for* it.
- *Example:* A legal team builds future-back planning exercises around AI's exponential growth. This prepares all lawyers and paraprofessionals to start to shift their value from production to insight much faster than peers in other legal departments.

7. Celebrating "productive failure"

- *Why it helps:* Failure during chaos that yields learning becomes a strategic asset.
- *Example:* An edtech start-up's legal department chatbot pilot's failure to answer frequently asked legal questions taught them how to better use data for real-time engagement. The second-gen product is being developed using learnings from the first "failure", to make it much more focused and user-friendly by leaning into conversations and collaborations with end users.

Another tool we use to help lawyers convert chaos in their projects or careers is the Four Zones of Curiosity (seen earlier in chapter three and explained in detail in chapter 13).

References

1 Ed Catmull, *Creativity Inc* (Random House, 2014) pp198-203.

2 Adam Morgan and Mark Barden, *A Beautiful Constraint* (Wiley, 2015).

3 The term originates from ancient Greek theatre, where gods were literally lowered onto the stage using a crane (the "machine") to intervene and resolve plot complications. It's now used generally as a term for any unexpected plot twist that resolves a complicated situation.

4 Catherine McGregor, *Business Thinking in Practice for In-House Counsel* (Globe Law and Business, 2020).

5 Ed Catmull, *Creativity Inc* (Random House, 2014) p200.

6 Beck's Cognitive Model of Depression: Evolution, Modern Evidence and Critical Appraisal. Panagiotis Tsolakis, *Psychology*, Vol.16, No.1, January 2025. www.scirp.org/journal/paperinformation?paperid=138847

7 Gross, J. J. and John, O. P. (2003). Individual differences in two emotion regulation processes: Implications for affect, relationships, and wellbeing. *Journal of Personality and Social Psychology*, https://psycnet.apa.org/record/2003-05897-016

8 The "Juukan Gorge Rio Tinto" event refers to the 2020 destruction of the 46,000-year-old Aboriginal rock shelters in Western Australia by the mining company Rio Tinto to expand an iron ore mine. The incident caused widespread outrage, led to public apologies and resignations from Rio Tinto executives, and prompted a government inquiry with recommendations for future protections and a reconstruction of the site. In response, the company has since committed to reforming its practices and has reached an agreement with the Traditional Owners.

9 Andrew Huberman, www.hubermanlab.com/episode/tools-to-enhance-working-memory-attention

10 Carol Dweck, *Mindset* (Do Not Use, 2017)

Chapter 6:
Agile Juggler – balancing consistency and ability

The Agile Juggler mindset – the ability to balance consistency with agility – has become increasingly vital in the Exponential Age, where the pace of technological, societal, and market change is accelerating. The need for this attribute is supported by organizational, leadership, and neuroscience theories. Perhaps the most striking application of this mindset came during the Covid-19 pandemic, where the world seemed to turn on its head – in many cases, literally overnight. Companies that had eschewed homeworking for years suddenly found themselves pivoting to this or being faced with going out of business. What amazed many of us was the speed at which this happened – the consistency of business as usual was maintained whilst the agility of a whole new way of working was applied.

How individuals responded during the pandemic also demonstrated the key aspects of Agile Juggler in action. Unexpected illness amongst colleagues, some of whom might be out of action for much longer than usual, led to individuals being called upon to cover for colleagues with little notice whilst also undertaking their own tasks.

The ability to socialize during the various pandemic-related lockdowns was non-existent but many quickly pivoted to virtual drinks, pub quizzes, game nights and so forth, so that social interactions could be mimicked virtually.

Whilst we hopefully won't face another global pandemic any time soon, this ability to maintain consistency but also be agile will be needed as we advance into the Exponential Age.

For lawyers, especially in-house lawyers, the Agile Juggler mindset is no longer optional. In-house teams that succeed in the Exponential Age will be those that can deliver legal consistency (that builds trust) while embracing operational agility (that unlocks speed and innovation). The future legal department is both a compass and a surfboard – anchored in principles, but fluid enough to ride waves of change.

The Exponential Age requires both stability and speed

In this time of fast-paced change, organizations must simultaneously maintain core operational excellence while adapting quickly to external change. This means understanding where there is need for stability and which areas and operations are ripe for innovation. In their 2014 book, *Exponential Organizations*, Ismail et al.[1] reflect on the need for organizations to develop both a stable internal core and an agile, externally focused edge. This is part of what is described as a new business paradigm where success is dependent on adaptability, and figuring out what needs to be core and what can be agile and flexible in your business model. Successful Exponential Organizations use "interfaces" and "dashboards" to ensure consistent operations while leveraging rapid experimentation.

A shared aspect of the Exponential Organization, according to Ismail et al., is the Massive Transformative Purpose. This stays as your North Star and helps provide consistency while other aspects, such as how this is achieved and who does it, can flex as needed to be competitive.

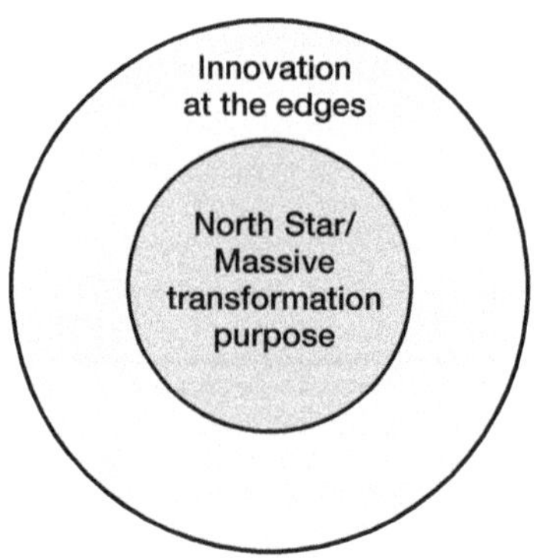

Figure 10: Massive Transformative Purpose. Source: Exponential Organizations, Ismail et al.[2]

For a legal department, this could be the core of what it does as a stable backbone (clear purpose, governance, and standards) while maintaining dynamic capabilities to pivot quickly, such as providing guidance on sudden expansion and being aware of ways to be creative to gain advantage whilst not letting go of that backbone.

Too often, lawyers think of stability and agility as polar opposites, whereas they are actually two sides of the same coin. This combination of stability and agility should also not be ruled out because of the ethical obligations of a lawyer. Sometimes, lawyers resist change by playing the trump card of "I have to be an officer of the law". Of course, you always need to ensure the legality of an action. Yes, there can be agile actions where haste can lead to unwise decisions, including those that are unethical and even illegal. But these actions are more likely than not actually the product of ingrained mindsets and bureaucracy that were resistant to change.

There is no "one-size-fits-all". Legal and ethical obligations are not antithetical to agility and innovation. Some of the changes in law that have resulted in the overturning of injustice are the result of agile thinking. Take, for example, the landmark Supreme Court case of *Brown versus the Board of Education*. This 1954 decision effectively overturned a previous Supreme Court ruling (*Plessy v. Ferguson*, 1896) which, in deciding that racial segregation did not violate the Constitution, upheld the toxic doctrine of "separate but equal".[3]

A conventional legal strategy might have focused narrowly on proving that schools for Black children were materially unequal. Thurgood Marshall and the NAACP Legal Defense Fund – who represented the Brown family, whose daughter had been refused a place at her nearest school due to segregation – shifted the argument from tangibles (buildings, books, funding) to intangibles – the psychological and social harm of segregation on Black children. This was a radical and innovative reframing, because it challenged the very premise of "separate but equal", not just its application.

This agility can be evident throughout legal practice and trials that may not be as groundbreaking as *Brown v. The Board of Education*. In his prior role as a deputy district attorney in trial, Lloyd had to simultaneously monitor four moving targets – the witness, jury, judge, and opposing counsel. By balancing the consistency of his case theory with the agility to read the room, he showed how to move from a rigid focus on the script to a responsive strategy to ensure he didn't lose the case.

To take an example from another high-stakes profession, a great analogy for the Agile Juggler might be a hospital's emergency department, which can simultaneously provide non-urgent medical care and keep those patients stable whilst also dealing with intensive emergencies when needed.

What can be achieved once you realize that it's not only possible for consistency and agility to co-exist, but it's also preferable?

Ambidexterity – exploit vs explore

At the heart of the Agile Juggler skill is a dynamic balance. Many of the Exponential Age Mindset Attributes require leaders to hold opposing forces in tension, because this is the defining nature of the Exponential Age itself.

Operationally, Agile Juggler is the ability to manage the pull between exploiting existing capabilities and exploring new opportunities. It is the mindset that allows leaders to hold competing demands – maintaining consistency in Business as Usual (BAU) while generating fresh, creative ideas – without dropping either.

For in-house legal leaders, this tension is constant – managing rising workloads while still applying adaptive strategy, and balancing the pace of innovation with the demands of the core business. Just as exponential organizations are both stable and agile, legal departments can also find many of their greatest opportunities for innovation within their everyday BAU work.

It's a common struggle we find frequently when coaching new managers. In his coaching practice, Lloyd sees new managers struggle to simultaneously juggle letting go of substantive expertise, managing up to senior leadership, and guiding direct reports. By balancing the consistency of building a high-functioning team with the agility to provide concise answers with imperfect information, he shows them how to move from directing action to asking the questions that empower their people.

In their influential 2004 *Harvard Business Review* article, Charles O'Reilly and Michael Tushman posited that ambidextrous organizations can simultaneously pursue incremental innovation and disruptive change.[4]

This sounds great, but how do you find the time when you feel like you need another few hours in the day just to get the normal stuff done? Time management sounds like one of the simplest tasks but it is actually a preoccupation for nearly every executive we have coached. The starting point is how you think about it.

The neuroscience of adaptive thinking

Cognitive flexibility – the ability to shift between tasks or mental frameworks – is essential in environments of complexity and volatility. The COVID-19 example mentioned at the start of this chapter provides a great illustration of cognitive flexibility in action. Those who transitioned more effortlessly used their cognitive flexibility to adapt to new challenges and opportunities around their daily routine.

Much of this is down to how our brain is wired. Neuroimaging studies have shown that cognitive flexibility depends on a network of frontal and "striatal" brain regions. The frontal regions are associated with higher cognitive processes such as decision making and problem solving. The striatal regions are linked with reward and motivation. The good news is that we can train our brains to be more flexible. Part of this is by considering different options and ideas. Cognitive Behavioral Therapy (CBT) – where assumptions are demystified and analyzed and replaced by alterative hypothesis – is an example of this. In my day job as an executive coach, my role is to be a catalyst and use techniques such as powerful questions and perspective shifts to get a client to consider different perspectives.

For lawyers, the Agile Juggler attribute is going to be crucial as many different demands compete for their time. This is even more true for general counsel. This role has expanded in scope exponentially over the last ten years, particularly in the US. Being a general counsel now is about much more than having just a legal focus. The ability to display cognitive flexibility is fundamental – am I dealing with the Board and working as a general counsel, giving strategic advice? Is there a specific question I need to weigh up the probability of regulatory enforcement on? Am I being a strategist with my operations and budget to do more with less?

For many in-house lawyers, this cognitive flexibility is already inherent in the role. Many in-house lawyers we work with speak about having to translate between outside counsel and the business, switching from the language of legal to that of commerce. What else is that than cognitive flexibility? The need to be an Agile Juggler is more imperative in environments with ambiguous, fast-changing variables – which is basically every workplace these days!

Leaders in particular will benefit from "metacognition" – the ability to reflect on and shift between mental models. This is akin to the skills described in our attribute of Bias Jiu Jitsu (chapter 10) – knowing not only how we understand and receive information but how others do so as well. It can also encompass an awareness of how we learn or how we need to show up as a leader. We have always found this more fluid concept based in metacognition much more helpful than the more static notion of leadership style, which implies something fixed. It's more, what sort of leader do you need to be for this specific context and how do you need to show up? This is more relevant than ever in a VUCA (Volatile, Uncertain, Complex, Ambiguous) world, where one set of leadership competencies may not be enough for every variable.

Leaders – VUCA and strategic responsiveness

The VUCA world demands that leaders be both consistent and adaptable. Ironically, this is actually where lawyers are likely to excel. Pretty much every

GC I know says that they are the calmest head in a crisis and that this is where they and their team add the most value. Bob Johansen, the futurist who has pioneered ideas around success in disruptive times with the Institute for the Future and his work with the Army War College, advocates for leaders to be clear but flexible, especially in the face of VUCA conditions. He recommends a mindset that can "pivot without panic". How this is achieved is via practicing voluntary fear exposure:

> *"In a world of disruptive opportunity, leaders will need to learn how to practice voluntary fear exposure. They will need safe zones to practice their leadership skills and develop their capacities, knowledge, discipline, practices, perspective, and worldview."*[5]

This idea really resonated with us both as we realized that through our training on the Exponential Age Mindset Attributes and tools, this is what we are doing – allowing leaders (and future leaders) to try out these new leadership skills in a safe place.

When we think about the leaders who have most skillfully embodied the attribute of the Agile Juggler, what stands out is their ability to adopt a true "both/and" mindset. Rather than seeing leadership challenges as an either/or choice, they hold the tension between apparent contradictions and use that tension productively. This ability to live in the space of paradox is at the heart of many Exponential Age Mindset Attributes – balancing long-term purpose with short-term responsiveness, maintaining clear structure while remaining flexible, and managing risk effectively while simultaneously driving innovation. In essence, Agile Jugglers don't collapse contradictions into compromise – they use them as creative fuel to expand what is possible.

Practical implications for leaders

The Agile Juggler mindset is a must-have for leaders as it enables them to plan for the future yet also be responsive to what is happening right now. How can you apply discipline in decision making yet also be open to agility and innovation? In legal, this might be a clear opportunity to define where the legal department's clear purpose lies and what is therefore immovable versus where there is flexibility. This could be encapsulated in the statement, "Just because it is different or new does not mean it is wrong".

This is an important distinction for lawyers as they move into the Exponential Age. The tension between "new and different" and "wrong" is one

I come up against frequently when coaching lawyers, especially those who have moved into leadership. Clients often report difficulty with delegation because of the uncertainty of letting go. "They won't do it the way I do it." Our coaching response is, "They might do it differently, but will they do it wrong?" Those aren't the same thing. An in-house lawyer needs to know the core values and purpose of their role (consistency) while being able to respond to market signals (agility).

What this looks like in action is the prioritization of people and relationship over process and documentation. Yes, both process and documentation can be improved, but often what is needed to supercharge that is a conversation and an understanding about what the aims and objectives are for all of those involved. The process and the documentation are only a means to an end. We often encounter this when we ask lawyers to reflect on the biggest purpose of a contract – it's not the contract document itself; it is to create income whether by buying or selling.

Dimension	Consistency (Stability)	Agility (Adaptability)
Strategy	Clear purpose and values	Responsive to market signals
Operations	Standardized processes	Rapid experimentation
Leadership	Disciplined execution	Cognitive flexibility
Culture	Trust and reliability	Curiosity and learning mindset

The Agile Juggler mindset in in-house legal teams

In-house legal leaders must juggle the need for legal and regulatory consistency with the agility required to support fast-moving, digitally-driven business transformation. This balancing act is central to delivering legal services that are both trusted and transformative. This requires, as with all our attributes, a cultural mindset shift and behavioral changes. These are not necessarily lincar. It may bc that you and your legal teams need to start doing things differently in order to start thinking differently, rather than waiting for a mindset shift whilst carrying on as you have always done.

From reactive to proactive

The most important shift is moving from purely reactive to proactive. Focusing only on responding keeps legal teams firmly in the sphere of business as usual and does not allow for the additions of both incremental innovations and disruptive changes. To be an Agile Juggler, risks need to be taken. That means being proactive about joining the dots and hypothesizing into a more strategic realm. In my experience, lawyers often struggle with this challenge as, when starting out in private practice, their whole *raison d'etre* was being reactive. This mindset and behavior, learnt at a formative age, can be hard to unlearn.

Look at the area of overwork and lack of resources. A legal team that is purely reactive just keeps responding and stays in the space of overwork and lack of resources. A team embracing the Agile Juggler mindset looks for opportunities and tries to take a step back to consider how the holistic issue of overwork can be innovated, not just dealt with.

Do lawyers spend too much time going back and forth on the same two clauses in a contract? Do we need to work collaboratively with the sales team to examine those clauses and their purpose to unearth why these issues continue to arise? Are these specific clauses leaving value on the table for the company?

Of course, if you are an overworked in-house lawyer, you may say this is easier said than done. In our experience as coaches, productivity and time management is a constant issue. But it is amazing how many people do not embrace simple hacks that could help.

For legal leaders, this is a key function of your leadership. How will your team be able to embrace its own Agile Juggler if you are trapped in a purely reactive mindset, and not role-modeling it yourself? It's also the main work of leadership to be able to zoom in and zoom out and embrace the opportunity as well as the here and now (see chapter three on Zoom Master).

Don't find the time, make the time

Take some strategic time. If you are not doing this, you need to. It's the real work of leadership. It may be helpful to categorize strategy time, which is more operational (how do we fix this?) versus truly blue sky thinking (where does the legal team need to be in the next five years?).

Set yourself up for success with this strategy time. Don't try and set aside two to three hours. That might be great to work towards, but if you are moving from purely reactive into Agile Juggler you are setting yourself up to fail. Start small but be consistent and build. The habit of 15 minutes of strategic thinking every few days is better than four hours every few months!

Use your team and stakeholders. Begin with the simple productive tool of "Stop, Start, Continue". This is a simple, actionable framework for identifying areas of improvement, used by teams and individuals to facilitate reflection and action after a meeting or project. It involves creating three lists – what to Start doing (new actions), what to Stop doing (ineffective actions), and what to Continue doing (successful practices). We're always surprised by how many teams find they are doing dead work when they apply this framework. An IT leader on one of our training sessions took a strategic look at what his team did and found that many hours were spent updating a SharePoint site that no one actually used. As a leader, he gave his team permission to stop immediately.

Using productivity matrixes like the Eisenhower Matrix can be helpful. A great hack is to ensure that the axis values work for you. The classic Eisenhower Matrix has the X axis value of "urgent/not urgent". I generally advise lawyers to change this to "Priority to me/Not priority to me" or to "Priority to business success". The urgent value may work for some, but if you are already trapped in a cycle of reactiveness, that may not help you get out of it!

What using these techniques ultimately leads to is more anticipatory legal partnering, where lawyers can be part of the strategy. Many legal teams have challenges with getting that seat at the table, but if you show how you can define strategic direction and innovate within your own team, perhaps peers and leaders will start to wonder what you can do for them. Again, this is where ensuring there is space at the edges for innovation and creativity is fundamental.

Legal leaders who role-model this mindset and behavior will also empower their teams to move into the realm of Agile Juggler. What is crucial for teams is feeling that they have permission to do this. Whilst some on the team may more naturally gravitate towards this mindset, others will need permission or coaching to get to it.

What this looks like in practice

It's moving from a focus on "Here are the legal risks" to "How can we help shape the opportunity?". From "We can't do that" to "Here's how we can do that responsibly". Moving into a "We can if..." space whilst keeping the North Star of ethics and responsibility. Moving from legal as a service provider that is purely reactive to legal being a strategic enabler.

In the Exponential Age, legal teams need to contend with rapid innovation cycles such as increasing implementation of AI, new uses of data, and new digital assets. The business-as-usual consistency challenge is how to keep these in line with the North Star of legality and responsible business, especially when existing legal frameworks may lag behind emerging business models. Agile Juggling here could be a move to interpreting law more dynamically while advising proactively on emerging risks. Key ideas here to aid our juggle are also drawing on Duality Master (see chapter 8) and looking at what can be learned from other instances where the law has lagged behind adoption and developments from other industries. We can also apply the Can If framework here to interrogate what is possible whilst ensuring we keep the consistency of our North Star.

The Agile Juggler mindset can also usefully be brought to bear on another Exponential Age reality – constant regulatory flux. Compliance functions can feel overwhelmed or trapped in a reactive state. Embedding legal and compliance early in the business cycle and ensuring that communication and relationships are enhanced to do this is fundamental. One of my coaching clients is a compliance officer who always makes her interactions with business stakeholders connective and memorable. She often uses props to ensure the message gets across, even ones that might raise some eyebrows – such as a Paw Patrol figure to embody the need for "wearing your compliance hard hat". It may seem silly, but it sticks!

Another Exponential Age intricacy to Agile Juggler is multijurisdictional complexity. Fragmented advice, whether from internal counsel or external counsel or a blend of both, can lead to slow decisions. This is where the balance of Agile Juggler is key. What is the consistency of your core legal standards and how can this be harmonized with an ability to empower local actions and decision making?

A final Exponential Age factor to juggle is rising stakeholder expectations, leading to legal being seen as blockers or brakes. This is where communication and relationship building are key, as well as demonstrating to business stakeholders the Agile Juggle of what needs to be consistent and where there is room for innovation. This is where the shift is needed from a "no" to a "how" mindset through risk-calibrated solutions. The use of tools such as the Can If Framework and Six Dimensions of Business Opportunity can help members of a legal team make this juggle successful.

Organizational ambidexterity in legal

Legal teams need a clear North Star (e.g., integrity, protecting the license to operate) and the ability to rapidly reconfigure to support new markets, crises, or Board priorities. Being very clear on non-negotiables and how legal uses these to protect and maximize the profitability of the business is a significant strategic aspect of the Agile Juggler. Having clarity for both team members and the business on what is non-negotiable while being able to show this does not preclude innovation or creativity.

Taking inspiration from O'Reilly and Tushman's *Harvard Business Review* article of 2004, how can this be applied in legal teams? This comes through a blend of where the tried-and-tested can be maximized and used to its optimum efficacy but not at the expense of exploring innovative solutions.

For example, create a proven playbook for risk management for contracts or IP protection whilst also exploring innovative solutions such as aligning these with AI governance and using / introducing blockchain contracts.

Example:

- Use standardized NDAs and compliance training (consistency).
- Partner on smart contracts or pilot regulatory sandboxes (agility).

Agile legal operating models

Although Agile Juggler is not strictly about Agile methodology as it is usually understood in business, the adoption of Agile principles can be an effective way to operationalize this in your legal team.

Key Agile principles such as cross-functional squads, prioritized legal sprints, and dynamic resourcing to serve evolving business needs can ensure the balance between what is "business as usual" and the innovation/ creativity space.

Legal professionals can adopt Agile methodologies by breaking down legal tasks into smaller, manageable steps, allowing for quicker delivery of results and facilitating feedback loops. Utilizing project management tools and techniques like Kanban Boards can help visualize workflow and track progress.

Conducting regular retrospectives is also helpful and is a key aspect of other Exponential Age Attributes, specifically Chaos Converter, where we learn from challenges and failure. Teams can reflect on their processes, identify areas for improvement, and adapt their approach.

What further helps this is fostering a culture of collaboration and communication. Open communication channels and regular meetings can help teams stay aligned and address issues promptly. An innovation that has helped some of our legal team clients is creating more focus and structure in meetings and limiting the amount of time given up to reporting on workload. Share this reporting in advance and make the actual meeting a chance to get shared insights for a key strategic challenge or a specific issue that a team member is facing where they are stuck.

Aligned to greater team connectivity via agility is also prioritizing client needs and feedback. Actively seeking client input throughout the legal process ensures that the final outcome meets their expectations.

Apply discipline in decision-making, while allowing experimentation at the edges. This can be clear communication with teams or stakeholders as to what needs to be escalated and what can be decided by individual contributors or even taken ownership of by the business.

Using scenario thinking to plan multiple futures while keeping today's operations aligned is a key discipline to introduce. For leaders, this can be done via the incremental start small "strategy time" outlined above. For teams and for business stakeholders, finding times to bring people together to do this starts to shift mindset and skillset and, in the case of business clients, how the legal team is seen.

Example:

- Maintain core service level agreements (SLAs) and legal policy guidance (consistency).
- Use a legal front door, where teams create a centralized, digital system for businesses to manage all incoming requests to their in-house legal department, serving as a single, organized entry point instead of scattered emails or messages. This enables structured intake of legal requests, automated routing, status tracking for both the business user and the legal team, and self-service options. Kanban boards and adaptive intake systems give the legal team more agility to juggle multiple demands than a reactive mindset based on answering every demand as it comes in.

Cognitive readiness in legal leadership

General counsel and senior lawyers must lead with strategic foresight, toggling between immediate legal clarity and long-term risk scanning. This is the opposite of "head in the sand" mentality. Rather than worrying that AI will take our jobs or about where AI won't work, focus on how it can be utilized safely now and where it can enhance. This also encompasses aspects of Bob Johansen's ideas that Exponential Age leaders need to engage in voluntary fear exercises and map out alternative scenarios to allow for preparedness and proactivity, rather than feeling as if change is simply happening to them.

Example:

- Maintain clear positions on data privacy law (consistency).
- Proactively scenario-plan for emerging AI liability regimes, including how these can be optimized via use in legal (agility).

Legal Agile Juggling tactics

Consistency anchor	Agility lever
Legal policy frameworks	Exception-based escalation models
Contract playbooks	Fast-track deal support for critical innovations
Centralized compliance oversight	Embedded legal SMEs in product teams
Annual risk assessments	Quarterly "what-if" scenario mapping
Law firm panels	Flexible legal tech solutions or ALSPs

Why the Agile Juggler Attribute matters

If in-house teams cannot balance the consistency of the key tenets of their role with upcoming new challenges, other more agile options will step forward to fill the gap this opens. This may be a technology application, but it's more likely to be a service provider that is maximizing a can-do attitude that is technology enabled. Step forward many of the Big Four and major consultancies. Maybe the actual solutions are not as finished or tailored as these providers would have us believe, but if your CEO is convinced by the promise, it's a harder job to talk them back than if they do not even feel the need to read the promises in the first place!

References

1 Salim Ismail, Michael S. Malone and Yuri van Geest, *Exponential Organizations* (Diversion Books, 2014)

2 *Ibid.*
3 https://naacp.org/history-brown-v-board-education
4 Charles O'Reilly and Michael Tushman, "Organizational Ambidexterity" (*Harvard Business Review*, 2004).
5 Bob Johansen, "Leaders: Do you Fear the Future?" (2017) https://legacy.iftf.org/future-now/article-detail/-3c3ad9a317/

Chapter 7:
Supreme Storyteller – the value of a good story

It often seems like creativity is something most of us are encouraged to leave behind in childhood, unless we are forging a career in the creative arts. But storytelling is one of the most fundamental human traits and has been throughout history. From cave paintings to creating content for TikTok, storytelling is how we share ideas and create communities. It's also a skill that is fundamental in business and is going to become even more impactful as we move into the Exponential Age.

A seminal study by George Land carried out for NASA in the 1960s found that 98 percent of children aged four to five scored at a "genius" level for creativity, measured by divergent thinking (generating multiple solutions to a problem). When the same children were retested at age ten, only 30 percent scored as creative geniuses, and at age 15, just 12 percent. By adulthood, this number dropped to less than two percent. The study concluded that the decline in creativity was not due to its natural fading but rather the influence of traditional education systems, which emphasize rote learning and conformity, suppressing natural curiosity and divergent thinking.[1] This is a shame and is one of the reasons why Supreme Storyteller is one of the most popular attributes our workshop attendees pick as an area they need to improve. But it's a skill we already have. For most of us, it's just unearthing it from where we have buried it under facts and data. It's also recognizing that facts and data tell their own stories, if we let them.

The Exponential Age is marked by rapid technological advancements, shifting business models, and constant disruption. This demands new ways of thinking, learning, and engaging. In this era, storytelling is more critical than ever because it helps leaders and professionals, including GCs and in-house lawyers, navigate complexity, drive influence, and build trust in an environment of uncertainty.

Why storytelling matters in the Exponential Age

Making sense of complexity

- The pace of change in AI, blockchain, sustainability, and regulation means that professionals face more complexity than ever before.
- Data alone is overwhelming. Stories provide context, helping people understand why something matters and how it impacts them.
- *Example:* A GC explaining AI ethics to leadership might say, "Imagine a company that implemented an AI-driven hiring tool. It worked well – until they realized it was biased against women and minorities. The legal and reputational fallout was massive. That's why ethical AI governance matters."

Engaging attention in an information-overloaded world

- With infinite content competing for attention, people tune out jargon and corporate speak but lean into stories.
- Neuroscience shows that stories activate more areas of the brain than facts alone, making them more memorable and persuasive.
- *Example:* Instead of presenting cybersecurity risks with statistics, a GC could say, "A CFO at another company once clicked on a phishing link disguised as an email from the CEO. The hackers got into the system, locked their data, and demanded millions in ransom. That's why our cybersecurity training isn't just a formality – it's business-critical."

Building trust and influence in a fast-changing world

- As hierarchies flatten and companies become more decentralized, command-and-control leadership no longer works. Influence is built through credibility and connection – which storytelling fosters.
- *Example:* A GC trying to push for stronger ESG policies could use storytelling to connect: "Years ago, a sportswear brand faced backlash for poor labor conditions in its supply chain. Consumers revolted, sales dropped, and it had to rebuild its brand from scratch. Let's make sure we're not the next company in the headlines for the wrong reasons."

Creating alignment in cross-functional teams

- The Exponential Age blurs traditional silos, requiring lawyers, technologists, and business leaders to work together. But each group speaks a different language.

- Storytelling bridges this gap by creating shared understanding and common goals.
- *Example:* When discussing the legal risks of entering a new market, a GC could say, "Imagine we're explorers heading into uncharted territory. We need a map (due diligence), a guide (local expertise), and safety gear (legal protections). Without those, we're just hoping for the best in a jungle of risks."

Driving cultural and ethical transformation

- As businesses adopt AI, automation, and new models of work, cultural transformation is key.
- People resist change when it feels abstract or imposed, but they respond to stories that make change personal and meaningful.
- *Example:* A GC leading an AI ethics discussion might say, "The CEO of a major healthcare company once said, 'We trusted our AI to diagnose diseases, but we never asked: can patients trust us?' If we don't embed ethics in AI decisions now, we risk breaking trust in ways that no policy can fix later."

Why do leaders need storytelling?

Leaders need to be able to tell stories to influence and inspire others. As you advance in your career, you are becoming a leader – irrespective of whether you have a leadership title. Your job is to lead people that you likely have some level of influence over, whether that is a team who report to you or colleagues that you need to buy into a project you are running.

To lead, you must influence. You need to bring what can be very different people along on a common journey via influence. The best way to do that is through storytelling. More importantly, storytelling that evokes an emotional reaction. But a crucial part of your leadership role will also be telling stories to people you do not have direct influence over and trying to persuade them to adopt a course of action. This becomes essential during transformation and change. It is therefore more important than ever during the time of increased change brought on by the Exponential Age. How do we make sense of the fast-paced changes brought about by technology? By telling stories.

This is why in our Exponential Age Mindset Attribute of Supreme Storyteller it is the ability to evoke an emotional reaction that will increase the probability of adoption of a new idea. *How* we speak about something needs to be as much, if not a greater focus, than *what* we speak about. Too often, lawyers can get hung up on the technical information they impart and not think about how to deliver that information for maximum impact. This is where storytelling comes in. In his coaching practice, Lloyd sees lawyers resist storytelling, priding themselves on logic while viewing creativity with suspicion. They often bury their audience in context, rules, and rationale, struggling to realize that accuracy alone does not guarantee influence. By balancing their command of the facts with the emotional resonance of a narrative, he shows them how to move from a dry recitation of the law to a compelling story that actually drives action.

Storytelling is a core skill for leaders and it's one of the competencies that the best leaders consistently draw on. There's a reason that politicians have speech writers – every speech writer knows the power of a story. Storytelling is the key modality for humans to communicate and to pass down the most crucial knowledge and ideas. That means we have adapted to receive information via a story more effectively than just a list of information. Storytelling is the most cognitively efficient way to get information into people's minds so that they can decide and act. If you tell a story, your audience will receive and process that information more effectively.

Not fluffy or frivolous

Too often we think about storytelling as fluffy or frivolous, a distraction from the important issues ("Just the facts, ma'am!"). But if you can craft a compelling and informative story that helps people understand where we are in a common framework, you can get them to start moving together in the same direction towards a common objective. As the new executive director of a legal diversity non-profit, Lloyd initially struggled to raise funds by appealing solely to logic. By balancing the abstract benefits of diversity with a visceral story of the future – imagining walking into a room filled with 500 attorneys of color – he showed donors how to move from a lack of vision to an emotional connection, ultimately asking if they wanted their firm to have a seat at *that* table.

As mentioned in earlier chapters, lawyers may be wary of creativity because, when it comes to the law, the phrase has too often had negative connotations. "Interpreting the law creatively" can be taken to mean ignoring it or using a loophole for unscrupulous ends. "Spinning a tale" often means telling an elaborate lie. But at its heart, storytelling is just arranging facts in a compelling and comprehensible manner – which lawyers are actually very good at!

Storytelling also makes the listener active. They relate to the story and link their own intrinsic motivations to it. They relate it to what it means to them and then connect that to how they can bring effort to find even better ways to move forward. If you are going to do any kind of leadership work where you need to apply influence – at any scale – then effective storytelling is a necessity. It will be an even greater necessity as leaders are responsible for steering their teams through increased change.

Managing vs leading

This might be a good point to revisit the crucial difference between managing and leading. As we tell our coaching clients, leading is a mindset and a set of behaviors. It is completely agnostic as to whether you have a title or a rank that is coded as senior or as a "leader" in your organization. You can lead at any stage in your career, no matter how junior. Of course, the reverse is true, and you can fail to be a leader in your behavior, despite having the most senior title and role!

In management, there is often a need to have a title or a hierarchy as there will be a focus on operations and on getting things done. It is about understanding the patterns of how processes overlap and how the individuals who are part of those processes work together. Management is most effective when it's a known quantity with very specific guidelines and boundaries. In our experience, this is often why management in a law firm for lawyers – say, as a partner or a practice area head – is very different from the leadership skills needed in-house. This is because of the different complexities and the fact that a lot more agility is needed in-house, due to the fast pace of change in many businesses and the range of stakeholders involved.

For lawyers who manage a team of associates as a partner, there is a very fixed hierarchy. Everyone is focused on the process of delivering work within the system of billable hours (or whatever the agreed system with a client is). This is more like a machine where everyone knows their place.

In many corporates, unlike law firms, there is a constant need to create new value, to innovate and to adapt to an increasingly dynamic environment. Of course, many corporate clients believe there should be more of these skills in their law firms than there currently are, but that is a whole other debate! Operating in an environment of new value creation, where what "value" means might change, means you need to bring people along with you on the journey, even though you might not actually know the destination.

In the Exponential Age, this need is more pressing. You, along with many, if not all your employees, will be facing existential change in the workplace. What people need more than anything at this time is a story that can help to explain the uncertainty such change brings. They want a narrative that they can insert themselves into, which gives them a personal point of connection and maybe even a sense of agency – so that they feel part of the change, and it is not just happening to them.

In leadership, you are getting into mission, vision, and strategy and how to operationalize others around that. In most instances, you do not know the specific path between where you are and where you need to go. Part of your role as leader is to recruit people to join you on the journey and bring the best of what they have, to help solve the problems that you will find along the way – problems you may have no idea of at the start.

Management and leadership are, therefore, a very different set of capabilities, and solve different problems. Both are necessary. In business, you do not want to have to lead on things that have already been solved – you want to manage those because that is an effective way to get great outcomes. You want to conserve that limited leadership capacity that you have in an organization to go and find the most interesting opportunities, to recruit the best people, and to get them moving on that. Leadership is focused more on the inspirational than the operational.

Just as you can be a leader at any point in your career, you can also be intentional about deploying storytelling at any point in your professional life. If you are going to be creative and find new ways to create value, being able to tell stories about what that looks like will be crucial to adoption.

Storytelling and the general counsel

In our years as executive coaches, we have both been surprised at how often communication is at the heart of many challenges for GCs and their teams. Indeed, we have often wondered whether communication in general, and storytelling in particular, should not be a compulsory skill for in-house lawyers as they advance in their roles!

Before the role

Central to getting a GC role is the ability to tell a story. How will you showcase your skill and experience to people who may not know or care about the intricacies of your legal experience? How can you tell stories that will show an interview panel that you have made an impact and can continue to do so on their business in a way that is broader than just legal? That may mean reframing your achievements in a way that will speak not just logically but emotionally to your interview panel and make them feel like they want to come on a journey with you as their GC.

The types of stories that are most impactful at this moment can be:

- How you work with the C-suite.
- When you have had to be the lone voice.
- How you and the legal team have made an impact on the business, shown in more than just legal terms.

Starting the role

The biggest focus when starting a legal leadership role is building relationships. This is the solid foundation for your role. What helps with building relationships? Stories!

The connection between building effective business relationships and storytelling lies in the ability to shape perception, build trust, and create alignment. The crux of the modern general counsel role is the need to bridge the gap between legal risk and business strategy. Supreme Storytelling is a powerful tool that allows GCs to communicate complex legal and risk-related issues in a way that resonates with business leaders, rather than alienating them.

It's also fundamental as you build a relationship with your team. When a new leader starts, it is inevitably going to be a time of change and uncertainty for your team, which will be amplified if there is uncertainty in your organization or industry. You will need your team behind you even if that team might change, so you need to tell them the story of:

1. Who you are.
2. The GC you will be.
3. What this means for them.

The stories you tell in your initial days in the GC role can literally shape the rest of your tenure. But Supreme Storytelling is a skill that should be deployed throughout your role, as it will be key in enhancing business relationships.

How Supreme Storytelling enhances business relationships

Firstly, it humanizes the role of the lawyer. Business teams often perceive lawyers as roadblocks. A GC who shares real-world stories about past business successes (or failures) linked to legal decisions can reposition themselves as a strategic enabler rather than a naysayer. The exact language used can also help to shape this reality. (For more on this, dive into chapter 14 on the Can If framework.)

Secondly, it creates emotional engagement. Facts tell, but stories sell, as Bryan Eisenberg, a pioneer in online marketing, stated.[2] His quote reinforces the importance of leveraging the power of story when connecting with others. When you start a new role, you are effectively selling yourself. When you are a new GC, you're also selling your vision of what the legal department is and can be with you at the helm. In the day-to-day of your role, people will always relate to narratives far more than abstract (legal) principles. A GC who frames compliance, risk, or governance as a relatable business challenge rather than a set of rules will gain more buy-in.

Thirdly, the stories you tell can help business leaders navigate uncertainty. There's a reason that Supreme Storytelling is a key attribute in the Exponential Age. This is a way for us to make sense of and then navigate uncertainty and change. For a GC and their team, storytelling provides a way to illustrate the consequences of certain decisions using real or hypothetical scenarios, helping non-lawyers grasp legal risk in a practical, tangible way.

Finally, in shaping corporate culture, increasingly GCs play a key role in embedding ethics and integrity into an organization. Instead of just laying down rules, they can use stories (such as case studies from similar industries) to illustrate why ethical decision-making matters and how it impacts long-term business success. This ethical aspect of storytelling has always been there – fables and fairy tales all have a message.

Whilst AI is not going back in its box, we are still figuring out the ethical implications of much of its usage and deployment, so this cultural storytelling piece will become ever more important as GCs and their teams help organizations navigate this.

What do we mean when we talk about storytelling?

We want to take others on a journey with us to get them to a new destination. We can frame that as having an emotional response or creating change. Another way to think about it is transporting others to our reality or viewpoint. To do that effectively, we need to understand their context and where they are coming from. This is where the linked attribute of Champion Chameleon – the ability to craft communication to your audience – intertwines with Supreme Storyteller. However, we also need to distinguish between crafting the story and telling the story.

Tools to craft your story

There is a difference between crafting a great story versus telling a great story. Having a well-crafted structure will make the telling much easier – like scaffolding to support your storytelling. To effectively craft the story, we need to understand the basic structure of the story's journey.

What makes a great story can be defined in two words – human connection. A great story connects the writer and/or the teller with their audience and the audience with each other. It connects the audience to the characters so that we care about them. It also connects us to our own life and opportunities and challenges.

This can be refined into a simple structure of CSCS:[3]

- Character – we're introduced to them.
- Situation – we see their status quo.
- Challenge – they have an issue to be resolved.
- Solution – the issue is resolved.

Let's apply this to a couple of well-known stories.

Jack and the Beanstalk:

- *Character:* Jack, a poor boy who lives with his widowed mother.
- *Situation:* Jack is sent to sell the family cow but instead trades it for magic beans.
- *Challenge:* The beans grow into a giant beanstalk leading to a castle in the sky, where Jack must outwit a fearsome giant to retrieve treasures that can help his family.
- *Solution:* Jack climbs the beanstalk multiple times, steals magical items (a harp, a hen that lays golden eggs), and finally chops down the beanstalk to defeat the giant and live happily with his mother.

Star Wars: A New Hope:

- *Character:* Luke Skywalker, young farm boy living on the desert planet Tatooine with dreams of a bigger life.
- *Situation:* R2-D2's message from Princess Leia leads Luke to Obi-Wan Kenobi, who reveals Luke's connection to the Force and gives him his father's lightsaber. After his aunt and uncle are killed, Luke embraces the call to adventure and joins Obi-Wan on a mission.
- *Challenge:* Rescuing Leia and fighting the Empire. To do so, Luke leaves Tatooine with Obi-Wan, hires Han Solo, infiltrates the Death Star to rescue Leia, and escapes the station after Obi-Wan's sacrifice.

- *Solution:* Luke helps destroy the Death Star and is recognized as a hero by the Rebel Alliance.

The characters' challenge is solved but they are changed and so is the audience via hearing the story.

How can this structure work outside of fiction? For example, in an in-house legal department?

- *Character:* Contract manager.
- *Situation:* Too many contracts with incomplete information.
- *Challenge:* How to streamline this process and ensure the legal department does not waste time going back and forth with the business to check information, leading to delays in contracts, delays in sales, and therefore delays in revenue.
- *Solution:* Intake system with requirements to complete key information by the business before contract goes to legal. Leads to a smoother process with faster completion time.

How to tell a good story

There is obviously a significant overlap between crafting and telling your story. In telling your story, you still need to consider the different components you need for a successful story. How do you present these? The story needs to resonate with its audience and have a purpose. Why are you telling this story and who are you telling it to? Does how you tell your story need to change with each audience? (Spoiler: usually, yes!)

Who is your audience?

The most important part of storytelling is understanding who the audience is and their frame of reference. The storyteller needs to get into that frame and understand what that other person is seeing to offer them something that will make sense to them. Storytelling therefore must start with curiosity and empathy.

You need to think about who is listening and what their goals are. Just as when you look at something from different angles it can appear very different, so the purpose of a story might be completely different depending on who you are telling it to. That needs to be fundamental in creating your story to be a Supreme Storyteller.

For example, telling a story about the need for a new process for dealing with contracts more effectively and efficiently via a Contract Lifecycle Management (CLM) system might be very different depending on your audience.

The business stakeholder

This person has no interest in the contract process or how you manage it, just in getting the contract executed smoothly and quickly so business can be realized. Revenue will therefore be faster.

- *Anchor point:* The CLM system will change how we do things, but the net result will be more contracts delivered more quickly.
- *Key emotional point:* You and your team will look better to clients. You will get revenue incentives such as commission faster.

The GC

Their focus is on big picture strategic wins for the business and how this will affect legal's reputation.

- *Anchor point:* Delivery on contracts will be faster using less human resource. If contracts are processed faster the business will have access to more cash quickly via revenue being delivered faster.
- *Key emotional point:* Legal will literally be creating ROI for the company. What will that do for your standing in the executive?

In-house lawyers

Their focus is on the way this changes what they do.

- *Anchor point:* Frees up their time from repetitive tasks and being constantly stuck in a cycle of reactivity for business clients.
- *Key emotional point:* What could *you* do with more hours in the day?

Paralegals

There will be concern about how this will change their role and the transition to a new system. Will it make me obsolete?

- *Anchor point:* This is the next development for your role and it gives you strategic oversight over a huge volume of contracts.
- *Key emotional point:* This is a change you can take control of.

It's one thing if you are telling your story to these groups separately – it can be crafted to their particular perspective. The easiest of all is telling a story to one individual and you know the characteristics of who you're trying to effectively sell to. Is Jane a football fan? I can use a football metaphor. Stuart loves traveling with his young family, I can draw attention to the time this frees up to do that.

When you are working with a larger group, you start by taking shared viewpoints that unite and make up the group you are speaking to. Where it gets hardest is when you have a larger organization and you must create a communication strategy that has pieces that will hit the different psychographic profiles. For example, a global general counsel who has different cultural values displayed across her team and is responsible for legal, compliance, security, and government affairs. In this case, there has to be big themes so that there's something there for everyone, because she won't get to tell each of them an individual story. Maybe it's safety, fairness, or a key aspect of what defines the organization. Whatever it is, there needs to be recognition and an emotional hook, so that when somebody reads through it or hears it, they are seeing themselves in the story.

The purpose – why am I telling you this?

In training that we have run with companies where a presentation is the capstone project – often one that is presented to business leaders or Board members – the purpose is always crucial and is the thing to lead with. Why should they be listening to this?

The purpose of the story is the anchor point, and you need to come back to it repeatedly.

It is why your story exists. The most memorable stories have a message or a purpose, and the narrative explores that but ultimately brings us back to the purpose and what we should take from it.

Let's look at the fairytale of Jack and the Beanstalk again as an example of this. The central message is that via action and risk you can change your circumstances.

1. Jack dares to explore the unknown by climbing the beanstalk. His curiosity and ability to take a risk open doors to opportunity and adventure.
2. Jack outsmarts the giant and escapes with treasures, showing that cleverness can overcome even the most intimidating obstacles.
3. Jack's family is poor, but through action and risk, he changes their fortune. This suggests that *initiative and perseverance* can lead to better circumstances.

In business settings, particularly with business stakeholders, it is crucial to lead with your purpose. In watching in-house lawyers practice presenting to the Board, one of the most consistent pieces of feedback we hear from Board members is, "Why are your presenting to me? Why should I bother to listen?"

This needs to be stated in the first few seconds of your presentation (or conversation or email). One Fortune 500 GC shared with us that his CEO never reads more than the preview of an email shown on his phone, so he must make his key points in the subject line and the first two short sentences. It's worth remembering that when telling a story to a CEO too!

Lawyers can be at a disadvantage here because of their training, which focuses on setting up your argument and proving it. This means most lawyers are used to elaborating on their argument and then ending with their key point. This is something that must be unlearned in both business and private practice. Lead with what matters. You can return to it. Indeed, repetition is a technique you can use to increase the effectiveness of your story.

The rule of three

In presentation and storytelling, the rule of three is well-recognized. If you are looking to become a Supreme Storyteller in the Exponential Age, it is a tactic you should know and use. But why is the number three so effective in getting information across?

- *Groups of three create pattern recognition.* Our brains are wired to recognize patterns, and groups of three are the most easily recognizable and memorable.
- *Rhythm and flow.* The use of three elements can create a natural rhythm and flow in a story, making it more engaging. Three also has a natural balance which four does not achieve in quite the same way.
- *Emphasis.* Repeating a concept or element three times can emphasize its importance and make it stick in the audience's mind. Take, for example, former UK prime minister Tony Blair's speech about "Education, education, education" or the famous phrase about what's important for property – "location, location, location".
- *Structure and organization.* The rule of three can also provide a structure for organizing story elements, such as the three-act structure of a play or the three stages of a hero's journey. In the classic analysis of story structure, three is the organizing structure:

1. Exposition (or Situation).
2. Conflict (or Challenge).
3. Resolution (or Solution).

Politicians love using the rule of three in their speeches because it resonates so well. Famous examples include Julius Caesar's "Veni, vidi, vici" ("I came, I saw, I conquered"), Dr Martin Luther King Jr's "Free at last! Free at last! Thank God Almighty, we are free at last!" and Barack Obama's "I stand here today humbled by the task before us, grateful for the trust you have bestowed, mindful of the sacrifices borne by our ancestors". You don't need a speech writer to use this, though. In a training course we undertook with paraprofessionals in a large legal department on taking charge of their careers, one session was how to speak about your career. One of the best examples they came up with was "Boost, Build, and Breakthrough". This not only uses the rule of three but alliteration.

Alliteration

As in the example above, alliteration is using words that begin with the same letter. Like the rule of three, it creates a link between ideas in the listener's mind. It also creates rhythm and melody – for that reason, it's often used in poetry or dramatic dialogue. (Think of Shakespeare's introduction of the characters in Romeo and Juliet: "From forth the fatal loins of these two foes".)

It is also catchy, so is often used in branding and advertising.

Metaphor

A metaphor is using something to describe something else to get a point across. For example, "a rollercoaster of emotions". Emotions and rollercoasters are different things but if we want to convey the experience of changing emotions, the feeling of being on a rollercoaster gives us a sense of that. A metaphor can be crucial to get a point across to people who are not experts. It can be a fantastic way to humanize technical knowledge and bring it to life. What a metaphor essentially does is draw a picture or create a mini movie in the mind of your audience.

This is another reason why knowing your audience is important. Using a metaphor that is very specific to your business might work in some instances – in fact, can be useful to make them relate to the story more – but won't if you're presenting to a more general crowd.

Let's look at some popular metaphors:

- The elephant in the room.
- A rollercoaster of emotions.
- We're building the plane as we fly it.
- Opportunity is a door.
- He is a wolf in sheep's clothing.

A metaphor can be crucial in building a brand for yourself or your team. "If opportunity is a door, then we want to make sure we don't crash through it thoughtlessly. Think of the legal team as opening the door for business opportunity in the right way."

More than facts

When you know where you are starting from and where you want to get to, it gets easier to build the hardest part of the story, which is the compelling narrative that connects them.

Something we've observed is that people in business (lawyers especially) tend to think of a story as a recitation of facts, like reading a list. That is not a story. A story is a journey, which has visuals and emotions – Jack sells the cow for some "magic" beans. He feels like he has been swindled, because they don't do anything at first. But they grow a magic beanstalk. This climbs up into the sky to a giant's lair. He must outwit the giant to ensure success and happiness. There is tension – the giant will kill him if he catches him! We are rooting for Jack to succeed.

We need to weave elements into the story that activate both thinking and feeling for people, because that is what makes it "sticky", using the concept of "The Stickiness Factor". In his influential book, *The Tipping Point*, published in 2000, Malcolm Gladwell explained this "stickiness" is what makes a message memorable, impactful, and resonant.

Reinforce it with rhetoric

Additional techniques to create messaging – aside from the alliteration, which this heading illustrates – that bridge between the crafting of a story and its delivery are those associated with the ancient art of rhetoric. Rhetoric is the skill of effective or persuasive communication, especially in speaking or writing. It involves using language strategically to influence or convince an audience. Rhetoric was defined by Greek Philosopher Aristotle in the fourth century BC in his book of the same name.[4]

Aristotle defined the key components of rhetoric as:

- *Ethos*. Credibility of the speaker and their experience. Using the example above, our contract manager can create ethos by defining what their role entails and how much experience they have; how many contracts their team might process a month and so forth.
- *Pathos*. Appealing to the audience's emotions via empathy. In our contract manager example, that might involve quantifying the time saved by a new system and inviting the audience to think about what they would do with that extra time.
- *Logos*. Using logos involves providing facts and external data to validate claims. In our CLM example, it might be benchmarking how much other legal teams who use this process have speeded it up and streamlined it.
- *Kairos*. Kairos is an often-forgotten aspect of the components of rhetoric, which considers the timeliness and appropriateness of the message and the moment to deliver it. It's about delivering the message at the right time and in the right context. Going back to our contract management example, delivering the message in a one-to-one interaction with a junior salesperson who is just trying to get a single contract done would not resonate. However, if our manager delivered it in a strategy planning meeting for the whole sales team, that might mean greater success.

Brutus versus Mark Anthony

One of the best examples of a story that really grabs an audience emotionally in is the contrast between the speeches that Brutus and Mark Anthony give over Julius Caesar's body. Brutus uses reason and ideas. He is using persuasion, not influence. This is a speech designed to speak to the head not the heart. He uses only ethos and logos, not pathos and kairos – this is compelling but only up to a point. When it is followed by a full-on emotionally charged story steeped in the skills of influencing and relying heavily on pathos and kairos for its effect, as exemplified by Anthony, the heart wins over the head every time.

Brutus' speech is balanced. It literally weighs one idea or action against another: "Not that I loved Caesar less but that I loved Rome more."

Anthony's speech plays with a similar construct of balance but uses it to *unbalance* Brutus' speech. In this excerpt, he gives examples of Caesar's personal acts of generosity to him and to the people of Rome and balances these against the argument outlined by Brutus, thereby destabilizing that argument.

"When that the poor have cried,
Caesar hath wept:
Ambition should be made of sterner stuff:
Yet Brutus says he was ambitious.
And Brutus is an honorable man."[5]

Anthony's speech focuses on the visceral and emotional aspects of Caesar's murder – showing the wounds that have been inflicted by his friends. It is designed to appeal to the heart, not the head. In business, both are needed but too often the emotional impact of storytelling versus imparting information is forgotten.

Storytelling and influencing

Storytelling is at the heart of influencing. In order to both tell the best story and to influence, we need to know our audience. One of the things we have seen play out across the political spectrum in recent years is that it is often easier to sway people by appealing to their emotions than their logic. This isn't always a positive – but it's important to be aware of it.

A key emotion is feeling valued and that we can trust the person giving the information – that they have our best interests at heart. One reason social media influencers do so well is that they create a sense of community and a sense of trust between people they have never met. They do this by crafting a narrative or a story about themselves that their audiences relate to.

Instagram and TikTok are made up of micro stories that are great at grabbing people where they are or where they feel they want to be. Those telling the stories can then craft their messages to the community they want to reach. Those stories literally shape their audiences' worldview – to influence them.

Change management – influencing and storytelling

Change management needs stories to create influence that causes people to do something differently. The relationship between change management, influencing, and storytelling lies in their interconnected roles in driving organizational and behavioral transformation. Here's how they relate.

Change management and influencing

- Change management involves guiding individuals, teams, and organizations through transitions.

- Influencing is a critical skill in change management, as it helps gain stakeholder buy-in, overcome resistance, and align people toward a common goal.

Influencing and storytelling

- Storytelling is a powerful influencing tool. It helps convey complex ideas in a relatable way, making change feel necessary and achievable.
- A well-crafted story can engage emotions, making people more open to new perspectives and willing to act.

Change management and storytelling

- Storytelling can frame the need for change in a way that resonates with different stakeholders.
- It helps create a shared vision, making the change journey compelling rather than daunting.
- Leaders can use stories of past successes, future possibilities, and personal experiences to inspire commitment to change.

Change management is like gardening. Like a gardener, a leader planning change carefully plants, nurtures, and guides growth. They must understand the environment, anticipate resistance (weeds), and ensure the right conditions for transformation. *Influencing is the soil.* The quality of the soil determines whether change takes root. If it's rich and well-prepared (strong relationships, trust, and alignment), new ideas will flourish. If it's dry and compacted (resistance, lack of engagement, lack of trust), even the best plans struggle to grow. *Storytelling is the sun.* Just as the sun provides energy for plants to grow, storytelling fuels engagement and emotional connection. A compelling story can illuminate the purpose of change, making it more relatable and inspiring people to embrace it.

Without influencing (the soil), change won't take root. Without storytelling (the sun), people won't feel the energy to grow. And without change management (the gardener), the process lacks direction and care.

Examples of storytelling in a GC's role

Compliance and ethics – the cost of getting it wrong

Instead of just saying, "We need to comply with anti-bribery laws", a GC could tell a story: "I once worked with a company that ignored a small red flag in their third-party contracts. Five years later, that red flag turned into a full-blown regulatory investigation that cost them millions. Let's make sure we don't walk into the same trap."

This frames compliance as a proactive business strategy rather than a bureaucratic burden.

Risk and decision-making – choosing the right path

A GC advising on a major commercial deal might say: "I've seen companies take shortcuts to close a deal faster, only to spend years in litigation trying to undo those shortcuts. The best deals are not just the fastest ones, but the ones built on a solid legal and commercial foundation."

This helps business leaders think beyond short-term gains.

Building trust with the board – lessons from the past

A GC advocating for stronger governance might use a case study: "There was a CEO who dismissed governance concerns as "red tape" – until a shareholder lawsuit led to his removal. Strong governance isn't about bureaucracy, it's about protecting leadership from blind spots."

This makes governance feel like a shield rather than a constraint.

Handling internal resistance – relatable business scenarios

If business teams resist process-heavy legal requirements, a GC might reframe the discussion: "Imagine we're a Formula 1 team. The drivers (business teams) want to go fast, but without a pit crew (legal and compliance), they'd crash. Our job isn't to slow you down; it's to make sure you can win the race safely."

This shifts the perception of legal from a blocker to a crucial support function.

Key takeaways for GCs:

- Use storytelling to reframe risk discussions so that they align with business priorities.
- Make legal issues real and relatable by using metaphors, case studies, analogies, and past experiences.
- Turn abstract legal concepts into concrete narratives that highlight consequences and benefits.
- Engage emotions, not just intellect – people remember stories and human connection, not rules.

References

1 Dr George Land, TEDX Tuscon, December 2011, The Failure Of Success", https://youtu.be/ZfKMq-rYtnc?si=ZR4YwUjoFEWWLjUr

2 www.linkedin.com/posts/bryaneisenberg_if-you-want-to-kill-a-sale-heres-how-take-activity-7361026286317719553-j-s7/

3 Thanks to friend and fellow coach Larry Stubbings for introducing us to this way of framing storytelling. Larry is an amazing coach and workshop leader for storytelling skills. www.lawrencestubbings.com/index.html

4 This is also known by other titles: *On Rhetoric, Treatise on Rhetoric.* It was also not likely a real book and not intended for publication as it is a series of students' notes from his lectures.

5 William Shakespeare, *Julius Caesar*, Act 3 Scene 2.

Chapter 8: Duality Master – looking outside of your area of expertise

Being a Duality Master is having the ability to take knowledge from one pursuit and apply it creatively to another. This is based on knowing that some of the best ideas can be borrowed or stolen, and not only from obvious sources. Drawing on ideas from other areas also stops your brain from being constrained by "known" solutions.

This attribute sits firmly at the heart of creativity. Creativity is a fundamental competency that humans will need to thrive in the age of AI. The good news? We already have lots of it! The bad news is we often subdue this in our professional lives unless we are in a profession deemed "creative".

I have worked both in the creative arts and in areas not generally considered creative (such as professional services), and I firmly believe – and have seen for myself – that whatever we do benefits from applying creativity. For what is creativity, but the ability to think differently and bring disparate ideas to a problem?

AI can currently sort through vast amounts of data and come up with ideas, but these cannot match true human creativity. When a fan attempted to create a "Nick Cave style song" via ChatGPT, the singer/songwriter himself was understandably unimpressed. The result had captured the style, but none of the substance that makes Cave such a unique artist – one that has a decades-long, devoted fanbase. What is this substance? It is human experience and the ability to take this and transform it into something else. Said Cave:

> *"Songs arise out of suffering, by which I mean they are predicated upon the complex, internal human struggle of creation and, well, as far as I know, algorithms don't feel. Data doesn't suffer. ChatGPT has no inner being, it has been nowhere, it has endured nothing, it has not had the audacity to reach beyond its limitations, and hence it doesn't have the capacity for a shared transcendent experience, as it has no limitations from which to transcend. ChatGPT's melancholy role is that it is destined to imitate and can never have an authentic human experience, no matter how devalued and inconsequential the human experience may in time become."*[1]

What Cave defines in his response to the fan who used ChatGPT to create a "Nick Cave" song is the effort and search in creation. "It's a blood and guts business, here at my desk, that requires something of me to initiate the new and fresh idea. It requires my humanness. What that new idea is, I don't know, *but it is out there somewhere, searching for me. In time, we will find each other."* (our italics)

What this quote highlights is the search for a creative idea that will often come from looking outside of what we know or giving that familiarity a jolt. This is where the aptitude of Duality Master comes to the fore. It is going to be increasingly central to what drives the value and the spark that humans bring to business as it is something that technology will be unable to replicate.

What is at play here is divergent thinking, which is a core component of creativity and what it means to be human.

Divergent thinking

Divergent thinking is a method used to generate creative ideas by exploring as many potential solutions as possible. This is done by brainstorming in a spontaneous, free-flowing, non-linear manner, which generates myriad ideas through an emergent cognitive process. In neurological terms, this means that the more cognitive aspects of the brain are connecting with its more emotional parts. The more creative you force your brain to be, the more neurological connections it will generate. This echoes the lived experience of creativity. A famous proponent of this point of view was Apple co-founder Steve Jobs, who in his 2005 Stanford University Commencement address focused on the idea that learning a diverse range of things that, in the moment, may not offer the most practical benefit, is better long-term. Over time, these things add up to give you a broader base of knowledge from which to connect ideas:

> *"Creativity is just connecting things. When you ask creative people how they did something, they feel a little guilty because they didn't really do it, they just saw something. It seemed obvious to them after a while. That's because they were able to connect experiences they've had and synthesize new things. And the reason they were able to do that was that they've had more experiences, or they have thought more about their experiences than other people. Unfortunately, that's too rare a commodity. A lot of people in our industry haven't had very diverse experiences. So, they don't have enough*

dots to connect, and they end up with very linear solutions without a broad perspective on the problem."[2]

This literally defines divergent thinking. What is at play here is completely different to the "thinking" of technology tools, which is linear and needs the right prompts, questions, or instructions.

The creative skill of understanding not only the issue but how it can be viewed from different angles – or even connected with something disparate – is going to be the key not only to using technology effectively but also to developing the next generation of technology, including AI.

Reframing the problem to release creativity

Many researchers believe it is problem formulation that will define the creation and application of the next waves of AI. Unlike prompt creation, problem formulation is less about engineering language but more about understanding the whole situation and the context in which it exists, including being able to reframe the problem.

Problem reframing involves changing the perspective from which a problem is viewed, enabling alternative interpretations. By reframing a problem in various ways, you can guide AI to broaden the scope of potential solutions, which can, in turn, help you find optimal solutions and overcome creative roadblocks.

At its core, Duality Master is about reframing problems and solutions by drawing on a wider base of knowledge and diverse perspectives to find better ways forward. When James Dyson invented the vacuum cleaner to which he gave his name, he was frustrated with the way the suction power of the traditional vacuum cleaner diminished as the bag filled with dust. Trying to solve this problem in a linear way did not produce results. By reframing the problem through taking an idea from a completely unrelated industry and applying it, he created the innovation that made his fortune – by mimicking the centrifuge in sawmills that sucked dust out of the air and eliminated the need for a bag.

In coaching, the coach will help the client reframe a perceived problem by looking at it from a different perspective (or variety of perspectives). Some of these may be suggested by the coach – being open to others' suggestions is a key part of reframing, as they may offer perspectives you lack. This can create a catalyst for the client to come up with a completely unthought of solution or even see that the problem is not as significant as they believed.

The key is moving beyond one way of thinking and understanding. It is this broadening of perspective that is at play in Duality Master.

How does Duality Master apply to lawyers?

How can lawyers apply this? Creative thinking techniques such as Duality Master are not as far removed from the lawyer's mindset as some might think. Lawyers are trained primarily to think via looking at the facts of a case and at the precedent of prior judicial decisions. But how those can be interpreted or reinterpreted, particularly by bringing different evidence or ideas to bear on them, is where creativity comes into play.

Legal training is rigorous in getting students to think about problems and refigure them in different ways. Where it is less analogous with creative thinking is in giving a broader and bigger perspective beyond the original context to get new ideas and to view the problem in a different way, which can create innovative solutions.

Going wide

It's often obvious to look for ideas in teams or disciplines that are close to our own. For example, the discipline of legal operations largely evolved out of financial specialists being embedded within legal departments in financial services companies to slow down spiraling costs, particularly with outside counsel. That involved taking ideas from one discipline – financial management and accounting – and applying them to the similar one of managing cost with outside counsel.

Where Duality Master really flexes its power as an attribute is when those working on issues look to very different arenas for ideas and solutions.

In their article in *Harvard Business Review* in 2014, Marion Poetz, Nikolaus Franke, and Martin Schrieier posit that it is in seeking ideas from further afield where innovation lies:

> *"When you're working on a problem and you pool insights from analogous areas, you're likely to get significantly greater novelty in the proposed solutions, for two reasons: People versed in analogous fields can draw on different pools of knowledge, and they're not mentally constrained by existing, 'known' solutions to the problem in the target field. The greater the distance between the problem and the analogous field, the greater the novelty of the solutions."*[3]

The key is to find ideas that are related in their core factors, even if the specifics or the application are completely different.

Doing this in and of itself is incredibly useful, as it will force you to get to the crux of an issue by boiling it down to its key general components rather than its specific context. This is where the significant difference between the human mind and the machine mind is found. For generative AI queries, the key is to be as detailed and specific as possible in prompts or questions. In the discipline of Duality Master, we are going broad and wide to try and identify new ways of solving problems.

As a coach, this is what we like to do with our clients when we "bottom line" a problem or try to put it in its broadest terms possible. The client may tell a very involved story featuring lots of different people, but as a coach, we must try and find the broadest way of looking at that issue. This is for two reasons:

1. To open the client's mind to different ways of considering the problem, which is easier to do if it is conceived in the broadest brushstrokes.
2. If the issue is taken out of the specific context and framed more broadly, it may open the client's mind to other instances when this has come up for them – and the solutions that were then applied.

Can If – harnessing the power of Duality Master

The Can If process (discussed in detail in chapter 14) is a crucial tool for stretching into the attribute of Duality Master because it forces focus on a problem whilst marrying this with an outward-looking mindset – where, if one avenue of possibility does not work, we look to the next avenue, which may yield results.

Just as problems often have multifaceted interlinked aspects, Can If pushes us to look beyond one solution. Many of the paths in the Can If map force us to look beyond the obvious and even potentially beyond our own disciplines to find solutions by looking at a challenge via a range of different proposed pathways such as "We can if:

- We access the knowledge of..."
- We mix together..."
- We think of it as...".

In an exercise using Can If applied to a role-play scenario focused on environmental issues, one group of in-house lawyers unlocked a whole new way of solving legal issues by following the pathway that led them to other sources of knowledge – "We can if we access the knowledge of environmental scientists".

How legal departments can use Duality Master

Step 1: Make time and space

Many leaders do not allow themselves time and space to think about the bigger picture. One of the biggest challenges we face when coaching general counsel, particularly those new to the role, is getting them to recognize the need to block out time to think about challenging problems and allow their mind space to make connections with other ideas.

Some years ago, I heard Sacha Romanovitch, the first female CEO of Grant Thornton, speak about how she kept a two-hour slot sacrosanct twice-weekly on her calendar for thinking and strategizing. This was a revelation to me, partly because of the way she framed it – the work of a leader is to think about the big issues and solve problems, and you need time and space to do that. This can be a challenge for many lawyers, who are schooled in being reactive to client demands. They need to literally unmake this mindset.

Step one, therefore, is to create the time and training your mind needs to be able to make connections. This might not be just sitting at your computer figuring out if there is a link between your supply chain issue and Bram Stoker's *Dracula* (which, after all, has a major plot point centered on shipping crates internationally!). It might be making a connection with a colleague in a completely different area in your business to hear about their strategies.

Step 2: Bottom line your issue

Once you have created the time to think, you need to be able to "bottom line" your issue. What is the essence of your problem?

For example:

> *"My company is facing a challenge with getting its business unit in Malaysia to undergo mandatory legal and compliance training. The business unit leader is a salesperson who thinks this is a 'check the box' waste of time. Admittedly, the historical training we had is not that compelling. My AP lead legal counsel is too deferential to him. I'm worried that with this combination of an opinionated leader, an unconfident lawyer, and a lack of focus on how we do things, we are potentially courting risk."*

What are the key aspects of this problem?

- The business team and its leader do not see the value of training (understanding).
- The lawyers may not understand the specific challenges of the business unit (understanding / connection).
- There is a lack of discussion (connection / communication).
- The training is boring and irrelevant (understanding / communication).

So, we have three general issues – lack of understanding, connection, and communication. The potential outcome could be enhanced risk factors.

Another solution is to look outside of our own understanding and history to see if there are examples of others who have solved similar issues.

The Duality Master in practice

We mentioned Dyson and his sawmills, but there are numerous other examples in business of game-changing ideas coming from a source completely removed from the original issue. Utilizing a completely different idea is a way of reframing perspective, which provides the opportunity for a groundbreaking new insight on the issue.

Failure is not an option – outsourcing at NatWest

The outsourcing technology and IP legal team at UK bank NatWest wanted to tackle failure directly, as it was limiting innovation and preventing the bank from meeting customer needs while shifting toward greater digital engagement.

The team's lead lawyer, Kenny Robertson, realized there was a big issue holding the team back – its fear of failure. As he probed more, he realized that he had this fear as well. It seemed to be a common issue in the industry. He had been reading a lot about how innovation in arenas such as technology was fueled by a mindset that saw failure as part of the process – the "fail fast and fail forward" mindset. But it would be hard to adapt this to the area of law if the idea of failing was such a taboo. Robertson had the idea of bringing in some speakers from other industries where failure was even more high stakes than an in-house legal department. He found a surgeon and an airline pilot – jobs where the cost of failure could literally be life or death.

Both speakers shared that failure was not something to be ashamed of, to hide, or to hide from. These key insights transformed the legal team's relationship with failure. They saw that the value in a failure – even a catastrophic one – was learning what went wrong and why. Doctors and surgeons will – as part of a key process in understanding – present to colleagues on cases that went wrong. This is in order to actively source feedback and suggestions about what could be done differently to prevent such things happening again. Air accidents and incidents are routinely investigated by the relevant authorities to ascertain causes, with the results shared to improve future aviation safety.[4]

Doing things differently

What this looks like in practice is partly rooted in understanding that the *accepted* way of doing things is not the *only* way of doing things.

More CLOs and GCs are going to need to embrace this mindset in the Exponential Age in the same vein as James Dyson or Steve Jobs to maximize the power of making creative connections.

One of the key issues that we see currently with many legal leaders is recognition of the need for AI and similarly transformative technologies and processes – but a lack of understanding that the fundamental operating model and structure within which these are applied will need to change. It will not merely be layering extra tech onto what we already have, but "blowing up the box". In Gary Magenta's book of the same name about disrupting the customer experience, a phrase that resonates and is repeated throughout the book is, "What is our purpose and what are we willing to throw away to remain true to it?"[5] Mastering this is at the heart of the Duality Master.

References

1 Nick Cave, the Red Hand Files www.theredhandfiles.com/chat-gpt-what-do-you-think/

2 "Steve Jobs on Creativity", *FS Blog*: https://fs.blog/steve-jobs-on-creativity.

3 Marion Poetz, Nikolaus Franke, and Martin Schrieier, "Sometimes the Best ideas Come from Outside Your Industry", *Harvard Business Review*, 21 November 2014: https://hbr.org/2014/11/sometimes-the-best-ideas-come-from-outside-your-industry

4 Catherine McGregor, *Business Thinking in Practice for In-House Legal Teams* (Globe Law and Business 2020) pp305-317.

5 Gary Magenta, *Blowing up the Box* (Root Inc, 2020) p59.

Chapter 9:
Champion Chameleon – the empathic part of communication and influence

Champion Chameleon is intrinsically linked to Supreme Storyteller and Bias Jiu Jitsu. It is a chameleon-like communication style that allows you to communicate effectively with all learning styles and the ability to craft communication to your audience, whether that's many people or just one. Having the awareness of Champion Chameleon is also a fundamental building block of influencing skills.

Champion Chameleon in action

"My CEO is a crook." This was the bold declaration from one of my GC coaching clients who was new in role. This was certainly serious, but his delivery of this proclamation was colored by emotion. The obvious question might be, "Why do you think that?" But a more useful question, informed by my coaching experience, was "What's making you reach that opinion?".

The GC felt he was not listened to. His emails detailing the best way forward and giving the legal whys and wherefores seemed to go unanswered, often unread. His CEO was not keen to meet with him regularly. The GC felt unseen, unheard, and devalued. There was a lot of frustration bubbling up in him. To his mind, a CEO who ignored his lawyer was gearing up to enact business tactics that were inadvisable and maybe illegal. But was this actually true?

I asked him to tell me about his CEO. This was a man focused on results and sales. They were working in a fintech start-up that was growing but had a lean management team. The CEO was very busy. A key detail for me was that the CEO had never worked with a GC before – his prior companies had been so small they had no dedicated internal legal support.

What was the CEO's communication style? He rarely answered emails and preferred a phone call or WhatsApp message. He always liked meetings to be to the point and was not good at "small talk".

To me, this seemed less like impending malfeasance, and more a clash of communication styles and expectations. And an illustration of why being a Champion Chameleon is so important in the Exponential Age.

What would change if the GC could see things from his CEO's perspective – time poor and dealing with a function he had no experience with? We explored the emotions that the CEO might be feeling. In doing this, the GC had a significant insight – "He just doesn't know what to do with me!".

The action plan we put in place was succinct communication to demonstrate to the CEO how the GC could help him achieve what was important to him. Rather than framing the legal and regulatory advice purely as such, the GC made a conscious effort to always frame this through the key driver for his CEO – getting to profitability.

He also started to think about how best to communicate with his CEO. He moved his scheduled meeting with the CEO from a weekly to monthly hour-long catch-up, but got in the habit of popping into the CEO's office or making sure he encountered him in the corridor or the coffee room to give him short updates or ask a to-the-point question. He also moved from email to text as his preferred mode of communication. Part of this strategy was an education piece, with the GC telling the CEO what he could do and what he could help with. The relationship took time and is still not quite where the GC would ideally like it, but it has improved – the power of the Champion Chameleon attribute in action.

Why we need the Champion Chameleon skill in the Exponential Age

The Exponential Age is an age of increased change and, as mentioned before, humans generally do not deal with change very well. When trying to persuade people of the need to change, an understanding of what is important to them and demonstrating empathy is crucial to successful influence. Champion Chameleon is not only analogous to the influencing competency of the Exponential Age Attributes but also intimately connected to the other key competencies of curiosity and creativity.

If we are curious about others and how they see the world and receive information, we are more likely to be able to connect with them effectively. Better connection means we can communicate with them in a way optimized to get our message across in a way they will hear. Understanding others and therefore how to best connect with them is also linked to greater creativity by helping us see things from different angles and use this to come up with more innovative ideas.

This is fundamental because it builds trust and credibility. When you demonstrate that you understand your audience, they're more likely to see you as competent and empathetic. People are more open to influence when they feel seen and respected. They are then more likely to listen to you but also really hear what you are saying. Effective tailoring aligns your message with what motivates your audience – which increases the chances they'll act on it.

Therefore, Champion Chameleon is an essential skill for leaders. It's also an essential skill for lawyers – particularly in-house lawyers. Yet it's one that many lawyers struggle with. Often, this is not even done consciously, as they are not necessarily aware of its importance and its absence from their lives.

Let's go back to basics and explore why it's important to tailor communication to your audience, and why this is even more crucial during the Exponential Age.

Tailoring your communication to your audience

People are more likely to pay attention and respond when they feel the message speaks to their needs, priorities, or concerns. A common in-house legal dilemma is getting messages over to commercial teams whose driving motivation is sales and revenue.

A message crafted purely through the lens of regulatory necessity does not go very far with this audience. However, being able to explain how regulatory compliance might aid revenue generation would be received in an entirely different way. The inextricable link to Bias Jiu Jitsu can be felt here. If I have a certain way of seeing the world, it may be impossible for me to see the way you understand the world, if that differs from my own perspective. Effective communicators must close that gap as much as possible. A message that resonates gets absorbed – one that doesn't gets ignored. If I make my message personal and crafted to what you care about, you will listen. When we can give examples taken from our participants' lived reality to illustrate our concepts in our training sessions, what we are saying becomes more real. They are then much more likely to see how our ideas and related tools can be used to help improve their own roles and professional lives.

"Don't lawyer me an answer"

One of the starting points here is understanding how we communicate. How can we improve clarity and reduce misunderstanding? The biggest issue with some lawyers is that they use dense language and legalistic concepts that do not make sense to most people – certainly not to those who are not lawyers. Add to that the fact that their audiences may not be interested in even trying to understand this language and you have a significant issue. There's even a term for this – "legalese" – which is now mostly used pejoratively. A CEO once summarized this for a GC contact of mine when he said, "Don't lawyer me an answer".

I belong to a group of senior female executives – many of whom are general counsel. When undertaking a pulse survey on their biggest complaints about client service from law firm lawyers, there was a significant focus on poor communication and a lack of empathy to the in-house lawyer's perspective. Many of the group bemoaned the fact that they had to translate dense legal opinions into bite-sized relevant business advice – feeling that when they found outside counsel who would do this, these were lawyers worth keeping! One of the most amusing comments – which neatly illustrates the gap between those who firmly shun the Champion Chameleon perspective – was the GC who wished her external lawyers "would stop using Latin!" Use of Latin is only required if you happen to be advising an ancient Roman!

The biggest learning most in-house lawyers mention is the need to synthesize their communications immensely to get the message across to busy business colleagues. We talk more about this in chapter 11 on the Superlative Synthesizer, but it is also a component of the Champion Chameleon attribute. Using the right language, tone, and level of detail helps avoid confusion. Tailoring helps bridge knowledge gaps – you wouldn't talk to a technical expert and a senior executive in the same way. Too much technical or legal language doesn't clarify the message – it makes key stakeholders less likely to really comprehend or not even be inclined to try and understand.

A key aspect in presenting to business stakeholders is how you structure your message. Most lawyers are taught to lay out the argument or the evidence and then share their conclusion. Unfortunately, most senior executives do not have the patience for that. In many of our programs where the capstone project has been a presentation to a public company Board member, the overwhelming feedback is "Lead with your key point". Business people want to know why they are listening to this. The presenter needs to grab their attention in the first few seconds.

Champion Chameleon equals champion influencer

There's a strong link between the attribute of Champion Chameleon and being an effective influencer. Take a zoom out to look at the wider perspective. When we think of communication, we often focus on the act of speaking and what is being said. In Champion Chameleon and in influencing, there is an important aspect of listening and receiving information at play.

We are more likely to be influenced by people we trust. How do we feel trust? We feel that the other person understands us; they have our best interests at heart; they see us, and they hear us. Influence is central to change management. Therefore, ensuring those we want to influence trust us and feel seen and heard is a massive part of this.

The hostage negotiation perspective

At the cutting edge of influencing is doing so in a real life-or-situation. You may think your contract life cycle management tool is important, but it's never going to be as stressful as trying to make someone release the cashiers from the bank they are currently robbing! Some years ago, I heard the former head of hostage negotiation at the Metropolitan Police speak at a conference. What he said resonates with me still. Hostage negotiators are trained to diffuse situations where there is a credible threat to life – including, sometimes, the perpetrator's own life. It's easy to think that what they *say* must be incredibly important. However, most hostage negotiators say the crux of their job is in how they *listen*. It is in being able to effectively hear and see the reality of the hostage-taker that allows them to diffuse the situation.

Hostage negotiation techniques offer valuable lessons for communication, emphasizing active listening, empathy, and emotional intelligence to build rapport and de-escalate tense situations. By understanding and responding to the emotional needs of the other party, negotiators can foster a more conducive environment for productive dialogue. Some of the significant ideas from hostage or crisis negotiations that are also pertinent to a business context are listed below.

Demonstrate active listening and empathy

Demonstrate deeper listening skills and really focus on what the other person has to say. Pay close attention to not only what is said but also the underlying emotions and motivations. What are they saying and how are they saying it? What are they not saying or avoiding saying? When we were training as coaches, the different levels of how to listen were one of the first aspects we focused on. Too often in this time of multiple stimuli from social media and our devices we have lost the ability to really listen and focus. There are three levels of listening:

- Level 1 is surface-level listening. This is what most of us use daily. Our listening might only be at 25 percent. We are much more focused on what we are going to say. It is more about just waiting for the other person to stop speaking so we can get our point across! This is also the level of listening we engage in if we are distracted by other stimuli such as phones and email.
- Level 2 is more active listening. We are present and are focused on what the other person is saying. We might even demonstrate this by repeating key components of what they are saying to show we are really listening.
- At Level 3 we are completely focused on the other person. It's not just about what they say but how they say it and their body language. Our intuition might pick up key indicators about their mood and emotion. In the coaching context, this is the goal, as you feel completely connected to your client on an emotional level. When we can really get into this mode of listening as coaches, we can start to feel the emotions our clients feel and can sometimes even anticipate what they are going to say.

Demonstrate tactical empathy

- Demonstrate understanding and validation of the other party's perspective, even if you don't agree with it.
- Utilize paraphrasing and reflection. Repeat and rephrase what the other person is saying to ensure understanding and show you are listening attentively.

Build rapport and trust

- Establish a connection. Focus on finding common ground and creating a sense of shared humanity.
- Be genuine and honest. Avoid manipulative tactics and maintain transparency in your communication.
- Show respect and dignity. Treat the other party with respect, even when you disagree with them.

Manage emotions and attempt de-escalation

- Identify and address underlying emotions. Acknowledge and validate the other party's emotions, even if they seem irrational.
- Use silence strategically. Allow the other party time to process information and express their thoughts without interruption.

- Control your own emotions. Remain calm and composed, even when dealing with a challenging situation.

Apply strategic communication techniques

- Use labeling and mirroring. Reflect the other party's emotions and words back to them to show understanding.
- Focus on mutual goals. Frame the situation in terms of shared objectives to create a sense of collaboration.
- Be patient and persistent. Negotiation can be a marathon, not a sprint. Be prepared to endure prolonged communication and setbacks.

Understand nonverbal communication

- Observe body language and speech patterns.
- Pay attention to subtle cues that may reveal the other party's true intentions and emotions.
- Adapt your communication style as required. If something isn't working, pivot.
- Adjust your tone, pace, and body language to match the other party's communication style.

SAFE communication

Many hostage negotiators will use the SAFE model to navigate discussion around the hostage taker's demands. SAFE stands for Substantive (instrumental) demands, Attunement (relational) concerns, Face (identity) concerns, and Emotional concerns. This may seem irrelevant in lower-stakes situations, but exploring the Champion Chameleon attribute shows how it can be applied in a legal and business context.

Substantive demands are tangible wants and needs. Substantive goals in hostage negotiation cover a range of requests – from peripheral demands, such as food and drink to meet the hunger needs of the hostages, to central demands, such as requests for a car or a plane for escape. In interactions with business clients for an in-house lawyer, these could be the aspects that the business feels are fundamental to them such as delivery of contracts, getting a deal done, and being able to conduct business in a new jurisdiction.

Attunement demands have to do with the relations between the parties involved. In hostage situations, these include threats to the hostage-taker's power and control, as well as the need for the hostage negotiator to convey empathy and build trust with the hostage-taker. At the beginning of a negotiation there is a period where the hostage negotiator must rebuild trust as the starting point is unequal – the hostage-taker will already feel threatened. In a much smaller way, some business clients – especially those who are less attuned to dealing with lawyers or who are drawing on stereotypes of what in-house lawyers do or do not do, seeing them as "the department of no" – will need a period of attunement. For the most effective GCs and their teams, this is an ongoing process. But the process of attunement with key business stakeholders and building a relationship where there can be trust is one of the most important undertakings in the in-house lawyer's role.

Face concerns are those that promote, protect, or defend from threat our own identity as well as the identity of the other party. This is very much linked to attunement but can often be what stops attunement from happening – whether this is a business situation or an actual crisis negotiation. Face concerns are primarily ego-driven – about, as the name implies, saving or losing face. In the in-house legal context, this could be a business stakeholder who is so focused on seeing legal as a blocker they do not see the value of the advice the lawyer might bring regarding the wider business context. Conversely for in-house lawyers, this can be the lawyer who is so fixed on their identity of being "the lawyer" and only seeing issues through the lens of legal risk that they cannot calibrate the broader business perspective of commercial opportunity.

Emotional issues can hinder the other issues where one or both parties is in a state of heightened emotion. It can feel justifiable to feel hurt and angry as a lawyer if you feel your concerns and your expertise are being ignored. But Exponential Age Mindset Attributes such as Champion Chameleon teach us that focusing on our own emotional reaction roots us in our own response and blocks us from seeing the other person's perspective, which is fundamental to successful influencing.

Case study – a new GC uses Champion Chameleon

A new GC was in her first role in a global manufacturing company. Happily, she had a great relationship with her CEO and most of the other executive committee. However, the head of supply chain, who we'll call Mark, was a different story. He failed to answer emails even when she copied the CEO in. She was not alone as most of her colleagues also found him difficult. But Mark's role was a key one and crucial to the success of the business. He frequently needed to give answers that he was not giving.

A significant aspect of the challenge for the GC was that she saw this interaction through only what was important for her and how she was trained to interact with others. When she worked through the steps outlined below, she was able to tap into her Champion Chameleon and communicate with Mark in a more effective way. Yes, he sometimes went off grid in times of high stress but there was a more effective communication channel opened by understanding what was important to him and how he would best receive information.

In our coaching sessions, I encouraged the GC to put herself in Mark's shoes and understand what that might feel like – not only to consider what he was thinking but try to tap into what his emotions might be.

We then considered in that emotional state what types of outreach the GC would like. She realized it was immediate and to the point. After the session, the GC started to reach out to Mark via WhatsApp instead of email. She realized that Mark's preferred mode of communication was WhatsApp. He rarely answered emails and phone calls and face-to-face interactions were difficult due to time zones.

In terms of how the ask was framed, he needed a mix of high level – getting engaged with *why* his input was needed or why he should be bothered – and then more specific asks, which he could just cut and paste into a message to people on his team. The GC now consistently flipped her message. Rather than saying, "I need this update" or "Head office needs to know X", she changed the messaging to say, "Getting this update is going to make things easier for your team in X jurisdiction and will get goods moving faster".

Her relationship with Mark was never perfect but, by meeting him more where he was at, it became less frustrating for her and more effective.

Why did she have to change her communication style – why couldn't he? To be effective in Champion Chameleon, as with the other attributes, you need a certain level of self-awareness, which Mark did not have. He was a legacy hire who felt threatened by changes and expansion, so was retreating into his shell like a tortoise. As someone who was growing her leadership expertise via coaching and whose first GC role was certainly not going to be her last, there was more reward for my client to become more proficient in her Champion Chameleon. Importantly, as we discuss in the attribute of Bias Jiu Jitsu, by leaning into Mark's cognitive biases, she was able to use these to get what she needed.

Toolkit: Techniques for supercharging your Champion Chameleon

1. Know your audience:
   - Understand their roles, priorities, pain points, and motivations.
   - Ask yourself, What do they care about? What do they need from me? What do I need from them?

2. Match the level of detail to the listener:
   - Executives want high-level insight, summaries of outcomes and risks.
   - Operational staff might need step-by-step guidance or specifics.

3. Use the right tone and language:
   - Formal vs informal, technical vs plain language.
   - Mirror the tone your audience is most comfortable with (without being inauthentic).

4. Lead with what matters to them:
   - Flip the message to focus on *their* interests first, then yours.
   - For example, instead of, "We need to change this process", try, "Here's how this change will save time for you and reduce error rates".

5. Anticipate objections and questions:
   - Be proactive about addressing what might cause resistance or concern: "Yes, there might be a period of learning where this is going to be slower but once the team are used to it, we can half response times".
   - This shows respect for their perspective and prepares the ground for a smoother conversation.

6. Choose the right format and medium:
   - Quick texts, WhatsApp, Slack, or Teams message for informal updates.
   - Well-structured emails for clarity and record-keeping.
   - Face-to-face or video for sensitive or high-stakes conversations.

7. Use storytelling and examples:
   - Abstract ideas become powerful when illustrated with relatable scenarios or data points.
   - This is especially helpful for bringing dry or complex topics to life.

Practical ways to boost your Champion Chameleon

Below are several tailored training and coaching exercises that focus on building both written and verbal communication skills for in-house lawyers. These exercises are designed to help legal professionals translate complex legal language into clear, actionable insights for business teams and decision-makers.

Exercise 1: Stakeholder mapping and audience analysis

Objective:
Enhance the lawyer's ability to identify, understand, and prioritize the diverse internal audiences they interact with.

Exercise details:

- *Preparation:* Provide participants with a fictional yet realistic company scenario that includes multiple stakeholders (e.g., executive leadership, HR, compliance, IT, sales).
- *Activity:* Ask the in-house legal team to create a stakeholder map. This should identify key decision-makers and outline their main concerns and communication needs.
- *Discussion:* Facilitate a session where teams present their maps and discuss differences in perspectives. Ask:
  - How would the legal communication differ when addressing each stakeholder?
  - What key messages are most relevant to each group?

Coaching point:
Emphasize the importance of aligning the legal message with the business priorities of each stakeholder while keeping it concise and jargon-free.

Exercise 2: Plain language legal writing workshop

Objective:
Translate dense legal language into clear, plain language that can be understood by non-lawyers without sacrificing accuracy.

Exercise details:

- *Preparation:* Distribute excerpts from actual legal documents or contracts that are typical within your organization.

- *Activity:* Have participants work individually or in small groups to rewrite these excerpts into plain language summaries. Encourage them to focus on clarity, eliminating unnecessary legalese and structuring the text in an easy-to-read format.
- *Peer review:* Pair up participants to exchange drafts and provide feedback on readability, tone, and messaging.
- *Presentation:* Each group can then present one before-and-after example, explaining their choices and the intended audience impact.

Coaching point:
Stress that clarity enhances trust and efficiency in decision-making. Remind participants that good legal communication should empower the business audience rather than overwhelm them with technical details.

Exercise 3: Role-playing negotiation and board meeting scenarios

Objective:
Develop verbal communication skills by practicing how to deliver legal insights during high-stakes meetings and negotiations.

Exercise details:

- *Preparation:* Create detailed scenarios where in-house lawyers must present risk assessments or legal opinions to executives (e.g., during a Board meeting or a strategy session with business leaders).
- *Activity:* Role-play sessions with one participant playing the in-house lawyer and others assuming the roles of various stakeholders (e.g., CFO, CEO, department heads).
- *Simulation focus:*
  - Presenting legal risks in a manner that is both assertive and aligned with business goals.
  - Answering challenging questions and addressing concerns without reverting to legal jargon.
- *Feedback:* After each role-play, hold a debriefing session to discuss what worked, areas for improvement, and effective techniques for managing difficult questions.

Coaching point:
Highlight how posture, tone, and pace can affect the message. Encourage the

use of visual aids or summary slides that break down legal risks into actionable items.

Exercise 4: Legal issue storytelling

Objective:
Teach in-house lawyers how to use storytelling techniques to turn complex legal matters into compelling narratives that resonate with business audiences.

Exercise details:

- *Preparation:* Provide a case study or a recent legal event from within the industry.
- *Activity:* Ask participants to develop a short narrative that explains the case's legal issues, outcomes, and impacts on business operations. The narrative should include:
  - A clear beginning that outlines the context.
  - A middle that highlights the challenges and key legal points.
  - An end that provides recommendations or lessons learned.
- *Presentation:* Have participants present their narratives to small groups.
- *Discussion:* Facilitate feedback on clarity, engagement, and effectiveness in driving home the business implications of the legal matter.

Coaching point:
Encourage the use of metaphors and analogies to simplify complex concepts. Stress that a well-told story makes it easier for non-lawyers to grasp the essential points and implications.

Exercise 5: Active listening and questioning skills workshop

Objective:
Enhance interpersonal communication by improving active listening and strategic questioning skills.
Exercise details:

- *Warm-Up:* Conduct a brief exercise in which participants pair up and share a personal anecdote. The listener then summarizes the key points to ensure accurate understanding.

- *Role-play:* Simulate a scenario where the in-house lawyer must gather detailed business requirements from a department head or a project manager. One plays the lawyer, asking open-ended questions to uncover underlying concerns and goals.
- *Debrief:* Discuss the types of questions asked, non-verbal cues observed, and the effectiveness of the listening process.
- *Reflection:* Ask participants to note how practicing active listening has influenced their ability to ask sharper follow-up questions that yield actionable insights.

Coaching point:
Reiterate that effective legal advice often starts with understanding the full context of a business issue. Listening actively and questioning strategically can reveal nuances that make the advice more tailored and impactful.

Exercise 6: Simulation of crisis communication

Objective:
Prepare lawyers for high-pressure situations where immediate, clear, and concise communication is essential.

Exercise details:

- *Scenario setup:* Design a crisis scenario such as a data breach or regulatory investigation that involves multiple legal and business stakeholders.
- *Activity:* Divide participants into teams where one group acts as the in-house legal team, and the other represents the company's crisis management team. The legal team must craft initial statements and subsequent updates addressing legal risks, steps taken, and next actions.
- *Execution:* Simulate a series of rapid updates (e.g., press releases, internal memos, briefings) and allow for real-time feedback from peers playing other roles.
- *Analysis:* Post-simulation, review the language used, the clarity of the updates, and how well the message aligned with the crisis management objectives.

Coaching point:
Focus on the necessity of balancing speed with clarity. Ensure that even under pressure, legal communications remain straightforward, empathetic, and confidently delivered.

Implementing the training program

Integration with regular workflows:

- Schedule these exercises as part of quarterly training sessions.
- Use them during onboarding for new in-house lawyers to set the standard for effective communication.

Follow-up and continuous improvement:

- Collect feedback from participants regarding which exercises were most helpful.
- Act on the feedback rather than just collecting it – people will be more willing to offer honest feedback if they think it will yield results.
- Offer periodic refresher courses and update the scenarios based on current business challenges and legal trends.
- Encourage a culture of peer feedback, where lawyers can share experiences and discuss how they adapted their communication for better business impact.

Chapter 10:
Bias Jiu Jitsu – different ways of understanding

Bias Jiu Jitsu is the understanding of how other people see the world combined with a self-awareness of how we ourselves see things and any biases we may bring to decisions.

Understanding how others see the world is a fundamental aspect of influencing. It's one of the reasons why listening is such a key leadership skill and one that will become even more important in the Exponential Age. We will all bring our own biases to how we see the world. This will largely depend on how we have been conditioned to see it through our formative years and beyond.

As discussed in chapter nine on Champion Chameleon, hostage negotiators point to the fact that listening effectively is much more important than what they say. This is because this gives an insight into how the hostage-taker is seeing the world. Understanding their viewpoint is fundamental in being able to steer them away from their destructive course of action.

Whilst Champion Chameleon focuses on how we communicate most effectively to others, its linked competency of Bias Jiu Jitsu is how we understand others' ways of seeing the world and how that interacts with how we see the world. Most importantly, how we can interrogate both others' view and our own for biases that might hamper curiosity and creativity.

Jiu Jitsu as a concept is extremely relevant here.

The Gentle Art

Jiu Jitsu (or jiujitsu or jiu-jitsu – there are variant spellings) is a Japanese martial art. While it has roots in ancient India, it evolved in Japan as a method for Samurai to defend themselves against armed opponents when they had lost their long swords or katana. It was later popularized in Brazil.

Jiu Jitsu roughly translates from Japanese as "The Gentle Art" or "The Art of Gentleness". The effectiveness of Jiu Jitsu is based on leveraging your opponent's strength against them, in a similar fashion to Judo. By teaching you to understand how your opponent is going to attack and what their strengths and weaknesses are, Jiu Jitsu often employs techniques that might seem counterintuitive, such as staying close to your opponent or leaning into them. However, these are always undertaken with a broader understanding that this will give you the advantage and set up a move that will lead to submission.

Around the time of starting this book, I began practicing Jiu Jitsu. In part, I was attracted by the self-defense possibilities it offers for a petite woman – who will likely never be able to compete with an opponent on pure strength. But practicing Jiu Jitsu also requires blending the physical and the mental, in the way that Bias Jiu Jitsu (similarly to many of the other Exponential Age Mindset Attributes) gets us more adept at the key qualities needed in the Exponential Age – curiosity, creativity and influencing.

Understanding our own biases

Understanding our own and others' biases will be mission critical for leadership in the Exponential Age because rapid technological and structural shifts demand not just adaptability, but metacognition – the ability to examine how we think, decide, and relate. This quality of metacognition in its more obvious Exponential Age application will be central to formulating the most effective questions for generative AI and fundamental to teaching AI in ways that – hopefully – do not replicate the worst human biases.

Disrupting bias is a concept widely used in inclusion training, but it has a much broader business application rooted in the same impulse – that of questioning the status quo.

Bias is the enemy of adaptability

In the Exponential Age, change is constant and non-linear. Leaders who are unaware of – or don't care about – cognitive biases (e.g., status quo bias, confirmation bias) may resist disruptive innovations or new ways of working simply because these feel uncomfortable or unfamiliar. This has been central to the ideas of innovation for many years.

When training using the Exponential Age Mindset Attributes, we often use the famous example of Kodak. This once household-name company failed to see the opportunity of digital technology and photography, or more broadly the opportunity of digital technology to capture memories. Digital technology took away the wait time and the limits of the analogue technologies of film. Capturing memories became more immediate and almost limitless. The bias of not being able to conceptualize a different way of seeing the world – one in which everyone has a digital camera in their pocket via their phone – took Kodak from a market-leading Fortune 500 company that had been listed there for 74 years to a struggling company delisted from the Fortune index in 2004 and forced to diversify to stay alive.

Biases can cause leaders to undervalue emerging trends (like GenAI, remote work culture shifts, or ESG evolution) and overvalue legacy models, leading to poor strategic decisions.

As we write this book at the end of 2025, two of the biggest trends we think are ripe for applications of Bias Jiu Jitsu in legal departments and corporations more generally are the application of GenAI and what this will mean for how lawyers work and how they think about their roles, and the shift to remote work culture as a result of COVID-19.

Let's take the shift to remote work culture first. Since the early days of lockdowns, we have seen a normalization of the expectation for remote working for many employees. Five years on, many companies are settling on a compromise of requiring a certain number of days in the office per week – usually three. However, some companies, such as investment banks and law firms, are moving to a full five days back in the office. But many employees are simply not willing to go back. Some relocated during the pandemic and have no wish to move back to overpriced cities and long commutes. I have spoken to leaders who struggled to recruit candidates when a role was advertised as being fully in-person but easily attracted quality candidates when it was offered as partially remote.

The increase in digital technologies means that we can work very differently and potentially from anywhere, but there is a clash where the biases of many employers – driven by equating presence with productivity or needing to justify the ROI on corporate HQs – potentially produce a challenge that could result in talent management issues.

As Generative AI and other emerging technologies reshape how organizations operate, in-house legal teams face a profound shift in how they define value. For many general counsel and their teams, the long-standing equation of *doing more* and *reacting faster* with being successful is no longer fit for purpose. Gen AI will make some tasks dramatically easier while simultaneously increasing expectations in other areas.

To thrive, legal teams will need to adopt a more proactive, strategic mindset – one that embraces new ways of working, challenges old heuristics, and lets go of biases such as equating personal worth with visible output or viewing digital tools as "cheating".

This is not simply a technology upgrade – it is a mindset transformation.

Legal functions that learn to leverage AI to anticipate issues, create capacity, and operate at the speed of the business will be best positioned to lead in the next era of legal work.

Research has noted a specific gender bias in legal around the use of AI, with female lawyers more likely to view its use as "cheating". This is less about the more universal notion of gender bias in AI, which is when algorithms are trained on male-dominated or stereotyped data, and thereby replicate and scale those biases, from recruitment tools that favor men to healthcare systems that misdiagnose women. This specifically legal AI use bias was expressed by women lawyers over concerns that they will be held to higher scrutiny if they use AI. Given societal bias, mistakes made by a woman lawyer using AI might be judged more harshly than the same mistakes made by a man, according to a 2024 survey.[1] If women feel they have more to lose if AI goes wrong, this may slow their adoption of useful technologies.

Innovation requires cognitive diversity – bias blocks it

In the Exponential Age, to ensure we maximize the key mindsets needed to thrive – curiosity, creativity, and influence – we need diverse perspectives.

Innovation thrives on diverse perspectives, yet biases (such as affinity bias, or groupthink) can cause leaders to surround themselves with like-minded individuals or dismiss ideas from non-traditional sources. Recognizing and mitigating these biases helps leaders consciously build diverse teams and foster environments where contrarian or novel thinking can thrive. That's why the legal teams that will thrive in the Exponential Age will recognize and empower the perspectives of professionals who are not lawyers as well as those who are. In most legal departments, there still exists a fundamental bias against non-lawyers. Even the common nomenclature of lawyer vs non-lawyer reinforces a perspective where the primacy of the lawyer and their way of understanding the world is seen as the main one, and other perspectives are merely a corollary to this.

As we started using the Exponential Age Mindset Concepts and Attributes in our training, this also coincided with several opportunities to train paraprofessionals (non-lawyers) in legal departments. The key concept that informed this training was "empowerment" – to realize the full potential of their ideas and the benefits these could have to the legal department. Interestingly, many of the participants in these trainings were much more adaptable and less biased – partly because they were not set in a fixed way of understanding the world, which we sometimes find lawyers to be. A key skill needed for lawyers in the Exponential Age is Bias Jiu Jitsu and being able to use this to disrupt themselves.

Exponential change triggers threat responses – bias intensifies under stress

Exponential change is change at a rate we have never seen before. Of course, the challenge with this is that our brains prefer routine and lack of change. Neuroscience shows that, under pressure, our brains revert to instinctive patterns and biases – just when we need reflective thinking the most.

When faced with such levels of change, our brains automatically default to the easiest ways of thinking about the world, and this generally means our biases, which feel like comfortable and safe spaces. Leaders must be aware of how bias shows up under ambiguity (e.g., favoring short-term thinking, reverting to hierarchy), and develop emotional and cognitive regulation tools to lead with clarity. We have found that many of the tools we use in our training, if nothing else, force participants to take a step back from the normal way they view the world and gain some objectivity.

In moments of stress, crisis, or when we encounter unfamiliar problems, our reptilian brain often takes over and triggers a subtle fight-or-flight response. Utilizing a tool or framework that introduces objectivity and distance – such as Can If (chapter 14), the Six Dimensions (chapter 12), or intentionally applying the Exponential Age attributes – helps interrupt that instinctive reaction.

These tools create a pause, allowing us to literally and figuratively take a breath and see the situation more clearly. They also reduce the risk of slipping into default biases like "We've always done it this way," enabling more thoughtful, adaptive decision-making.

AI and data reliance can amplify bias

Whilst we need to disrupt old ways of thinking and employ our Bias Jiu Jitsu to supercharge our Exponential Age mindsets and their attributes, we also need to be aware of the potential for biases baked into many of the new technology developments we are working with.

As decision-making becomes more data-driven and integrated with AI, leaders must understand how their own biases can influence the design, interpretation, and ethical use of data and algorithms. Unexamined biases can also creep into AI systems themselves – bias awareness is essential to responsible AI leadership.

In an era where decision-making is increasingly driven by data and embedded in AI systems, it's vital that leaders recognize how their own biases shape the design, interpretation, and ethical use of data and algorithms. Yet biases don't stop at the human interface – they can also become embedded inside the algorithmic systems themselves. Awareness of bias is therefore essential for responsible AI leadership.

In the UK, the case of *App Drivers & Couriers Union (ADCU) member Pa Edrissa Manjang v. Uber Eats* is a stark example. The driver was locked out of the platform in April 2021 after multiple failed facial recognition "selfie" checks. He claimed the system unfairly targeted him because he is Black, arguing that the algorithm had a disparate impact on ethnic minority drivers. The UK Employment Tribunal refused Uber's attempt to strike out the claim on grounds of no reasonable prospect of success, recognising that the process and data-logic behind the system were unclear and potentially discriminatory. Recently, Uber Eats reached a settlement with the driver after the claim, bringing further attention to how biometric tools used in employment or platform contexts may embed bias and lead to unlawful discrimination.[2]

In addition, several UK/European cases have examined how AI-based tools used for recruitment, shortlisting and performance management can lead to unlawful discrimination (via disparate impact) under equality legislation. One recruitment case study prepared by the law firm Lewis Silkin details how an AI tool shortlisted candidates, and the unsuccessful ones raised claims under the Equality Act 2010.[3]

The law is still developing in this area but even if a tool does not use protected characteristics (race, gender, disability) directly, proxies (such as names) can still trigger indirect discrimination. Courts/tribunals are still navigating how to apply existing non-discrimination law to algorithmic systems, but liability is emerging and could create unforeseen exposure without use of bias mitigation. The opportunity for legal teams in leading the development of governance frameworks (data governance, vendor contracts, bias-impact assessment) is also one of positioning themselves as strategic enablers of trustworthy AI in their organizations. An imperative that has business impact and is a message that many stakeholders can get behind more readily than when it is framed as legal governance.

Empathy and inclusion are strategic imperatives

Empathy and inclusion are not just nice to have – they are strategic imperatives. In diverse, global, hybrid workplaces, leaders must be attuned to how unconscious biases affect inclusion, psychological safety, and team performance. It's only by understanding social and cultural biases that we can develop empathy-based leadership, which is increasingly vital for engaging and retaining next-generation talent.

As mentioned in chapter nine on Champion Chameleon, we need to really amplify our curiosity and our ability to actively listen to do this. To go back to our analogy, the sensei in my Jiu Jitsu studio emphasizes the ability to think like your opponent to be able to anticipate their move and counter it. In practice, this becomes much more like the third level listening in coaching we mentioned earlier, where your empathy is largely unconscious and instinctual. In a combat situation, even a staged one, you don't have much time to stop and think!

The technique that legal leaders and their teams will need to employ to effectively do this is to be able to listen and understand all perspectives.

In the Exponential Age, it's particularly important to have empathy for the perspective of those who are frightened and threatened by Exponential Age change and do not see a place for themselves in it. A significant role for leadership is being able to understand why your team feels this way and to introduce tactics to interrupt these biases.

The mindsets and behaviors that Lloyd and I teach are designed to be optimal for the age of increasing technology, yet we do not reference technology that much during the actual training or overuse technology focused examples. This is deliberate to separate the perception of technology and attitudes around it from the mindsets needed to develop those. For many who are less used to using new technologies, over-indexing on said technologies will introduce the fight or flight trigger and activate many of their biases – most of which may be directed against themselves. "I'm too old / not clever enough to understand these new technology tools." "I'm smart enough and I don't need technology – it won't do the job as well as I can."

These are all mindsets that are mitigating against the learning mindset, but they can be disrupted when we introduce empathy and understanding and give people ways in which they can lean into and combat their own biases. In Jiu Jitsu, for example, I can overcome my own worry that "I'm too petite to beat someone bigger and stronger" and instead recognize how I can use the strengths I do have – agility, good reflexes, forward thinking – to be more effective.

In the same way, if people seem a little worried in our training, we give positive reinforcement of how the skills they already use can be implemented in the Exponential Age. I often do this via perspective shifting – a common coaching tool. In the first session of one of our paraprofessional training programs, one of the participants looked both worried and skeptical. At the start of the session, she shared that all the potential change in the legal department scared her.

I made sure to pay her extra attention, and illustrate the ways in which she was already demonstrating Exponential Age mindsets. I also, via thoughtful questioning, laid the foundations of a path to show her that she could apply this in new and different ways. For example, I reminded her: "During Covid, you had to do your own work but also be able to handle the work of those colleagues who might have been out sick. That's Agile Juggler in action. Also, you are already balancing professional demands and your home life. That's the mindset we need when new ways of working and thinking about work are coming in."

This empowerment undercuts the bias we all have against change – realizing this isn't necessarily actual change but just an extension of something we have already done. At the end of the session, this participant came up to me and said, "Catherine, I was worried about all the change but I'm not anymore". Moments like that reinforce why we love what we do!

Exponential change demands a learning mindset – bias fights it

A key mindset for the Exponential Age is "unlearning to relearn". Biases often lock people into outdated schemas or overconfidence in past success. Leaders need humility and curiosity – recognizing bias helps them challenge their assumptions and embrace continuous learning.

Heuristics shape perception of change

- *Why it matters:* In a fast-changing environment, outdated mental models can lead to misreading signals or underestimating disruption.
- *Example:* A leader relying on past industry cycles might miss early indicators of AI transforming their – or their competitors' – business model.

Biases distort decision-making under pressure

- *Why it matters:* The exponential pace of change increases ambiguity, making people more reliant on heuristics like confirmation bias or availability bias.

- *Example:* Leaders might favor familiar solutions even when data suggests new, unconventional approaches are more viable.

Team alignment requires awareness of diverse mental models

- *Why it matters:* Teams interpret strategic goals and threats differently based on their roles, experiences, and cognitive shortcuts.
- *Example:* A legal leader may focus on risk containment, while a product lead sees only innovation opportunities – leading to conflict unless these perspectives are reconciled.

Innovation requires disrupting established thinking patterns

- *Why it matters:* Breakthrough ideas often come from challenging the very ideas that made a company successful in the past.
- *Example:* Kodak's failure to capitalize on digital photography wasn't technological, it was cognitive – leaders stuck to their mental model of film dominance. Compare this to Fujifilm, which recognized the inevitable decline of the film industry and took decisive action. Between 2000 and 2010, the demand for photographic film dropped by 90 percent, but Fujifilm was already reinventing itself. It leveraged its expertise in chemistry, optics, and imaging to enter new, unrelated markets.[4]

Adaptive leadership demands meta-cognition

- *Why it matters:* Being able to think about how we think (metacognition) is critical for learning, unlearning, and guiding others through uncertainty.
- *Example:* Leaders who regularly question their assumptions foster a culture of psychological safety and curiosity, essential in times of transformation.

Ethical and societal impacts are interpreted through heuristics

- *Why it matters:* As exponential technologies raise novel ethical dilemmas (e.g., AI, biotech), leaders must recognize how values and cultural filters shape reactions.
- *Example:* Public trust in data use varies widely across cultures and generations – leaders need to understand these frames to communicate and govern responsibly.

Bias Jiu Jitsu tools

Tool 1: Personal reflection and cognitive journaling

Tactic: Encourage leaders to regularly record high-stakes decisions and the reasoning behind them. Later, they can review outcomes and compare what they assumed versus what actually happened.

Purpose: Builds self-awareness around habitual thinking patterns and over-relied-upon shortcuts.

Tool 2: "Assumption hunting"

Tactic: Before finalizing major decisions, ask:

- What assumptions are we making?
- What if the opposite were true?
- Where might we be wrong?

Purpose: Surfaces hidden thought patterns like status quo bias or optimism bias; challenges mental models.

Tool 3: Cognitive diversity check

Tactic: In key discussions, actively include people with different functional, generational, or cultural perspectives and label the bias risk (e.g., groupthink, availability bias). Bring in a colleague from a completely different area who may have a completely different viewpoint to hear your team's plan and identify any biases that might be a problem.

Purpose: Forces teams to see problems from non-dominant frames, widening their lens.

Tool 4: Red team / blue team debates

Tactic: Assign one group to challenge a preferred decision using a contrarian frame (e.g., risk-focused, customer-focused, long-term focused).

Purpose: Highlights how heuristics affect framing and legitimizes dissent.

Tool 5: "How might they see it?" exercise

Tactic: Role-play how a customer, regulator, employee, or competitor would view the issue.

Purpose: Disrupts egocentric bias; encourages perspective-taking to counteract narrow viewpoints.

Tool 6: Experimentation mindset
Tactic: Frame strategic initiatives as experiments with hypotheses rather than final answers.

Purpose: Reduces the anchoring effect and allows for adaptive learning rather than fixed decision paths.

Tool 7: Data vs intuition calibration
Tactic: Before acting on a gut feeling, compare with data or previous benchmarks – then log the result.

Purpose: Helps leaders understand when their intuition aligns with reality and when it misleads.

Tool 8: Exponential signals radar
Tactic: Create a monthly or quarterly ritual to scan weak signals (start-ups, patents, societal shifts) with a "beginner's mind" lens.

Purpose: Counteracts normalcy bias and keeps leaders from clinging to linear thinking.

Tool 9: Feedback on thinking, not just outcomes
Tactic: In after-action reviews, ask, "What mental model drove this decision?" not just "What happened?".

Purpose: Creates a culture that values cognitive process improvement, not just performance.

Tool 10: Reverse mentoring or peer coaching
Tactic: Pair senior leaders with junior staff or external peers to expose blind spots in assumptions and challenge heuristic patterns.

Purpose: Broadens viewpoint and questions "This is how we've always done it" reasoning.

References

1 Victoria Basham, "Artificial Intelligence 'could deepen gender divide' in law" *Global Legal Post*, 4 December 2024 www.globallegalpost.com/news/artificial-intelligence-could-deepen-gender-divide-in-law-1430647169#
2 www.equalityhumanrights.com/media-centre/news/uber-eats-courier-wins-payout-help-equality-watchdog-after-facing-problematic-ai
3 www.lewissilkin.com/en/insights/2023/10/31/discrimination-and-bias-in-ai-recruitment-a-case-study
4 Oliver Kmia "Why Kodak Died and Fujifilm Thrived: A Tale of Two Film Companies" 14 December 2022: https://petapixel.com/why-kodak-died-and-fujifilm-thrived-a-tale-of-two-film-companies

Chapter 11: Superlative Synthesizer – getting to the point

The ability to synthesize and simplify. Keeping it simple and keeping it relevant. Say no more...

This attribute, perhaps more than any of the other nine, has particular significance for lawyers, whether in-house or in private practice.

Over-complication of ideas, verbose messaging, and dense language is a well-worn stereotype about lawyers. However, like most stereotypes, it also has a grounding in truth – in many cases, a very firm grounding! But for in-house lawyers, particularly those in senior roles, less is certainly more in communication. Most executives do not want to hear or will not tolerate excess communications.

Synthesization in the Exponential Age

The ability to synthesize and communicate information clearly and succinctly is increasingly critical in the Exponential Age, and not only for lawyers. This isn't just a practical workplace skill – it's becoming a strategic leadership imperative. As technological advances gain pace, the ability to effectively sift through information and focus on what is important will become even more crucial.

Cognitive overload – too much information

In one of my former roles in a legal and business media company, I worked with a woman (let's call her Vera) who was responsible for editing one of our titles. One summer, she went on holiday for a month and during that time role-modelled admirable wellbeing behavior by not checking her work email. On her return, she had thousands of emails. She immediately deleted all of them. Her reasoning was that if it was urgent they would have contacted someone else or they would email again. At the time, I was horrified. But as the amount of information we receive on a daily basis expands all the time, I now wonder if Vera was a genius ahead of her time!

I've seen a less chaotic version of this behavior modelled by the artistic director of a London theatre whose out of office message states that anything received during his absence will be deleted without being read and to email again after his return date.

The rate of change and expansion of technology means the amount of information available – particularly online – is also increasing exponentially. This leads to cognitive overload from information abundance. According to Eppler & Mengis,[1] too much information can impair decision-making, reduce productivity, and increase stress. Performance increases in relation to the amount of information – up to a certain point.

Eppler and Mengis display this as an inverted U curve. Performance peaks at a certain critical mass of information and then declines. This means overexposure to information will likely make us dumber, not smarter. In the Exponential Age, leaders and teams face a deluge of data, dashboards, and real-time updates. The ability to distill complexity into clarity becomes vital to avoid decision paralysis. This is significant for lawyers, who often become unable to make decisions unless they feel they have all the information. But does all the information sometimes become too much information? According to Eppler and Mengis, there is a very delicate balance between when enough becomes too much. And this research was carried out 20 years ago – before smartphones and social media took over the world!

Most lawyers would argue that the more information they have before making a decision, the better. In our experience of training leaders – including lawyers moving into leadership – we would disagree. One of the most important competencies we train aspiring leaders in law departments in is being able to make a decision quickly. Being able to "call it definitively" is a skill that leaders have always needed. This is going to become more and more valued as the amount and rate of dissemination of information expands. Therefore, the information shared needs to be able to cut through the cognitive overload – especially for those business stakeholders who are already drowning in information.

The skill of being able to make decisions quickly is seen in its most definitive application in areas such as the military, aviation, and medicine, where split-second decisions can literally be a matter of life or death. In all high-stakes decision-making situations, critical and creative thinking is key to solving problems and establishing the framework and conditions for leaders to make effective decisions. A common factor in military, aviation, and medicine is situational thinking – the need to understand both the big picture and the detail but crucially be able to situate the detail within the context or situation of the bigger picture – literally our Zoom Master attribute in action!

To help us get to situational thinking, concise and relevant information is needed. Enter Superlative Synthesizer – showing the interdependency of our Exponential Age Attributes.

Accelerated decision cycles

It's not only that we have more information coming at us on which to base our decisions, but that those decisions need to be made even faster. That's why succinct and focused communication is paramount. It's not only helpful for those who listen to the information but will result in better outcomes for organizations.

A 2020 study by McKinsey found that organizations that make decisions quickly and execute faster outperform their peers by a wide margin.[2] However, to do this effectively, those in those organizations need to deliver fast, to-the-point and high-quality communication.

Interdisciplinary collaboration

In the evolving landscape of business and technology, the essence of leadership is shifting from command of information to the capacity to connect meaning across disciplines, platforms, and people. This is the same impulse that drives creativity and is evident in Duality Master (chapter eight). It also draws on the need to see beyond our immediate concerns or be trapped in silos – therefore drawing on the Zoom Master attribute (chapter three). This changing nature of what great leadership looks like in the Exponential Age is demonstrated in research by Edmonson and Harvey, which makes it clear that cross-functional collaboration depends not only on accuracy of communication but also on its sensitivity to context.[3]

Leaders today must therefore act as translators – integrating diverse perspectives, synthesizing insights, and articulating meaning in ways that resonate with audiences as varied as regulators, technologists, and frontline teams. As challenges such as AI ethics, climate technology, and cybersecurity demand input from multiple disciplines, the ability to frame problems with clarity and coherence is no longer optional – it is a defining hallmark of strategic leadership.

This is already true in many ways for in-house lawyers and will be even more so as the boundaries of law are pushed beyond what we know by what we have yet been unable to imagine. In this time of boundary pushing and great unknowns, clear and concise communication is more crucial than ever.

Building and sustaining trust

Equally vital is the ability to build and sustain trust in digital environments. Mayer, Davis, and Schoorman's foundational model of trust[4] identifies ability, benevolence, and integrity as the pillars of credibility. In an era where hybrid and digital-first work have become the norm, these qualities are expressed primarily through communication. Leaders no longer rely on physical presence or positional authority to inspire confidence – their trustworthiness is judged through their precision, transparency, and consistency across digital channels. Leaders who can foster psychological safety and alignment through words alone will maintain influence and cohesion in increasingly distributed organizations.

Adding AI to the mix

The integration of artificial intelligence introduces yet another dimension. There is a clear division of strengths – machines excel at processing scale and speed, while humans remain indispensable for interpreting nuance and conveying meaning. This divide is certainly where the promise lies for legal departments. As generative AI automates tasks from drafting to data analysis, the distinctive human contribution shifts to synthesis, sensemaking, and empathetic communication. Leaders who can navigate ambiguity, interpret machine outputs, and articulate insights in ways that inspire trust and action will not be displaced by AI – they will be amplified by it. We see this at work in what we do where we often use AI to generate the first draft of a case study but then use our own experiences and creativity to add the nuances and more layers of meaning.

Together, these dynamics point toward a profound reframing of leadership in the digital era. Authority is no longer measured by access to information but by the ability to create alignment and shared understanding in the face of complexity. Leaders who can synthesize across domains, build trust through transparent communication, and differentiate themselves from machines by exercising empathy and judgment will set the standard for influence and impact in the years ahead.

Strategic sensemaking

No matter how comfortable we get with living in ambiguity, there are moments when we do want it all to make sense. Karl Weick's Sensemaking Theory (1995)[5] emphasizes that organizations thrive when leaders help others "make sense" of complexity, especially during times of ambiguity.

That's a fundamental role of leadership in the Exponential Age – even if we don't know what the sense is. Sometimes the value can be sharing the fact we are all sitting in uncertainty. This is shown in the example in chapter four, where a leader leaned into the Joyful Tightrope attribute and shared with her team her uncertainty around their future. They surprised her with their response, which embraced creativity and problem solving.

It's also something that gets to the fundamental value of in-house lawyers in the Exponential Age due to the breadth of knowledge and understanding across the organization that they will have.

Why does this matter? In the Exponential Age, environments are often VUCA (Volatile, Uncertain, Complex, Ambiguous). Leaders must filter, frame, and communicate insights to anchor others in purpose and direction.

The conciseness conundrum for lawyers

Why do so many lawyers struggle with being concise and to the point?

Having spoken to many lawyers during the course of my career – and the fact that Lloyd has been one – we think there are several factors at play here. Some are rooted in the psychology of those who choose to become lawyers, and some are a result of legal training and how success is framed in the early part of their careers. There can also be a certain degree of insecurity around their role in the earlier stages of in-house and a desire to assert relevance through oversharing information or showing all their working, when it isn't needed.

The psychology of lawyers

Most lawyers are very smart. We've talked about the idea of work or personal "superpowers" – for lawyers, their superpower is being able to understand a broad range of facts and use these facts to construct a coherent argument with a core thesis. Lawyers are keenly observant and can understand not just facts but their context. These are all skills that are incredibly useful, whether in-house or at a law firm. However, the downside of these is too much information and generally way too much context setting.

Throughout their formative career and training, most lawyers have been praised for these very skills. No one is praising a junior lawyer or law student for their ability to synthesize a 15-page document into a one-line text that is a recommendation, not an analysis. Yet in business, it is the latter skill that is more valued.

In one of our training programs, Lloyd and I carried out a cybersecurity breach simulation with a legal team leadership group. We split the team into groups of four who had to present on different aspects of the scenario to faculty who were comprised of executives in the business. Catherine happened to sit in with the group working with the organization's chief operating officer (COO).

The lawyers all did the same thing as they presented their different components to the COO. They set out in detail the context of what was happening, but they did not get to the point. The COO's response was more or less the same every time: "Why are you telling me this? What are you asking me?" He wanted a highly focused operational communication. "There's been a cyber breach – we need to shut the network down." Not a detailed explanation of why it had happened and all the different variables of what could happen.

Another example we've mentioned in an earlier chapter is the Fortune 500 GC who said that he'd had to develop the skill of putting his message for his CEO into the subject line of an email. The CEO did not generally read his emails unless the subject line was compelling enough to inspire him to open it – truly Superlative Synthesizer in action. Over the course of his tenure in-house, this GC literally had to unlearn what had been coded as success in the early parts of his career. This can be a struggle for many lawyers and is often harder the more the lawyers love their area of subject matter expertise. They cannot understand why not everyone wants to hear and understand the minutiae of the technical workings!

Not to overlabor this point, but it can be one of the most significant derailers of lawyers in a business context. It is often even more amplified in law firms than in-house. Most in-house lawyers I know speak of having to "translate" their external counsel memos into business speak. The term "translate" is significant here as it can therefore feel like the business and the lawyers are literally speaking different languages.

This is going to be even more high stakes with the advent of generative AI, which is trained on large language models but can scour these efficiently and synthesize succinctly. Lawyers will be using this but will also need to match AI's level of Superlative Synthesization.

Will we even need lawyers in this brave new world? As detailed in earlier chapters, even the most advanced AI's creative and strategic engagement with information is not anywhere at the same level as we write this book in 2025.

Of course, if you are reading this in the future, this may seem like a quaint, outdated statement – but for now it holds. Lawyers won't be replaced by AI but will need to partner with AI. In my use of AI, I have found it is naturally a Superlative Synthesizer. It speaks the language of business. Human lawyers will need to do the same and effectively calibrate when headlines are necessary and when and how more detail is communicated.

Tell me more, tell me more

One of the consistent pieces of feedback that lawyers receive when presenting to executive leadership or the board is that there is too much information. We usually reference the song *Summer Nights* from the musical *Grease* at this point. We explain that with executives, the aim should be to give them enough that is relevant and compelling that they will actually want to hear more. "Tell me more, tell me more." Then you have an audience that is actively listening.

This information overwhelm is often compounded by PowerPoints. We have all heard the phrase "Death by PowerPoint". (If you haven't, or even better, if you haven't experienced this, then you are truly blessed!) What is often at the core of this is a lack of understanding of how people process information.

Your audience will always read faster than you speak. If your slides are exactly what you are saying, when they finish reading their attention will go elsewhere – likely to any other devices they have to hand.

The most effective PowerPoints are highly visual and will summarize the idea at the highest level. Maybe it is literally a picture, not words – a radical concept for many lawyers we have worked with but one that some have embraced to surprising effect. A lawyer on one of our programs presented to a Board member who had sat on multiple Fortune 500 Boards. The lawyer's mostly visual PowerPoint received high praise, with the Board member saying that it was the best presentation he had seen in his entire career.

Why clarity and conciseness are essential for in-house lawyers in times of ambiguity

Ambiguity has become the defining condition of modern business. From shifting AI regulations and ESG disclosure rules to cybersecurity crises and geopolitical shocks, uncertainty is now the backdrop against which legal departments must operate. In such environments, the ability of in-house lawyers to communicate clearly and concisely is not just a professional skill

– it is a strategic differentiator. When information is incomplete and pressure is high, clarity builds trust, enables swift decision-making, and anchors organizational stability.

Reducing cognitive load

Cognitive load theory, developed by John Sweller in 1988, shows that individuals process and retain information more effectively when complexity is minimized.[6] In times of ambiguity, employees and executives are already stretched by stress and information overload. Legal teams that produce lengthy, jargon-heavy memos can inadvertently increase confusion instead of offering guidance.

Example: Instead of sending a 15-page legal analysis on AI data use, an in-house lawyer distilled the essentials into a two-page risk briefing with a simple traffic-light system – green for low-risk uses, yellow for pending policy decisions, red for prohibited practices. This clarity made it easier for business leaders to act quickly and responsibly. It also provided an effective quick reference guide for the business team in the future.

Enabling rapid decision-making

Daniel Kahneman's research on decision-making under uncertainty[7] demonstrates how clarity accelerates action by preventing "analysis paralysis". Ambiguity slows organizations down; lawyers who frame choices concisely help the business move forward.

Example: During a cybersecurity breach, a GC didn't overwhelm leadership with technical detail. Instead, they said, "Here are three immediate legal obligations – notify regulators within 72 hours, inform customers, and preserve evidence. The decision needed now is whether to disclose publicly before we have full forensic results." This framing empowered decisive action at the right moment. In a time of crisis where the brain's amygdala and hypothalamus may be triggering the body into crisis response mode, listeners may literally not be able to process anything beyond very concise, to-the-point communications.

Building trust and credibility

Mayer, Davis, and Schoorman's model of trust identifies ability, benevolence, and integrity as the core dimensions of credibility. In volatile times, stakeholders equate clarity with confidence.[8] Legal leaders who hedge with dense legal caveats risk eroding trust, while those who communicate complex realities in straightforward terms are perceived as competent and reliable.

Example: With AI governance rules still unsettled, a CLO briefed the Board as follows: "The law is evolving. Here are three likely regulatory scenarios, and our recommended stance is to align with the strictest now to avoid rework later." Such precision inspires confidence even when the legal terrain is still shifting.

Anchoring psychological safety

Amy Edmondson's work on psychological safety[9] demonstrates that clarity reduces anxiety and makes it safer for employees to act and speak up. In times of organizational change, ambiguous communication fuels rumors and fear. Concise, transparent updates steady the culture.

Example: During a restructuring, the legal team leadership communicated in plain terms: "This adjustment affects only one division. Other units are unaffected. We will comply with legal requirements and provide enhanced severance." Clear but empathetic language prevented misinformation and reassured employees. A caveat for this is ensuring you align clarity and empathy. Do not lose empathy in such situations.

The distinct role of in-house lawyers

For in-house lawyers, clarity is not just a matter of style – it is a form of risk management. Business colleagues rely on legal to interpret complexity and to signal priorities when everything feels urgent. In times of ambiguity, lawyers who can strip complexity down to its essentials become the most valuable strategic partners in the room.

- In *AI adoption*, clarity means telling teams what they *can* do safely while a full policy is developed.
- In *ESG disclosure*, clarity means mapping overlapping regulatory regimes into a single path forward.
- In *crisis response*, clarity means identifying the *first three actions* that matter most.

Clarity as a strategic asset

Ambiguity is not going away – it's increasing. What is going to distinguish effective in-house lawyers in the Exponential Age is their ability to provide guidance that cuts through noise, accelerates decision-making, and inspires confidence. Clarity and conciseness are not about dumbing down complexity – they are about distilling it into actionable insight. In times of uncertainty, clarity is both a leadership trait and a competitive advantage.

Summary: Core arguments

Exponential Age pressure	Communication need
Information overload	Synthesize key points to reduce noise
Accelerated decisions	Communicate clearly and quickly to enable action
Interdisciplinary work	Translate across functions and levels
Digital collaboration	Build trust through clear and concise messaging
AI integration	Stand out through human sensemaking and communication
Strategic uncertainty	Create shared understanding through narrative and framing

References

1 Eppler and Mengis (2004), *"The Concept of Information Overload: A Review of Literature from Organization Science, Accounting, Marketing, MIS, and Related Disciplines".*

2 Aaron De Smet, Elizabeth Mygatt, Iyad Sheikh, and Brooke Weddle, "The need for speed in the post-COVID-19 era – and how to achieve it". McKinsey.com, 9 September 2020

3 Edmondson, Amy C., and Jean-François Harvey. "Cross-boundary Teaming for Innovation: Integrating Research on Teams and Knowledge in Organizations." Special Issue on Creating High Performance Teamwork in Organizations. *Human Resource Management Review* 28, no. 4 (December 2018): 347-360.

4 Roger C. Mayer, James H. Davis, F. David Schoorman, Integrative Model of Organizational Trust. *The Academy of Management Review*, Vol. 20, No. 3 (July 1995), pp. 709-734. https://doi.org/10.2307/258792

5 Karl Weick's Sensemaking Theory, outlined in his book *Sensemaking in Organizations* (Sage Publications, 1995) describes how people in organizations create meaning from experience to structure reality and respond to uncertainty. It emphasizes that sensemaking is a retrospective process, driven by extracted cues from the environment, and that it prioritizes plausibility over strict accuracy.

6 John Sweller, "Cognitive Load During Problem Solving: Effects on Learning," *Cognitive Science*, April 1988: https://doi.org/10.1207/s15516709cog1202_4

7 Daniel Kahneman, *Thinking, Fast and Slow*, 2011.

8 See note 4.

9 Edmondson, A. "Psychological safety and learning behavior in work teams." *Administrative Science Quarterly*, 44(2), 350-383 (1999); Amy Edmondson, *The Fearless Organization* (Wiley, 2018).

Chapter 12: The Six Dimensions of Business Risk and The Six Dimensions of Business Opportunity

Integrating risk and opportunity thinking

We consistently find that integrating risk and opportunity thinking is a hallmark of Exponential Age leaders:

- *Systems thinking.* Viewing risks and opportunities across interdependent dimensions rather than as isolated issues (e.g., financial constraints shaping strategic pivots, political lobbying influencing reputational positioning).
- *Cultural mindset shift.* Embedding a "Can If" mindset – seeing constraints as innovation triggers – into leadership behaviors.
- *Data-driven decision making.* Using real-time risk dashboards and scenario planning to turn risk signals into opportunity hypotheses.

In our training, we have developed this integration with lawyers via the Six Dimensions of Business Risk and the Six Dimensions of Business Opportunity.

The Six Dimensions of Business Risk emphasize the interconnected aspects of risk in all situations and that risk is not merely bad – it can be an opportunity. This is further refined through the Six Dimensions of Opportunity, which reframes The Six Dimensions of Business Risk purely in terms of opportunity. Both are driven by curiosity and creativity. They both align well with the attributes of Zoom Master, Bias Jiu Jitsu, Champion Chameleon, and Duality Master – the ability to see beyond the day-to-day functions of a legal team.

The Six Dimensions of Business Risk

1. *Business risk.* To what extent does the company have adequate financial resources to remain in business despite adverse economic conditions or an unforeseen catastrophe?
2. *Political risk.* To what extent does the company engage in lobbying to prevent a potentially adverse government (federal, state, municipal, or regulatory) decision or course of action that could hurt its ability to remain profitable and grow?

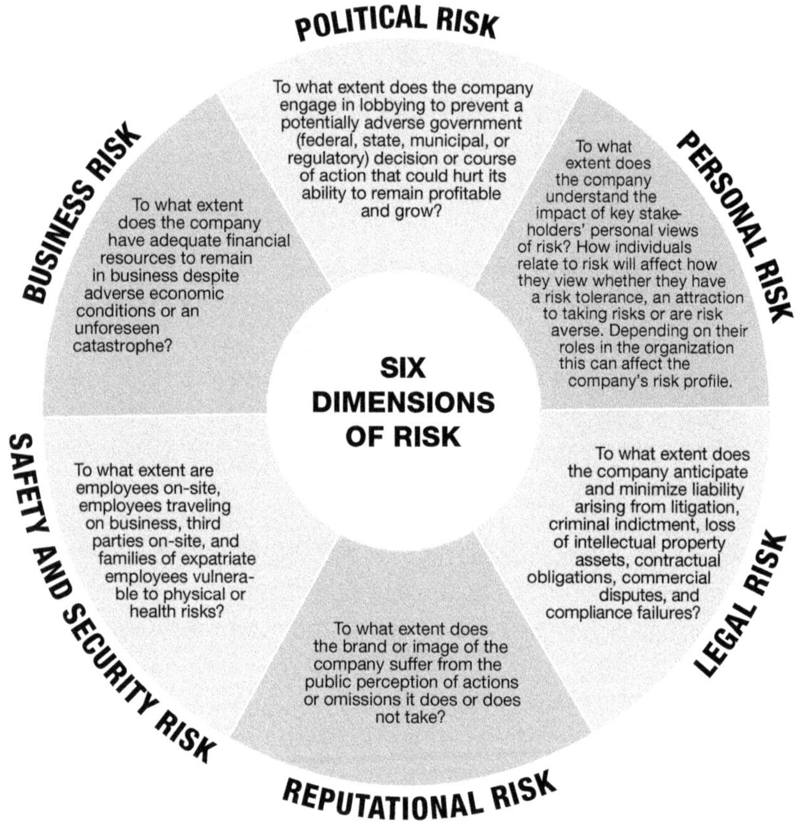

Figure 11: The Six Dimensions of Business Risk. Source: Chief Legal Executive LLC.

3. *Personal risk.* To what extent does the company understand the impact of key stakeholders' personal views of risk? How individuals relate to risk will affect how they view whether they have a risk tolerance, an attraction to taking risks, or are risk averse. Depending on their roles in the organization, this can affect the company's risk profile.
4. *Legal risk.* To what extent does the company anticipate and minimize liability arising from litigation, criminal indictment, loss of intellectual property assets, contractual obligations, commercial disputes, and compliance failures?
5. *Reputational risk.* To what extent does the brand or image of the company suffer from the public perception of actions or omissions it does or does not take?

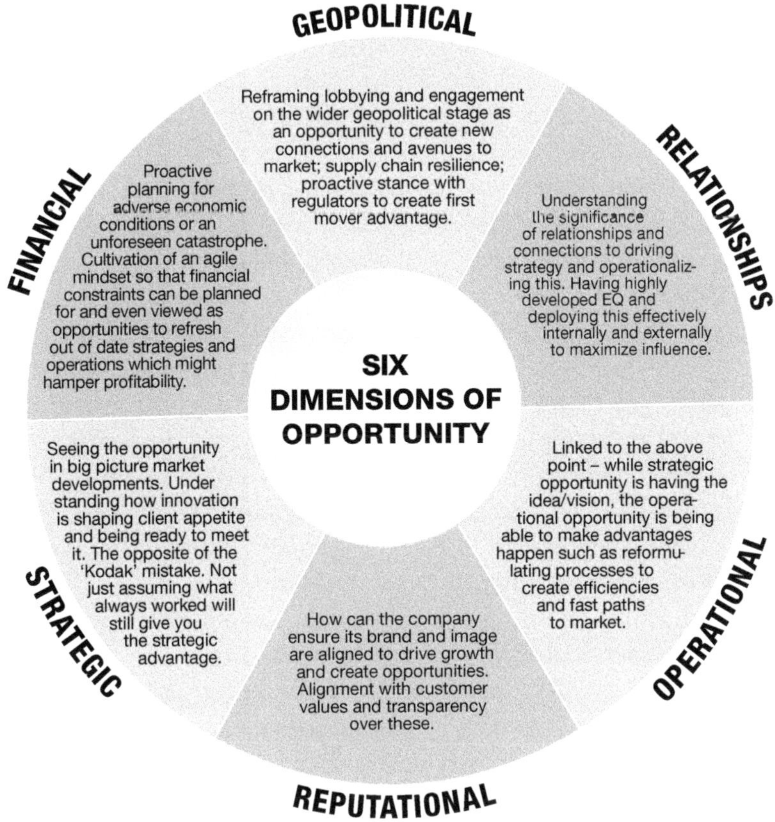

Figure 12: The Six Dimensions of Business Opportunity. Source: Chief Legal Executive LLC.

6. *Safety and security risk.* To what extent are employees on-site, employees traveling on business, third parties on-site, and families of expatriate employees vulnerable to physical or health risks?

The Six Dimensions of Opportunity

1. *Financial opportunity.* Proactive planning for adverse economic conditions or an unforeseen catastrophe. Cultivation of an agile mindset so that financial constraints can be planned for and even viewed as opportunities to refresh out-of-date strategies and operations that might hamper profitability.
2. *Reputational opportunity.* Ensure brand and image are aligned to drive

growth and create opportunities. Emphasis on alignment with customer values and transparency.

3. *Operational opportunity.* Transform operational risk into advantage by reformulating processes to create efficiencies and faster paths to market.
4. *Relationship opportunity.* Understand the significance of relationships and connections to drive strategy and operationalize it. Leverage high emotional intelligence (EQ) internally and externally to maximize influence.
5. *Geopolitical opportunity.* Reframe lobbying and engagement on the wider geopolitical stage as an opportunity to create new connections and avenues to market, enhance supply chain resilience, and take a proactive stance with regulators to create first-mover advantage.
6. *Strategic opportunity.* See the opportunity in big-picture market developments. Understand how innovation is shaping client appetite and position the company to meet it – avoiding the "Kodak mistake" of assuming the past guarantees future advantage.

The interconnectedness of risk and opportunity

The Six Dimensions of Business Risk is a framework for analyzing a range of business risks in any situation. It was developed via conversations undertaken by Lloyd with public company Board members on the key aspects of risk they saw coming up in a variety of business situations.

We initially used the Six Dimensions of Business Risk to train both in-house lawyers and law firm senior associates to analyze issues with a broader framework than just legal risk. During our use of the Six Dimensions of Business Risk, we emphasized the fact that every risk carried an opportunity. We found that in our training, we needed to keep emphasizing the need to look at opportunity as a requisite part of leadership development. Increasingly, it is this ability to operate as a business opportunity maker that sets the most innovative general counsel apart from the rest.

As a result of this insight, we developed the Six Dimensions of Business Opportunity to make it more obvious to the lawyers we were training where some of the significant areas of business opportunity lay and how these could be categorized. We found that, in practice, making the lawyers we worked with explicitly look for opportunities rather than just risks helped them to access a more creative problem-solving mindset. This was expedited using the Can If problem-solving framework (see chapter 14).

Another practical aspect that helped was to counsel participants against taking the risk event as the starting point when reframing it as an opportunity. For example, rather than saying, "We have a regulatory risk to consider, which could become an opportunity to work proactively lobbying key decision makers in government", it helped ideas to flow and the energy of the communication if participants led with the opportunity: "We have a great opportunity to work with decision makers in government to drive our strategy forward". As mentioned in this chapter, the Sapir Whorf hypothesis of the link between what we say and how we think comes into play again here. But why is the understanding of the link between risk and opportunity even more pressing in the Exponential Age?

Risk, opportunity, and resilience in the Exponential Age

The Exponential Age – characterized by rapid technological advancement, interconnected markets, and volatile geopolitical shifts – creates a business environment defined by high uncertainty, complex interdependencies, and accelerating change. Research from McKinsey[1] emphasizes that organizations that thrive in this environment share two key capabilities:

1. *Dynamic risk awareness.* Continuously scanning for emerging risks across multiple dimensions rather than in silos.
2. *Opportunity reframing.* Viewing disruptions (economic shocks, regulatory changes, reputational crises) as potential catalysts for strategic and operational innovation.

The McKinsey research calls for resilience as a defining characteristic needed in this age of fast-paced change. But this resilience is a balance of being able to take risk and recognize opportunities:

> *"Firms cannot afford to be either inflexible or imprudent. Those unwilling to take sufficient risk will not respond or innovate to meet changing circumstances. But at the same time, those too focused on financials, growth, or expansion may take on risk that kills their long-term success."*[2]

Businesses need to display resilience to navigate what McKinsey defines as "the surprise gaps" – these are the events that could be seen to correspond to Nassim Nicholas Taleb's Black Swan events, which seem to defy preparedness – which will increasingly be a hallmark of the Exponential Age, as the rate and pace of change increases. (We talk more about Taleb's ideas later in the chapter.)[3]

What is needed is a new type of resilience – one based on a new understanding and application of both risk and opportunity. This resilience in the Exponential Age comes from rethinking risk as a capability, not just a control mechanism, and doing the same with opportunity via embracing both as interconnected and therefore dynamically looking for the opportunity in every risk situation and vice versa. It is this interconnectedness of risk and opportunity that will define business going forward.

If either is out of balance it can create challenges. When creating a magazine such as *Inside Counsel*, Lloyd discovered that his ability to generate vision and strategy was actually a liability. He severely over-indexed on the opportunity while placing far too little emphasis on the operational risks. He was, by his own admission, high on "hopium". Consequently, he developed beautiful financial forecasts based on optimism rather than reality, which meant the team frequently ran out of money while there was still crucial work left to be done.

In his work with in-house counsel, Lloyd encountered the exact opposite challenge. In-house lawyers rarely get high on "hopium"; instead, in many instances, they over-index on risk to the total exclusion of opportunity. They tend to lock onto standard risk factors – such as legal, financial, or operational threats – while overlooking corresponding dimensions of opportunity such as innovation, efficiency, or market expansion. Business leaders are desperate for solutions, but when lawyers primarily provide barriers by exhaustively listing what could go wrong, they risk being marginalized. Often, they are quietly pushed to the periphery of strategic decisions without ever knowing why.

Lawyers who are going to thrive in business will need to embrace the mindset and skillset of the symbiosis of risk and opportunity. This will be defined by being more proactive in suggesting solutions as well as identifying risks – being able to offer a view based on the known situation and communicating this in an effective way with the biggest potential for influence.

The new risks

Part of this dynamism will be a new way of thinking about risks, and understanding that risks and opportunities will change constantly in the Exponential Age. We only need look at the threat of data breaches, which are a huge risk for a whole range of companies. On the flip side, using data provides one of the biggest business opportunities – one not even fully realized yet.

The need for a new way of thinking about and applying risk is at the heart of Azeem Azhar's 2021 book on the exponential age.[4] Many of his central ideas are highly relevant for lawyers. Azhar introduces the concept of an "exponential gap", where technological advancements outpace our capacity to understand and manage their consequences. This gap contributes to challenges like political polarization, rising inequality, and the unchecked power of large corporations. What this means is there is a need for new risk management approaches that can keep pace with rapid technological changes and address the associated challenges. Given some of the challenges will never have been seen before, the associated risks may be difficult or even impossible to fully appreciate.

This means that traditional risk frameworks, often based on linear assumptions – "if this then this" – are inadequate for addressing the exponential nature of technological change. This requires a shift towards more dynamic and adaptive risk assessment methods – one that can encompass the duality of risk and opportunity.

The Six Dimensions of Business Opportunity

One of the main reasons we introduced the Six Dimensions of Business Opportunity as a companion to the Six Dimensions of Business Risk was the lack of ability of many lawyers at the mid-level in-house to move beyond a risk-based way of thinking.

The characteristics of this risk-based way of thinking were focused on the negative aspects of risk. However, all risks – whether large or small – will contain an aspect of opportunity. This is where categorizing risk in the investment world comes in. The higher the risk – true of early stage investing in particular – the bigger the reward. For example, if you invested in Google in its first round of angel investing in 1998, you were taking a huge risk – however, encapsulated in that risk was the potential for a huge opportunity. If you had invested $1,000 in the nascent Google then and kept your investment through the IPO, it would now be worth tens of millions of dollars.[5]

As lawyers move up the in-house career path, they must become better at calibrating the interrelationship of risk and opportunity and be able to clearly communicate and work towards the opportunity, not just the risk. This is going to flex dependent on the industry, the stage of the company, and the amount of regulation the company faces. In one company where we worked with training leaders two levels below the GC, we used The Six Dimensions of Business Risk and Opportunity a lot. This really resonated with the GC, who in his interview had been explicitly told by the Board and the exco that they were looking for a general counsel who saw opportunities more than risks.

When we use a phrase like, "A GC who sees more opportunities than risk", we often witness a knee-jerk reaction from lawyers who see the notion of abandoning risk-based thinking for opportunity-based thinking as being akin to abandoning all legality. This is transparently not the case. The lawyer will always have to know where the line or the edge is – that is where they add value. However, this does not mean you always stay six feet away from the edge and ignore the business wins that might be gained by taking you (safely) closer to the edge.

The wheels

To adapt how we view risk we need a focus on the interconnectedness and associations of different risk factors, such as technological, economic, social, and political forces. A framework like our Six Dimensions of Business Risk helps lawyers do that via not framing everything through just legal risk. When lawyers are asked to apply the range of dimensions of risk, it starts to give them a much more holistic approach. It is this holistic approach that is needed to understand and manage risk in the Exponential Age. The main reason for this is the interconnectedness of risk factors. This was emphasized for us by having the risks framed as a circular wheel, not a list or a flow chart. This was deliberate. Circular or radial representations – with central hubs and interconnected nodes – encourage viewing information as a complete, interlinked system, rather than just isolated items. This mimics the ways in which most of our brains work.

A non-linear layout aligns with our brain's associative thinking, making it easier to see the big picture and how elements interconnect rather than being buried in a hierarchical list. It reduces cognitive load by visually grouping and connecting ideas in proximity, allowing for better sense-making, creativity, and systems-level reasoning. Based on educational research and cognitive theory, such formats consistently outperform lists or linear diagrams in supporting holistic understanding and associative thinking versus linear thinking. Studies have also shown that mindmapping improves reading comprehension and information retention, because it organizes complex concepts spatially, highlighting connections that linear lists obscure.[6] Unlike flowcharts or lists that focus on sequential or unidirectional relationships, circle-based or conceptmap structures support bidirectional links, feedback loops, and emergent patterns essential in systems and associative thinking. It is this sort of thinking that is still emergent in technology and where human minds still have the edge.

Linear versus associative thinking

A non-linear model of approaching problems takes us away from linear or purely cause and effect-based thinking and more into the realm of associative thinking.

The key differences between the two forms of thinking are summarized below.

Linear thinking

- *Structure:* Follows a clear, sequential path from premise to conclusion.
- *Reasoning:* Employs rules of inference and deduction.
- *Example:* If A implies B, and B implies C, then A implies C (deductive reasoning).

Associative thinking

- *Structure:* May not follow a linear path. Connections are made based on shared elements or past experiences.
- *Reasoning:* Relies on patterns, similarities, and previous knowledge to link ideas.
- *Example:* Seeing red might make someone think of fire, blood, or a specific type of flower, all based on learned associations.

Associative thinking will generally focus on understanding the problem versus just finding the one solution. This sort of thinking is what is needed to deal with problems and challenges in a much more volatile, change-heavy environment like the Exponential Age.

If we apply this to the case of risk, then understanding the range of risk factors and how they interrelate gives a much more nuanced analysis of what is going on and can even be extended to encompass how the risks can relate to the opportunities. This type of understanding is much more able to cope with volatility and fast-paced change. Nassim Nicholas Taleb[7] argues that systems – and by extension businesses – that embrace volatility strengthen over time. He asserts that antifragility is "beyond resilience or robustness" and that systems should be designed to benefit from disorder.

The Six Dimensions of Business Risk and The Six Dimensions of Business Opportunity provide a structured way to build these capabilities by mapping threats and opportunities holistically across financial, operational, reputational, and geopolitical contexts.

How the six dimensions of business risk and opportunity work together in practice for legal teams

The below is not exhaustive and obviously cannot consider every variable for each legal team and their business, but it does give some initial ideas as to how legal teams can adapt the ways that business stakeholders will exploit opportunity scenarios in the Six Dimensions of Business Opportunity and be able to reframe risk as opportunity.

Financial / business risk ➡ Financial opportunity

The risks at play here are adverse economic conditions, unforeseen catastrophes, or lack of financial resilience.

Reframing this as opportunity involves rethinking the conceptualization of volatility and uncertainty as necessarily bad. These are the same ways of thinking that drive our Exponential Age Mindset Attributes of Joyful Tightrope, Chaos Converter, and Agile Juggler.

Joyful Tightrope is a heightened level of comfort with uncertainty. Uncertainty is a defining feature of change, as we may think we know how change will work out but can never be certain. As the Exponential Age is defined by increasing change, it follows that being able to be OK with uncertainty will be a crucial skillset. Chaos Converter is the ability to find opportunity in chaos. That is not necessarily transforming chaos into order, but being able to welcome the opportunities that chaos gives us, our teams, and organizations to test ourselves and potentially open new opportunities to view challenges differently. Agile Juggler is the ability to balance consistency with agility. Law is a profession grounded in precedent, but the best legal professionals understand the need to be creative and not get locked into the status quo for the sake of it. This aptitude will be crucial as change becomes even more of a constant.

These three ideas that coalesce around the idea of embracing volatility, not trying to get rid of it or fix it, correspond well with the notion of antifragility outlined by Taleb. Antifragile organizations embrace constraints to drive innovation. Agile financial planning – like restructuring outdated cost models or entering new markets – can turn downturns into opportunities for efficiency and reinvention.

Dynamic forecasting in business and finance utilizes real-time data and frequent updates to adapt to changing business environments. This encapsulates optionality being applied in how lawyers create contracts with flexible contract structures and renegotiation clauses to capture upside opportunities.

Scenario planning for business and financial volatility can be used by legal teams to design legal frameworks that test business model resilience such as simulating regulatory shocks or dispute scenarios. A classic model would be real-time simulation of a crisis such as a cyber-attack or dawn raid.

Another agile financial planning technique is decentralized budgeting, where budgeting responsibilities are distributed away from central administration to individual departments or units within an organization. This creates opportunities to potentially increase innovation and adaptability in the face of changing market conditions. Legal teams can adopt this financial and business opportunity mindset in practice by empowering business units with legal playbooks that support autonomous decision-making within defined risk thresholds.

Rolling forecasts are a financial planning technique that will avoid over-optimization. This can be adopted by legal via implementations of contracts or risk structures that preserve "slack" via buffer time or contingency funds. This can also be applied in legal teams' own financial planning via contingency fees for external counsel.

Cross-functional agility is a business activity based on breaking down silos so that project teams are comprised of diverse skillsets from across different business units, meaning response times and creativity are enhanced. For legal teams, this might look like embedding lawyers in product and deal teams to increase accountability and situational fluency.

Reputational risk ➡ Reputational opportunity

Reputation has long been one of a company's most valuable yet fragile assets. As the old saying goes, it can take years to build and just moments to destroy. In the Exponential Age – where information spreads at the speed of a tweet[8] and stakeholder expectations evolve daily – this adage has never been truer. Today, reputational risk is no longer confined to a few traditional domains like public relations or crisis management. It now spans digital trust, ethical supply chains, employee activism, and environmental stewardship.

The risk side of the equation is well understood. Damage to public perception can arise rapidly from failures in areas such as ESG compliance, data privacy, poor governance, or a mismanaged crisis response. One incident – whether a leaked email, a missed sustainability goal, or an AI ethics breach – can cascade into regulatory scrutiny, customer churn, and shareholder pressure.

However, this volatile landscape also opens the door to opportunity.

Research from Edelman's Trust Barometer[9] consistently shows that companies that proactively communicate their values and operate with transparency outperform their peers in trust. Organizations that are *first movers* in openly addressing their ESG commitments, social justice positions, or sustainability strategies can build credibility before a crisis ever hits.

Sometimes the law can get in the way of the reputational lens. In a well-publicized example from 2015 (although the initial tragedy was years earlier), travel firm Thomas Cook faced the fallout from a decision where taking the strictly legal risk view led to a much bigger risk via a reputational crisis.[10] In 2006, British children Christi and Bobby Cook died due to carbon monoxide poisoning caused by a faulty boiler at a hotel in Corfu where they were staying as part of a Thomas Cook Package holiday. The company distanced itself from the tragedy as the hotel was owned and operated by another group. Thomas Cook ended up suing the Greek hotel operators for damages and received £3.5 million. Via a strictly legal lens, the company did not have liability. But in the court of public reputation, its lack of attention to the plight of the children's parents and inability to apologize or give the family any compensation was damning. The consensus was that Thomas Cook listened too much to its lawyers and not enough to its PR advisors. What could have changed if its lawyers (internal and external) had been more focused on the interconnection of different risk factors, not solely the legal one?

By framing reputational risk through the lens of *strategic opportunity*, in-house legal and compliance teams can help the business not only protect its reputation but actively enhance it. This might include guiding leadership on how to:

- Embed ESG disclosures as part of core corporate storytelling, not just compliance reports.
- Craft governance frameworks that support proactive, values-driven decision-making.
- Advise on transparent public communications around difficult decisions (e.g., layoffs, regulatory investigations, or supply chain challenges) to preempt reputational damage and instead foster public trust.

Rather than treating reputation as something to be defended in a crisis, forward-looking organizations – and the legal advisors who support them – view it as a dynamic asset that can be strengthened through consistency, authenticity, and courage.

Operational and safety risk ➡ Operational opportunity

Operational challenges – ranging from inefficient procedures and inconsistent workflows to potential health and safety vulnerabilities – often trigger concerns about compliance or downside exposure. However, when these risks are addressed proactively, they can evolve into *strategic opportunities* that drive agility, efficiency, and competitive advantage.

Research from MIT Sloan Management Review on grassroots automation powerfully underscores this shift.[11] The study demonstrates how empowering non-technical employees – those closest to day-to-day operational friction – to adopt low-code or no-code tools and build automated workflows can generate substantial value.

This was a powerful learning through our work with paraprofessionals in a large national US retailer of home goods. These were the people in the legal department who were closest to much of the day-to-day operational friction. Much of this not only had cause and effect in legal but throughout the wider business. Via ownership and democratization of innovations such as automation, this does more than reduce errors or regulatory risk – it *accelerates internal processes*, removing bottlenecks that might otherwise delay product launches, contract approvals, or compliance reporting.

We have seen this powerfully in action with our application of the Can If framework in our training. In one power company, the environmental group told us they now used Can If in all their health and safety reviews because this tool allows them to transform risk into opportunity and helps to create the mindset shift to do so.

For in-house legal teams, this dual-framed perspective offers a powerful new lens. Rather than simply applying legal guardrails to shield the business, legal partners can champion *process harmonization and automation* as engines of strategic differentiation. By collaborating with operations, IT, and compliance, legal can help design governance models that ensure safe, consistent process flows and, in so doing, help unlock faster time-to-market and better operational resilience. In this way, what once appeared solely as operational risk becomes a springboard for institutional effectiveness and competitive differentiation.

Relationship / personal risk ➡ Relationship opportunity

We all have our own personal relationship with risk. Some of us are more natural risk takers than others. Our upbringing may condition this. As I have got older, I have been encouraged by life experience to take more professional and personal risks – including more physical sports. My parents were highly risk-adverse and discouraged me from taking physical risks as a child. My husband, however, is a self-confessed adrenaline junkie, and encourages me to try things I have never done before – such as taking up skiing in my forties!

In any organization, there will be a whole range of different relationships with risk. Lawyers by training and professional norms will likely be less comfortable with risk, whilst sales professionals are often incentivized to take risks by bonus structures that focus on increased sales revenue. Different types of organizations will also have their own cultural relationship to risk. Insurance, by the nature of the profession, is likely to be more risk averse. In the technology space, Facebook's "move fast and break things" – an internal mantra until 2014 – exemplifies a culture built on risk taking.[12]

Maturity is also a factor – early- or growth-stage companies will likely take more risks to turn these into opportunities, whilst mature companies that have found their niche may find risk-taking, especially in the creative sense, much harder. However, maturity and scale can also lead to arrogance and complacency, as exemplified by many of the financial institutions implicated in the 2008 global financial crisis. Institutions like Lehman Brothers were considered too big to fail but now exist only as cautionary tales. So, it's a complex relationship and one as nuanced as the range of different personalities in an organization.

Personal risk manifests when key decision-makers or stakeholders are uncomfortable with uncertainty or change. Their personal risk aversion – whether due to past experiences, leadership style, or organizational culture – can block bold ideas, delay decision-making, or create internal resistance to innovation. This risk is particularly acute in hierarchical or siloed organizations where influence is concentrated and dissent is discouraged. The story of Kodak's lack of understanding around risk and opportunity when digital photography emerged is a great example of this.

Connected relationships are the opposite of personal risk. This involves being able to look beyond one's own boundaries of risk, whether that's risk comfort or discomfort, and relate to others how risk and opportunity can be co-created. Relationship opportunity emerges when leaders cultivate trust, empathy, and emotional intelligence (EQ) across internal and external networks. By understanding stakeholder motivations and risk perceptions, they can build coalitions that reduce resistance and enable change.

According to Deloitte's 2021 Resilience Report,[13] organizations with strong stakeholder networks adapt to disruption 33 percent faster than those without. More specifically, the report found that 87 percent of chief experience officers (CXOs) who said they have done very well at balancing all their stakeholders' needs felt that their organizations could quickly adapt and pivot in response to disruptive events. Cross-functional collaboration and influence turn personal hesitation into shared momentum. This is echoed in my experience training in-house lawyers to be leaders. A pivotal learning for many is understanding the strength of relationship building and collaboration to increase influence and therefore results. This can involve unlearning the much more siloed norm of many law firms, and indeed many in-house legal teams, and moving to a position of being stronger together.

In-house lawyers often encounter business stakeholders who are personally risk-averse, hesitant to pursue innovation, or uncomfortable with ambiguity (e.g., launching AI tools, entering new markets). This can stall initiatives or delay decisions.

Rather than defaulting to legal caution or simply reinforcing stakeholder fears, lawyers can adopt an EQ-driven, collaborative approach that builds trust and shifts the collective risk appetite.

Opportunity-oriented actions:

- *Stakeholder mapping and influence strategy*. Proactively identify key decision-makers and understand their personal risk tolerances. Tailor legal advice to speak to their concerns and aspirations.
- *Facilitated alignment workshops*. Convene cross-functional sessions to align on risk posture – helping stakeholders move from "What could go wrong?" to "What could we unlock?".
- *Use the "Can If" framework*. Frame options positively – "We can pursue this market *if* we do X", instead of listing barriers. (See chapter 14 for more on this.)
- *Co-create risk frameworks*. Involve the business in defining thresholds for acceptable risk, particularly in innovation, so legal becomes an enabler, not an enforcer.

Examples:

A legal leader working on new SaaS integrations knew that the IT team was nervous about GDPR risks. Instead of blocking the project, the lawyer worked with them to co-develop a compliant data transfer agreement and leads training to build their confidence, accelerating implementation.

A lawyer at an investment firm identified a whole new way of structuring funds that could lead to new revenue opportunities. He focused on opportunity-based conversations with a range of stakeholders whose viewpoints and relationships he mapped to ensure he created optimum stakeholder alignment around his idea.

Political risk ➡ Geopolitical opportunity

We live in a time of increased geopolitical risk. Global conflicts like wars in Ukraine and the Middle East create instability and unpredictability. This exacerbates geopolitical tensions and raises the risk of further conflicts, including state-based armed conflicts and proxy wars. The world is currently in a "geopolitical recession", where international institutions struggle to maintain order and reflect the balance of power, leading to instability and a higher risk of conflict. There is less of a sense of certain powers being the "police of the world" who step in and sort out conflicts. A deficit in global leadership and a decline in international cooperation are leaving the world more vulnerable to risks. This contributes to a fragmented and less predictable geopolitical landscape. The volatile nature of some major powers' foreign policies is contributing to global uncertainty.

Rising nationalism and populist influences are leading to increased protectionism, trade wars, and the potential fragmentation of the global economy and supply chains. A decline in trust in institutions and government is contributing to civil unrest, as seen in recent events like the Hong Kong pro-democracy protests, the Serbian anti-corruption student protests, and the US Capitol riot.

Political instability and conflict can disrupt trade, deter foreign investment, and negatively impact economic growth. Global debt, particularly in developing nations, and potential economic shocks like a downward spiral in US–China relations or a climate tipping point, further exacerbate political risk.

Rapid advancements in technology, particularly in areas like AI, present new risks and challenges to global governance and stability. The competition for technological dominance between major powers is intensifying, further contributing to geopolitical tensions.

According to geopolitical advisor Xenia Wickett, "Geopolitics is coming into the C-Suite through the GC because of risk".[14] Specifically, the need to calibrate new risks differently.

Political risk includes exposure to sudden shifts in regulation, government policy, trade agreements, or geopolitical events. These changes can disrupt operations, limit market access, or create compliance burdens – particularly in sectors like energy, tech, and healthcare. Companies that fail to anticipate or respond to political signals can suffer from regulatory penalties, reputational damage, or operational paralysis.

Geopolitical opportunity involves proactive engagement with policymakers, regulators, and international stakeholders. Instead of simply reacting to political events, forward-looking organizations seek to shape them. Companies that anticipate and engage with regulatory trends – especially in emerging fields such as electric vehicles, AI, or climate tech – can secure first mover advantages, influence policy design, and enhance supply chain resilience. The GC can be a significant influence and first mover in creating this opportunity via their own and their team's focus on regulation and relationship with regulators. Increasingly, in the US, the whole remit of government affairs, which has a significant role in creating policy opportunities, falls under the GC or CLO's remit.

In-house lawyers are often reactive to regulatory or political changes, focusing on compliance and damage control when new laws, tariffs, or sanctions emerge.

Lawyers can play a proactive strategic role by anticipating political shifts, engaging with regulators, and helping the business position itself as a thought leader or first mover in navigating change.

Opportunity-oriented actions:

- *Scenario planning with policy inputs.* Work with government affairs or external counsel to model legal implications of likely political shifts – then brief the business before crises hit.
- *Regulatory relationship building.* Develop channels of influence with regulators and policymakers – offering feedback, joining roundtables, or contributing to industry standards.
- *Leverage legal for market entry strategy.* Align legal advice with geopolitical trends (e.g., local content rules, ESG expectations) to help the business de-risk and optimize market expansion.

Examples:

An EV manufacturer's legal team identifies upcoming EU battery supply chain regulations. Rather than waiting for enforcement, they co-lead discussions with procurement to diversify suppliers and engage EU regulators to shape standards, gaining reputational and regulatory advantage.

A home goods supplier was reliant on China for many of its materials. The legal team started to brainstorm with outside counsel and consultants immediately after the 2024 US election to be prepared for trade tariffs and supply chain challenges.

Strategic risk ➡ Strategic opportunity

One of the key mantras we repeat when working on risk and opportunity with legal leaders is that *not* taking a risk can be just as dangerous as taking it. This will be increasingly true given the pace of change and technological advances in the Exponential Age.

Strategic opportunity comes from seeing the big picture and anticipating change before competitors do. This means scanning for technological disruption, shifts in consumer behavior, or emerging market trends – and responding not just with vision, but with timely action. Companies that fail to evolve risk becoming obsolete (as with the classic Kodak example). Those that act with foresight, adaptability, and purpose can lead their industries into the future.

Global management consultancy firm Bain & Company calls this the "Flywheel" concept to describe a self-reinforcing cycle that builds momentum and drives sustainable growth. In the scope of innovation, it could be leveraging disruption as a chance to reimagine products, services, and customer experience.[15]

Lawyers are typically brought in late to "paper over" strategic plans, focusing on downside mitigation (e.g., disclaimers, risk clauses) rather than shaping strategy itself.

By positioning legal as a strategic thought partner early, lawyers can shape initiatives to be both ambitious and feasible, helping the business see around corners and future-proof decisions.

Opportunity-oriented actions:

- *Early-stage strategy participation.* Embed legal in product, market, or M&A planning teams from the beginning – not as a gatekeeper, but as a value-adding advisor.
- *Trend spotting and legal signal tracking.* Track emerging legal signals (AI regulation, ESG mandates, IP trends) and feed insights into strategic conversations.
- *Develop innovation-friendly legal frameworks.* Draft IP strategies, ethical guidelines, and risk-sharing models that encourage experimentation without derailing compliance.

Examples:
A legal team at a fintech firm identifies early signals about open banking legislation. It briefs product leaders and co-designs a compliant open API framework that positions the company ahead of competitors as the regulation rolls out.

A GC at a fast-moving consumer goods company was concerned that her lawyers were not part of early strategic conversations. She positioned access for her lawyers by appealing to business unit heads that this was a learning opportunity for the lawyers. Her directive to her team was to ensure they did contribute and become active participants to show their value as strategic collaborators so the business units would continue to include them.

The new breed of general counsel – opportunity spotters

Increasingly, the most effective and creative general counsel we encounter are those who can situate themselves firmly on the nexus of being able to integrate risk and opportunity. We would argue that, in the Exponential Age, the relationship to opportunity needs to be even more highly defined. Let's return to the example of the GC who was told in his interview by the ExCo that he needed to be an opportunity creator. He was very keen that his aspiring legal leaders also understood the importance of this mindset.

Having lived both in the US and UK – and having worked with GCs from around the world – I have seen how countries differ in their approach to the GC role. In the US, I see a much more expansive version of the GC role, where GCs have become more firmly part of the C-Suite, than in the UK and Europe. I believe this is due to their ability to straddle the delicate balance between risk mitigation and opportunity intensification. Being able to do this effectively also means that the lead lawyer is more likely to be listened to when they really need to be.

This shows a strategic way of thinking that will mirror many other officers on the executive team. It also demonstrates that the legal function is committed to the same goals of success for the company. It also creates collaboration. All these factors will help when an effective challenge is needed, much more so than a stance of not venturing outside your swim lane. Of course, at the heart of this is also a relationship between the GC and other C-Suite. That is why we emphasize and re-emphasize the importance of relationship building in the early days of a GC role to ensure that the interrelationship of risk and opportunity can be maximized.

A relationship is a two-way street, so when interviewing for a GC role, it's fundamental to sow the seeds of effective collaboration and relationships that will lead to the optimization of risk and opportunity. Warning signs can include key personnel such as the CEO not being part of your interview panel. Reporting to any other function than the CEO can also be a red flag. Asking how the CEO sees the role of GC and what success in this role looks like to them can also give you a guide as to whether the conditions are right for you to be an opportunity focused leader.

Example in practice: EV car company

In mid-2025, we were engaged to provide training for the leadership hi-potential lawyers in an EV company in the US. The candidates for the training were two levels below GC, at associate GC level.

Given the market focus of the company and its expansive growth trajectory, the relationship between risk and opportunity was a significant area of focus for the GC. He wanted the team to become better at developing an opportunity-based mindset. An enterprise-wide leader mindset is characterized by being able to view the business via a strategic trajectory and partner with other areas of the business. It is the opposite of legal being isolated and focused as subject matter experts. Having a strategic mindset is inherently linked to being able to see opportunity and risk and balance the two effectively.

In our first session with the group, our initial interactive exercise focused predominantly on getting the lawyers to see the range of risk factors in business decisions beyond legal risk, as well as being able to see the range of opportunities.

We created scenarios for each lawyer, based on the last four 10-Q filings for the company, so they were real and compelling.

The lawyers were asked to firstly evaluate their scenario via the Six Dimensions of Business Risk and formulate a presentation of what they deemed to be the main risk scenarios. The additional challenge was that they only had two minutes to present this, leaning into the Superlative Synthesizer competency – a key component of executive communication.

Having done this, they were then asked to evaluate the same scenario via the Six Dimensions of Business Opportunity and present this – again in two minutes, but also utilizing the Can If framework for their suggested actions for the business. There was definite discomfort with this exercise and much more so with the second part, which was focused on opportunity.

One of the most noticeable differences was in how the participants framed their second presentation. The most traditional lawyerly response was to reiterate the risk dimensions and then suggest how these could be reframed as opportunities. What was much more compelling was those participants who led with the opportunity rather than with the risks, completely focusing on an opportunity lens. Starting with the opportunity set the tone for the rest of the presentation and gave it more energy and focus.

A common technique we use in executive coaching is prompting the client to reframe a challenge as an opportunity. This can be difficult, but the shift to the opposite perspective can often unlock something in the client's relationship to the problem. For those in this session who really leant into this exercise and focused on the opportunity, the same shift seemed to happen.

Risk and opportunity toolkit for legal leaders and legal teams

Using the Six Dimensions Frameworks together, GCs and legal team can:

1. Map risk to opportunity directly (e.g., a reputational crisis ➡ ESG leadership positioning).
2. Build cross-functional alignment by framing legal and compliance issues as enablers of strategic goals.
3. Strengthen influence with the business by using data and value stories to show how risk mitigation drives growth.
4. Foster resilience and adaptability – critical capabilities in the Exponential Age.

Mindset shift: From "What could go wrong?" to "What could we make possible?"

Traditional risk view	Risk–opportunity view
Avoid harm and liability	Balance downside with potential upside
Mitigate legal exposure	Enable strategic business moves
Say "no" to risk	Ask, "How can we manage this risk to unlock value?"

Tool	Purpose
Risk–Opportunity matrix	Visually map where legal risks overlap with business opportunities
"Can If" legal thinking	Help teams find ways forward with constraints (e.g., "We can do this if we...")
Pre-mortem workshops	Help anticipate not just what could go wrong, but what could go right – and what might block that
Legal opportunity tracker	Log where legal advice helped to unlock or accelerate business outcomes

Practical strategies to integrate risk and opportunity thinking

Strategy 1: Reframe legal advice through opportunity language

- Instead of, "There's a regulatory risk here".
- Try, "There's a risk here, but if we structure it this way, we can move forward with more confidence and even gain a first mover advantage", or "We can move forward with this new opportunity if we structure it in this way".

Strategy 2: Use the Six Dimensions Framework

- Map opportunities across dimensions like:
  - *Strategic:* Does this support long-term goals?
  - Reputational: Could we enhance brand trust?
  - *Operational:* Could this streamline or scale internal processes?
  - *Financial:* Could we reduce cost or unlock new revenue?
  - *Geopolitical:* Could a proactive stance with regulators give us market advantage?
  - *Relationships:* Understanding and acting on creating connections and influence to operationalize strategic effectiveness.

Strategy 3: Participate early in business planning

- Join strategy, product, or innovation meetings upstream – not just at the final contract stage.

- Ask, "What's the opportunity here, and what are the critical uncertainties we need to plan for?".

Strategy 4: Use opportunity-oriented legal triage

- Triage legal matters not just by urgency or risk, but also by strategic value potential.
- Example categories:
  - *License to operate:* Required legal infrastructure.
  - *Opportunity enablers:* Initiatives that unlock growth.
  - *Reputation levers:* Actions that can enhance trust or brand.

Strategy 5: Scenario-based legal thinking

- Facilitate cross-functional workshops that explore:
  - Best-case and worst-case outcomes of a deal or initiative.
  - The inflection points where legal can unlock advantage (e.g., IP strategy, compliance speed, smart negotiation).

Strategy 6: Create legal playbooks for opportunity zones

- Identify recurring scenarios where legal input creates opportunity:
  - Strategic partnerships.
  - ESG and sustainability disclosures.
  - New market entry.
  - Data monetization.
- Build templated frameworks, checklists, and pre-approved clauses to accelerate business responsiveness while managing legal exposure.

References

1 McKinsey Global Institute (2021). *The Resilience Imperative: Succeeding in Uncertain Times*. www.mckinsey.com/capabilities/risk-and-resilience/our-insights/the-resilience-imperative-succeeding-in-uncertain-times

2 *Ibid.*

3 Nassum Nicholas Taleb, *The Black Swan: The Impact of the Highly Improbable* (Penguin, 2008)

4 Azeem Axhar, *The Exponential Age: How Accelerating Technology is Transforming Business, Politics and Society* (2021) Diversion Books.

5 www.linkedin.com/posts/davidolivencia_1000-invested-in-google-in-1998-as-an-angel-activity-7117229040553402368-md4b/

6 Raphaela Brandner, 15 February 2024. Why mind mapping? 5 key benefits (+ templates) www.meistertask.com/blog/why-mind-mapping

7 Nassim Nicholas Taleb, *Antifragile: Things That Gain from Disorder* (2012).

8 An example of stickiness and how storytelling can fail, no matter how well-funded, if it doesn't resonate with its audience: no one is calling it an "X post".

9 Edelman is a PR agency that for 25 years has carried out a global survey on trust in institutions such as governments and corporates.

10 www.bbc.com/news/uk-england-32719823

11 Ian Barkin and Thomas H. Davenport, "Harnessing Grassroots Automation," *MIT Sloan Management Review* (September 2023).

12 https://en.wikipedia.org/wiki/Move_fast_and_break_things

13 www.deloitte.com/in/en/about/press-room/deloitte-report-reveals-how-organizations-can-better-prepare-for-future-disruption-climate-change-top-concern-among-business-leaders.html

14 Xenia Wickett, Keynote speech at Eagle Club Symposium, London, 23 June 2025.

15 Rob Markey, "Engage Employees Using Customer Service Tactics," October 2011: www.bain.com/insights/engage-employees-using-customer-service-tactics

Chapter 13:
The Four Zones of Curiosity

A tool that we often use in our training sessions to get participants to think more strategically about projects or their career is the Four Zones of Curiosity (seen earlier in chapter three). This can be a fantastic way to get individuals or teams to stretch into Zoom Master and bring in the competencies of Joyful Tightrope, Agile Juggler, and Duality Master.

We adapted this from Johari's Window, which is a tool designed to create self-awareness and communication for individuals and teams by getting people to think about how they process information and relate to others. The model was created by psychologists Joseph Luft (1916-2014) and Harrington Ingham (1916-1995) in 1955. (Its title derives from the combination of their name, like an early version of Bennifer!)

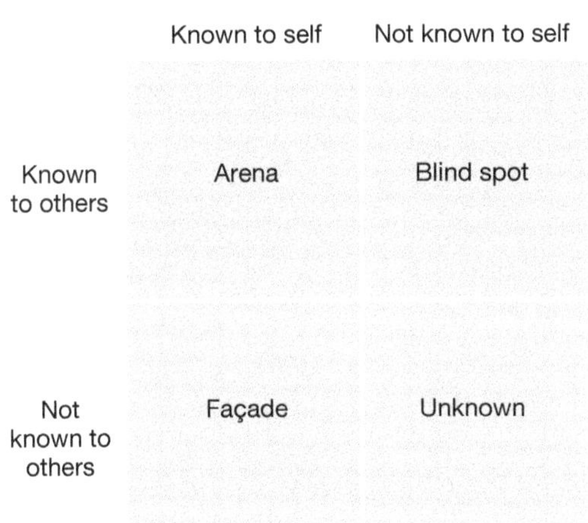

Figure 13: The classic Johari Window model.[1]

The window is divided into four quadrants: Arena (open), façade (hidden), blind spot, and unknown. The open quadrant is made up of information that is known to both the individual and others. The hidden quadrant is made up of information that is known to the individual but not others. The blind spot quadrant is made up of information that is known to others but not the individual. The unknown quadrant is made up of information that is unknown to both the individual and others. The goal is to move information from the unknown and hidden quadrants to the open zone, where it can be discussed and improved.

How our model differs is that it takes the initial concepts of open, blind, hidden, and unknown and applies them to strategic understanding, rather than communication.

- Zone 1 – today's projects.
- Zone 2 – tomorrow's projects that I am aware of, and my manager is aware of. These are tomorrow's achievements.
- Zone 3 – tomorrow's unknown projects. Uncommunicated and unmet are therefore tomorrow's challenges.
- Zone 4 – tomorrow's opportunities, currently unknown and unmet but offering the biggest strategic gains. Literally seeing around corners.

Why the Four Zones of Curiosity are important in the Exponential Age

When we coach clients through the transition to general counsel roles, we find a significant part of the mindset shift in becoming an effective general counsel is the ability to understand how what their "work" looks like has changed. It is not merely performing the role of a lawyer with additional leadership functions. It is performing the role of a leader where there may be occasional legal, compliance, and governance questions. The challenge for many newly minted general counsel is not getting caught in a cycle of increasing reactivity and being unable to let go of the doing that will not allow them to see beyond Zone One into even Zone Two, let alone Zone Four. It is the same process at work with AI adoption. It's not adding it onto what you already do but fundamentally reframing what that is from a new perspective of digital enablement.

One of the other red flags (in addition to a GC reporting to a CFO as opposed to the CEO) is a legal team full of subject matter experts (SMEs). Some are required, but that is why law firms exist. Legal teams with generalists are far more likely to make the mindset shift we are aiming for than a team of SMEs so dug into their own trench that they fail to see the wood for the trees. This is why we are both against businesses parachuting in 20 years-plus law firm partners into GC roles. They generally tend to just create a mini law firm in the business. Good CLOs are leaders and managers first then technical lawyers, not the other way around. Finding the legal technical expertise

Zone 1 **Known and met** *Focus is on my role and my team.* Known needs of GC/manager. Current projects. What I do now. Characterized by a siloed view. Reactive, detail-orientated mindset.	**Zone 2** **Known and unmet** *Focus is on my team and expanding what I do now within expected parameters that can help the entire legal team.* Known and unmet needs of GC/manager. Future projects in my sight. What I know I need to do. Peeking out of my silo to look at others around me in my legal team. Reactive but taking time to step back and look at the bigger picture.
Zone 3 **Unknown and unmet** *Focus on opportunities for the entire legal team and how they relate to the business.* Unknown and unmet needs of GC. Future projects I am not aware of. Connected view across the legal team and business stakeholders. View is looking at the legal team and how it relates to business then how my role connects to that. Strategic and operational.	**Zone 4** **Unknown and unmet** *Focus on the business and what I can do to provide strategic advances to the business.* Unknown and unmet needs of the business. Future strategies that I am not aware of. Focus on the business. View of what the business opportunities are and can be. Strategic and visionary.

Figure 14: The Four Zones of Curiosity. Source: Chief Legal Executive LLC

is easy. Understanding the nuances of the problem in the context of the industry and the business is not. And it is the law firms who will be able to do both who will thrive as the trusted advisors of clients in the Exponential Age.

Life in the different zones

Zone One

Zone One is what we are most comfortable with. It's our current role and tasks. For many people living in Zone One, this is the norm and may be all they aspire to. There is going to be a significant danger to this approach as the Exponential Age becomes more developed, in that this is the space where technology will be used more and more. The mindset associated with Zone One is reactive – the classic model of the in-house lawyer who responds to every request from the business and is constantly busy. This is where employees get burnt out but may also feel less engaged. It's also the place where people feel least connected to the overall purpose of what they do and how it connects to the purpose of their organization. This is the place where many legal teams and their lawyers currently reside.

It's also going to be much more uncomfortable as the various challenges of:

- Expenses increase.
- Volume of work increases.
- Complexity of work increases.
- Polarization of key stakeholders increases.
- Time allowed to complete work decreases.
- Headcount decreases.
- Budget decreases.

Zone One is going to be a box that increasingly faces more pressure. The choice is stark – give yourself the breathing room of another Zone or be squeezed unbearably.

In career terms, this is the place of effort but no development or stretch. It's also a place of comfort, which is why so many people want to stay here. This is where people log the years of service and may expect their tenure to mean increased pay and responsibility. This is now predominantly not the case in any organization.

It is also the mindset in career terms that focuses purely on being good at what I do and not expanding my repertoire. Of not being strategic about exposing the talents I do have.

The relationship of people who are solidly based in Zone One with the Exponential Age is one of fear and trepidation. This is the scenario whereby technology takes our jobs – because the jobs exemplified by these mindsets are ripe for the taking!

Zone Two

Zone Two contains the projects that most legal teams and their lawyers know they must work on. Focus on process and operations will fall into this category. For some, it might be starting to consider these metrics; for other teams, it will be increasing their sophistication and uptake. This will be where more obvious improvements and new projects will be implemented.

The viewpoint will be looking at how the legal team can more effectively service the business with the operations of the legal department being the heuristic lens through which projects and improvements are viewed.

In-house lawyers will be looking at what other legal teams are doing, rather than looking more laterally into other business functions. The GC or CLO focused on this space will be thinking about how they can be the best lawyer and not thinking of themselves as a business executive.

From a career perspective, this will be the space where individuals will start to stretch into logical development opportunities such as skills that their manager feels they need but they do not have.

Zone Three

This is the view of looking most broadly at how the legal team can be optimized in relation to the entire business. This is where projects such as looking at predicted regulatory advancements and what that means for business strategy are considered.

This is the space where the most effective GCs and in-house lawyers currently reside. Increasingly, in our work with lawyers who are aiming for GC roles, it's where we see those roles are going.

Lawyers in this space will be hyper focused on how the legal department can be most effective for the business – whether this is in operational effectiveness or advising beyond just what is legal or not, and considering culture and ethics.

From a career perspective, this is where an individual considers their job growing based upon what is possible now if they take the most expansive view of what they can do and how they can grow. To get to this understanding, they will need to expand their skills and understand how others view what the individual does and how they do it.

Zone Four

Zone Four is the space of innovation and where individuals and teams are operating at the highest level of the zoom out phase of Zoom Master.

It's also a space where creativity is firing, and the aptitude of Duality Master will be coming into play. This is the space where legal teams not only create value for the business but can definitively express how that value is created.

In career terms, this is where lawyers are comfortable with moving into lateral opportunities or seeing where there are opportunities for growth in skillsets or on projects that might not be purely legal.

In the US, many Fortune 500 general counsel have a much broader remit beyond just law. This is born of a more strategic viewpoint than staying in the zone that is known and comfortable. I work across the US/UK and Europe and am increasingly seeing more UK and European general counsel question whether they should add additional responsibilities to their remit, as it is outside of what they know.

Zone Four is that of the business executive who has legal training and can apply this across the needs of the organization.

This is a great space to be in, but it's a rarified atmosphere. If this is the only Zone you play in, you are in danger of being divorced from reality and the key operational challenges of getting things done.

The key to successful implementation of the Four Zones of Curiosity is understanding the relationship between the four different stages and how you as an individual or a team can move between them and relate these to each other.

An example of the Zones in practice

Contract management is one of the core opportunities for innovation from both a people and process point of view across most legal teams.

Zone One involves simply getting the contracts done that we need to do.

Zone Two would be starting to optimize that from a legal department point of view – such as introducing a Contract Lifecycle Management (CLM) tool.

Zone Three might be introducing self-service so that the business can take

Zone 1: Known Needs of Manager – Met (Communicated and Met – Today's achievements)	Zone 2: Known Needs of Manager (Communicated but Not Met – Tomorrow's achievements)	Zone 3: Unknown and Unmet Needs of Manager (Uncommunicated and Unmet – Tomorrow's challenges)	Zone 4: Unknown and Unmet Needs of Business (Uncommunicated and Unmet – Tomorrow's risks and opportunities)
Known processes focused on getting the legal work done as it has always been.	Streamlining process for greater efficiency and cost reduction.	Ensuring legal department processes align with the business for business results that drive value.	What are the business insights provided by the legal department that can increase business effectiveness and profitability?
Example: Identify all the leases we have with XYZ companies.	*Example:* Identify the solution to streaotiating leases.	*Example:* Reduce the number of leases that take up paralegal and attorney time and make the process faster leading to increased revenue via faster turn-around.	*Example:* Automate the lease process to maximize efficiency and to sort most favorable lease terms. Use intelligence on favorable lease terms to increase profitability for business.

control of high-volume, low-risk contracts, and legal can partner with business stakeholders to negotiate key terms when it's not a standard contract.

Zone Four would be when legal looks at the data and information from across its work on contracts and identifies places where the business is not agreeing to the best terms or is leaving money on the table.

The Four Zones of Curiosity in action

Most of our work on the Four Zones of Curiosity was created in tandem with the delivery of programs for legal operations professionals and for paralegals in legal teams.

Much of the most effective deployment was with the paralegal and paraprofessional segments in legal departments, who often found this concept much easier to align with than in-house lawyers did.

One of our first "A-ha!" moments with the Four Zones of Curiosity came when working through them in a discussion with a former paralegal to a legal team in a leading global company. We were speaking with this paralegal as an example of someone who had increased their remit and moved into a broader business role. The former paralegal now worked with the company's real estate group. One of her responsibilities was negotiating leases for its stores. In working through what she did using the Four Zones of Curiosity, we could see how to move from a detail-orientated focus to a much more strategic one – one where there was much more opportunity to display creativity and create ROI for the business.

Using the Four Zones of Curiosity in legal department training

Strategic project focus

In 2024, we were asked to create a program for paralegals at a leading global company. The remit was not only development of the paralegals within their roles but also showing them that thinking differently and more broadly about those roles could lead to other opportunities, including ones outside of the legal department and beyond the role of a paralegal. We decided that the best way to introduce these ideas would be to get the group more comfortable with a strategic view of what they currently did.

When we started working with the paralegal group, we commenced our work using the Four Zones of Curiosity by asking them:

- What are the high priority projects for your team?
- What are some of the impediments or challenges to achieving those goals?
- What are some of the opportunities to improve processes in achieving those goals?
- What would you like to see done to increase the probability of achieving those goals?

Sharing this information was a highlight of the session for many of the participants as they were interested to know their colleagues' challenges and found that there was a great deal of commonality in the challenges they faced.

Once participants had shared this information, we took them through an example of the Four Zones of Curiosity, using the lease negotiation example cited above.

We then asked them to try to map their projects into the Four Zones of Curiosity and see where the opportunities were to take their projects from Zone One to Zones Two, Three, and Four.

At first, it was easier for participants to get straight to Zone Four and identify the ideal state with the biggest strategic advantage. However, when we encouraged people to try to work backwards from Zone Four and consider the stages to get there, it helped participants see how their improvement idea could move from being a dream to an actuality. The value of stages Two and Three was in creating the operational foundations to get to the visionary and innovative stage of Zone Four.

Paralegal process example

The task we left the participants with was to do some more work on the Four Zones of Curiosity between session one and two of the program. This was a gap of about six weeks. During that time, we asked them to share the Four Zones of Curiosity plan with their manager.

Below is one of the examples that a paralegal came up with.

Zone 1	Zone 2	Zone 3	Zone 4
Identified the onboarding document available for our team's new hires.	Identified that the document should contain updated information and templates for new hires. Updated information and templates in the document will ensure new hire will have all available information on hand.	Transformed the onboarding document into a playbook with updated information and templates therein not only for new hires but also a place of reference for our team.	Potential to create a dashboard that would include interactive version of the playbooks from Zone Three with links to all the most up-to-date templates.

Four Zones of Curiosity and your career

In one of our subsequent programs working with paraprofessionals across a legal team, we utilized the Four Zones of Curiosity specifically as a tool to allow participants to think more strategically about their careers.

The seeds of this had been sown in the initial research for our first paralegal program, where a significant aspect was the research interviews we undertook with paralegals who broadened their remit or moved out of the legal department all together.

We found that five factors unified those individuals:

1. *Vision.* They saw an opportunity.
2. *Increased risk tolerance.* They took on a new responsibility in which there was no guaranteed outcome.
3. *Intentionality.* They took specific action (or series of actions – asked their manager, talked to others in the company).
4. *Increased influence with their manager.* They took steps to communicate more effectively and use storytelling techniques to enhance their executive communication.
5. *Sustained action.* Expanding job responsibility or scope of role as needed.

As we applied the Four Zones of Curiosity in different programs, including programs where the focus was individual career development, it was obvious that this tool could also be used by individuals to map how to be more strategic about their career. In a very basic version, it would look like this:

Zone 1	Zone 2	Zone 3	Zone 4
My job as I know it and the skills I have now.	My job as my manager sees it.	My career growth, based on what is possible in the near term.	My career growth, based upon the skills I will need to manage all future changes, imagined and unimagined.
I keep doing what I am doing. I may keep getting better and become an expert, but my view is focused on how what I do impacts the stakeholders I work with directly.	There may be gaps in competencies and expectations. These are communicated and known.	I may need to undertake new training, coaching, or development and flex into uncomfortable areas to grow. I will have a period of being a non-expert while I do this.	I remain open to consistent development and agility. I am OK with learning throughout my career and am not afraid of being a beginner. Curiosity and creativity define how I approach my role.
Example: Subject matter expert in a legal team.	*Example:* I perform my role technically well but my manager tells me I need to communicate more effectively and use technology tools to become more efficient.	*Example:* I want to become a people manager but I need to get better at communication and project management. I will undertake coaching and communication training.	*Example:* I love experimenting with technology. I tell my manager that I would like to grow my role. I am agile in how I apply this and communicate with a range of stakeholders to see what the opportunities arc and proactively bringing new ideas.

The Four Zones of Curiosity could equally be applied to the role of a general counsel.

Zone 1	Zone 2	Zone 3	Zone 4
The classic general counsel as "top lawyer" and legal department as "mini law firm".	The general counsel moving into more generalist "counsel" role	Business person with legal expertise	Enterprise-wide leader
I am the lead lawyer. I define my role via being a lawyer primarily. I am a business person secondarily. My stakeholders are my clients. My team is reactive. We are a cost center. Our function is to protect the business. We do lean primarily on legal risk.	I am the lead lawyer but I focus less on specific legal advice and more on joining the dots. I'm starting to take small steps out of my legal "swim lane" and speak up on non-legal matters. I'm focusing the team on being more reactive but starting to become proactive and demonstrating how we can show value.	I am a core part of the executive team. Others consult me on a wide range of topics that might be related to law but are becoming more tangential to proper legal advice. I can make decisions without all the information. I am focused on applying what I learn to my legal team as well. I may be taking on more responsibility beyond legal.	I will still wear my lawyer hat when needed for the business, but mostly I work as an executive. I have a big picture lens. I have a well-developed team of legal leaders below me who handle the day-to-day. I will have more responsibility than just legal. I focus on how to use what my team and I do to create ROI for the business and can demonstrate that.

Aligning the Four Zones of Curiosity with the Exponential Age Mindset Attributes

The Exponential Age Mindset competencies – Creativity, Curiosity, Influencing, and Visioning – and the Exponential Age Mindset Attributes encourage people to actively move towards Zone Four in how they approach opportunities and challenges.

General counsel and their legal teams in Zone Four

The default zone for many larger in-house legal teams has been Zone One. The thing that unites many disparate legal teams that are not prepared for the Exponential Age is that of legal exceptionalism. "We lawyers and the legal team are different and therefore we cannot operate under the same parameters as the rest of the company." In the worst cases, this leads to teams with outsized spend that is not needed and is totally divorced from any common understanding of ROI or strategy with the wider business.

The operational factor that leads to this exceptionalism mindset is silos.

One of the most common issues we encounter when training legal teams is that of communication (or rather lack of it) and siloes. Across legal teams, many stakeholders do not know what their colleagues are doing. There is often no common understanding of what people do and how they are doing it and very little knowledge management. This is where AI and technology will be able to help. But for those GCs looking at AI as a magic bullet, it is not that yet – and may never be. You must have the foundations built before AI can add to best practices.

According to leading operations and technology consultant Kevin van Tonder, most GCs fall on a spectrum ranging from custodian/guardian, legal solution provider, or manager (many GCs with an effective legal ops team fall into the latter). Says van Tonder:

> *"The most forward-thinking GCs align legal and business strategies to drive value creation/capture and are a competitive advantage for the business. For me, this gets into the business model and being able to use a tool like Porter's Five Forces Model to see where the legal team can provide that competitive advantage."*

To think like this, you constantly have to be thinking about Zones Three and Four of the Four Zones of Curiosity and flexing attributes such as Zoom Master, Agile Juggler, and Duality Master.

A question we often get about working in Zone Four is, "Does this potentially erode the general counsel and their lawyers' objectivity?". Will working as a strategic partner necessarily equate to "going over to the dark side"? This of course assumes a very black and white (or Jedi and Sith) viewpoint! However, the Four Zones of Curiosity Model and a focus on adding strategic value should *strengthen* corporate governance, not act in opposition to it.

There is a link between ownership, primary and secondary stakeholders, and the corporate governance strategy. A poor strategy erodes value and a good one drives and captures it. This is beyond just what is legal to what is ethical. This is a Zone Four GC.

GCs in Zone Four are proactively involved in reputation management – not just when there is a crisis but working with the C-Suite, HR, and communications team to actively put in place and manage a strategy. Legal should not just be one of the role-players in a reputation management strategy; they also need to be the conductor of that orchestra. It goes hand in hand with the governance strategy. Examples of when this fails or where legal does not work effectively in Zone Four combining business, legal and risk with effective influence could include Uber a few years ago under the controversy -ridden leadership of Travis Kalanick, or the UK Post Office "Horizon" scandal.

This is why I don't think that the current drive in the UK to extend the SRA's ambit to include in-house lawyers is a wise one. The result these GCs want could be achieved by enhancing their influence within an organization, not by hiding behind "independence" and the regulator. That is like bringing your big brother to a schoolyard fight. Nobody will respect you.

The strategic mindset and thinking about things in a Zone Four way is where leaders live – irrespective of whether they have a leadership title. As is evidenced in my previous writings, I am a tireless advocate for introducing leadership training earlier in careers, but also in encouraging employees to think about leadership as behaviors, not titles.

I don't think that many GCs understand the role and effect of different leadership styles (especially their own) on organizational performance. There is a phrase we once saw about GCs becoming more effective "conversation partners" with C-Suite decision-makers. Those who excel here make it easy for others to engage with them. That drives confidence and helps build that trusted advisor component beyond just legal matters.

Asking the right strategic questions

We have mentioned previously the need to ask the right questions in the

Exponential Age. To work effectively in Zone Four, you have to be asking Zone Four questions of your key stakeholders, particularly in the business.

Questions that the most forward-thinking in-house lawyers are asking their business leader colleagues could look like this:

- Looking ahead two to three years, how do you expect the business / industry to evolve? What does that mean for competition, new entrants, and substitutes? What does this mean for the work the legal team does and how they do it? Is the team structured correctly for these changes? Does it have the right capabilities and skills?
- Do we anticipate expansion in the next two to three years? What are your particular concerns?
- Do you anticipate that the legal team will require any additional business skills for the business to achieve its strategic goals in the next two to three years?
- What work does the legal team do where its effectiveness exceeds the importance of that work (in the eyes of the business) and vice versa? What work should the legal team be elevating because the importance of that work exceeds the current legal team's effectiveness in doing that work?
- What business insights would the business expect the legal team to extract from commercial contracts (beyond legal risk)? What insights can be gained that would support the business' position vis-a-vis their suppliers, for example?
- What are the three to five strategic goals that the business wants to achieve in the next year? How can the legal team align its objectives against these strategic goals and what does this mean for the work that it focuses on?

The coaching opportunity with your CEO

This brings us to our final observation. The most effective C-Suite leaders recognize that their GCs and CLOs are not simply legal guardians, but untapped strategic assets. A forward-thinking GC does not accept the confines of a corner office role – they rise to redefine the very boundaries of leadership. They do not simply react to legal issues – they actively shape business strategy.

The shift happens when the GC and business leaders co-create a broader remit that goes beyond legal oversight to include growth, innovation, and risk-opportunity thinking. By co-creating with business stakeholders, they transform the GC function into a hub of strategic foresight, innovation, and influence. This is the essence of the Zone Four CLO/GC – someone who navigates beyond risk avoidance into opportunity creation.

The challenge before you is clear – will you allow your role to remain linear, or will you define the exponential range of what a GC can be in shaping the destiny of the business?

Reference

1 https://en.wikipedia.org/wiki/Johari_window

Chapter 14: The Can If Framework

It's often far too easy to shut a new idea down by focusing on all the reasons why it can't work. A new challenge can spark our fight-or-flight mechanisms, and we want to distance ourselves from it. We metaphorically run away by putting a barrier in place – "We can't because..." "That's not possible...". Of course, not all ideas or solutions should be considered. Some might be illegal, unethical, too risky, or take a gamble on the organization's reputation. However, there's a world of difference between a response that shuts down *all* creative problem solving and one that stops an unwise avenue in its tracks but opens other avenues for exploration.

In business, that is often the difference between success and failure for a legal team. This is where the Can If framework can be an invaluable tool.

The department of no

The in-house legal department is often stereotyped as "the department of no" – the people who dampen business creativity, stop innovation in its tracks, hamper the ability to innovate the business.

There can be many valid reasons why the legal department says no. There can also be reasons why they are saying no that are less about the issue in question and more about how the business engages with the department. The classic one being bringing in legal too late and not involving them in the crucial strategic planning stages, so the team is unable to prevent mistakes being made – at which stage, a "no" may be the only way to avoid compounding the damage.

In our work with legal departments of a range of sizes and across industries, we have found that some lawyers and legal department professionals view a challenge as a dead end, while others view a challenge as the beginning of solving a puzzle.

We also find that the most successful and innovative in-house lawyers are the latter – those who are able to engage in creative problem-solving with their business stakeholders. It's these lawyers who will be more adaptive and therefore successful in the Exponential Age.

The influence piece

This is also where influence comes in. Studies on disagreement[1] or giving feedback in life and in business all point to the fact that a response that is simply negative can shut down the connectivity between different parties, because the side that has brought the idea is invested not only mentally but emotionally. A hard "no" is an outright rejection, which even on a limited level hurts the other party. A response that acknowledges the value of the other person's idea or effort is always going to be much more influential.

"I think we should do A."

"That's a terrible idea. We cannot do A."

Versus

"I think we should do A."

"That's interesting and it has valid points, but have you also considered the advantages of B..."

In the second example, the response starts by acknowledging the other person, their work, and their ideas. It comes from a place of empathy and is therefore going to be much more influential because the person feels we understand them and therefore our response is as much about them and having their best interests at heart.

A response that is more open also creates the possibility to collaborate and solve the problem together. It's the difference explored in the classic improvisation game, "Yes, and...". In improv, performers have to keep a scene going by saying "Yes, and..." – no matter how outlandish or silly the actions they have to follow are. Saying "No, but..." stops everything in its tracks.

Speaking as a former drama teacher, I have seen this in practice onstage. But in my time as a trainer and coach, I have also learned using improvisation games such as "Yes, and..." with professionals like lawyers can be incredibly valuable. These are often great tools to use in team-building. The challenge is always how to get all members of the team, especially those who might be more skeptical about such games, to take them seriously and be able to see them as ideas that can be carried over into their everyday role. "Yes, and..." also offers ideas that may hold the key to success as a business partner.

The challenge in our training is how to change the mindset of lawyers who do not automatically use this creative problem-solving mindset and how to get them to start to do so consistently in a way that would feel like something they could do. Even the most innovative lawyer could have challenges consistently saying yes, aligned to the danger that this would take away the important ability to veto unethical or illegal pathways.

A unique problem solver

When we started working with Carlos Brown, the visionary chief legal officer of Dominion Energy in 2022, we saw a lawyer with a uniquely creative problem-solving ability. This has been a major factor in Brown's success and ability to move from being a lawyer to a business executive. One of his key pieces of advice to others keen to develop their leadership skills is, "Think about your decisions as if you were the owner of the company".

Brown is often brought into an issue at the stage when others cannot see a way forward. What defines his mindset is that failure is not an option so how do we find a legal and ethical alternative? Some people understand that no doesn't have to mean never – it just may mean finding another way.

One of the challenges that we were discussing with Carlos was how we could train his direct reports to think like him. Moving from "No, but" to "Yes, and...".

When we shared the "Can If" framework with Carlos, he loved it as it encapsulated how he approached business problems.

We have found the Can If framework transformative in our work dealing with legal departments. Legal departments are characterized by having to impose legal constraints while simultaneously feeling hamstrung by their own constraints of budget, time, and headcount. Too often, this can feel like an insurmountable obstacle. This is not only true of legal departments but any business unit. In Lloyd's experience as a serial entrepreneur who has launched seven magazines, two non-profits, and a legal app over the last four decades, the conviction that "I can and I will" is baked into his DNA – often to a fault. He discovered that the difference between success and failure was rarely the quality of the idea or its timeliness. By balancing his innate drive with the specific expertise of "wartmasters" to expose flaws and "pathfinders" to direct the course, using the same ideas as those that drive "Can If" showed him how to move from blind optimism to the optimum course of action.

Success in business, particularly in regard to innovation, is about how business leaders view constraints. The more we can reframe a constraint as an opportunity, the more likely we are to succeed. At the highest level, businesses might actually impose constraints to further refine their thinking and test ideas.

The Can If Framework is cited in Morgan and Bardem's book *A Beautiful Constraint* and was inspired by conversations with Colin Kelly, head of research and development at UK-based bakery Warburton's. Kelly emphasizes the importance of the flow in problem solving – keeping ideas moving towards a positive solution. If blockers are expressed as "We cannot", "This is impossible because..." etc. they will block the flow of problem solving and halt people's thought processes to get to a solution. Kelly's idea of Can if came about from his experiences working in Russia in 2006. The conservative culture there meant the many innovative ideas he and his team had were always blocked by responses that were all a variant on "We can't do this because...".

The reasons would vary, but the focus was always that of "We can't because..." and this would inevitably halt the flow of positive ideas. Whilst many of the cultural factors that contributed to challenges in implementing the new ideas could not be changed overnight, one thing Kelly could impose discipline on was how people framed the problem and spoke about it. He reasoned that by being compelled to speak about a problem differently, this would also start to change how people thought about it.

Saying and thinking

The words we choose and how we structure sentences directly reflects and shapes our thought processes. The way we speak can reveal our underlying beliefs, perceptions, and even cultural perspectives, essentially acting as a window into our minds. While not completely dictating our thoughts, our words can significantly influence how we think about and interpret the world around us. This notion of linguistic relativity has been proven by the Sapir Whorf theory that how we speak can influence how we perceive the world and interact with it.[2]

By making his team in Russia start sentences with "We can if..." instead of "We can't because...", Kelly started to change not only what they said but how the team viewed problems, from something that stopped everything to something that was an obstacle for now – but could have a solution.

Using the Can If problem-solving framework with legal teams removes blocks to the flow of positive energy to finding a solution.

Why Can If is so powerful

According to Morgan and Bardem, the Can If framework finds the potential in what can seem like an overwhelming constraint. The below is adapted from their summary on pp.80-81 of *A Beautiful Constraint*.[3]

1. *It keeps the conversation on the right question.* This is about how something *would* be possible vs whether it *could* be possible. In an in-house legal context, this could be understanding the business client's end goals and how to work with them to get there, even if the initial idea has challenges (whether these are operational, legal, regulatory etc.).
2. *It keeps the oxygen of optimism continually in the process.* The focus is on finding a solution and that this will happen – it's not if but when.
3. *The narrative we create about ourselves is that we are people who find a solution, not people who find obstacles.* This can be incredibly reinforcing for legal teams, particularly if circumstances and the way they have historically interacted with the business pushes them into more of a blocker role. The language and mindset of Can If also positions connectivity between everyone solving the problem and posits the power of transformation.
4. *It is a method that maintains a mindset.* If one line of enquiry does not generate an answer, we move onto the next until we find one that does. Importantly, Can If is fueled by possibility.

Applying Can If

We have adapted and used the Can If map in our workshops and training with legal departments and other corporate teams as varied as IT, finance and supply chain in a variety of organizations. We have found it universally useful – indeed, often game-changing.

As a tool, it works well with the application of the Exponential Age Mindset Attributes because it makes people think about what is possible and how they need to think differently to *make* things possible; not to just use the skills and mindsets they are comfortable with now.

This tool is also incredibly transformative for lawyers in legal teams, particularly in the mid-level of the legal department. These are generally in-house lawyers who are working with business stakeholders but who, in their relationships with those stakeholders, may be pushed into a role of enforcement or saying no, partly because of incomplete information or because they are being left out of key strategic discussions. In our coaching practices, we see in-house counsel struggle to move beyond their self-conception as mere protectors of the business. They often cling to the mantra that "Lawyers give advice, clients make decisions", joking that colleagues who embrace business roles have gone to the "dark side". Lloyd believes that at the foundation of this resistance is usually a deep-seated fear of being wrong. By balancing their duty to identify risk with the courage to offer solutions, he shows them how to move from simply listing barriers to co-creating the outcomes their business partners crave.

Unfortunately, if a lawyer is always pushed into a position of needing to say no or flag up issues, it makes business stakeholders less likely to want to bring them in as part of the strategy. This consistently confines the lawyer to a purely reactive position, which may lead many to feel the best response is always that of least risk, thereby focusing on what is not possible rather than what is.

How we apply it

We introduce Can If to illustrate examples based on the legal team's experiences. At this point, we may offer an opportunity for participants to share their own examples of how they have used this, seen it used, or how it could be helpful in their role. This stage may come later, depending on the size of the group and their level of engagement with the idea.

To increase engagement and demonstrate application, we will often introduce a role-play based on challenges the group may face in their industry. The direction will be to use the Can If model to apply different solutions to a part of the challenge until you find the most suitable one. Each team member presents one major challenge based on their expertise or the expertise of the role they are playing, and comes up with a Can If statement and an action for each area:

Problem: "One of the challenges in getting to net zero and introducing more green energy sources is the lack of knowledge and amount of misinformation hampering efforts to introduce wind farms in communities."

Can If Statement: "We can if we collaborate with experts in green energy."

Action: "Let's find experts from nearby universities who we can collaborate with to create information for local communities."

The possible versus the impossible

Possible and impossible are two sides of the same coin. They are both ways of looking at the same set of circumstances, just from different perspectives. As Colin Kelly found in his work at Warburton's, and as we have found working with in-house lawyers, a change of perspective is partly due to simply changing the language we use to frame the issue.

A change of perspective is a very powerful tool for shifting mindset and therefore behaviors. It's often used in coaching, and a tool we frequently use in our own coaching practice. We can feel stuck when we believe there is only one way forward. To change perspective automatically gives us a different view. It also gives us greater objectivity. This is another example of the power of distancing ourselves from the immediate challenges that the mindset of Zoom Master gives us.

In coaching, the coach will suggest several different perspectives to explore. One example is to ask the client to find something in their surroundings that catches their eye, or the coach can even suggest something. This can seem quite bizarre to the client at first. What's the perspective of your table lamp!? But the very incongruity of considering what the perspective of the table lamp represents causes us to stop our usual flow of thoughts and start to consider something different. The table lamp might represent continuity – it's always there – or guidance – its light helps me see better. Perhaps I bought it on a fantastic holiday, so it reminds of that happier time. By taking a different perspective, a whole new host of thoughts are unlocked. The coach can then help guide the client to apply those ideas to the issue in question. In a similar way, the Can If map forces us to look at a challenge in a different way.

Taking a diversion

A good metaphor is that our problem solving can often get stuck on a particular path. Often, it's simply that this is what we are used to. This is how it's always been done, so this path is well-trodden. Our brains don't like forging new paths!

But taking the usual path can often result in a dead end. As Colin Kelly found, "We can't because..." is a block. Lawyers can get stuck on this track due to various factors:

- The reactiveness forced upon them by the scope and speed required in modern business.
- A natural aversion to doing things differently.
- The focus on precedent in legal training.

The Can If framework is literally a map that can guide people to different paths to solve the problem.

Let's explore the different paths it offers.

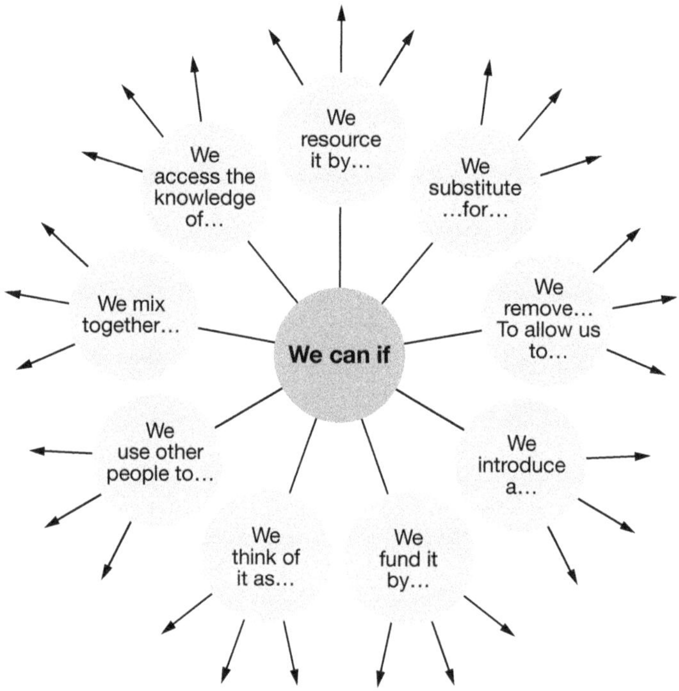

Figure 15: The Can If Map. Source: Adapted from Morgan and Bardem.[4] *Source: Chief Legal Executive LLC*

How it works in practice with legal teams

Below are some examples of the Can If statements in the figure in practice.

"We can if we think of it as..."

This is a great starting point on the Can If journey, by thinking in a new way about something that may have been taken for granted and created a specific mindset.

A classic one I have seen in many legal teams is when in-house lawyers make a shift from thinking of business stakeholders as clients to colleagues. The mindset of lawyer and client keeps the in-house lawyer more in the remit of outside counsel advisor. It can introduce a metaphorical and even literal separation between the lawyer and their business colleague. The very phrasing of Can If posits everyone working together as a team ("*We* can if"). We are in this together. I am not saying "*You* can if you...".

One of the best uses of Can If I've seen in practice was at one of our training programs with lawyers at a leading US energy company. One lawyer had thought about a routine issue regarding the boundaries of a lake the company owned and potential infractions of this by nearby property owners as an enforcement issue. But following Can If, he saw an opportunity to reframe this as an education and community building exercise.

Previously, the response to any infractions on the boundaries of the waterfront was to send out teams to tell the property owners what they had done wrong and to insist they stop. Our lawyer started to think about what would happen if this became a proactive process rather than a reactive one. He had noticed that when complaints were filed, a common theme was that the property owners were unaware of the restrictions and codes they needed to follow. The lawyer decided that he would ask IT to help create a portal to educate lake-front residents and work with local realtors to educate them on the restrictions, so they could make buyers and leasers aware of them. By reframing the problems as a different heuristic, it started to change the relationship between the company and local residents.

"We can if we use other people to..."

This has been at the heart of many legal innovations that looked at *who* did the work. One of the earliest strategies to focus on legal process and efficiency was the DuPont legal model, which examined whether all work needed to go to licensed attorneys and started normalizing much greater use of paralegals to cut costs.

This aligns to this pathway of the Can If model in thinking more broadly about a skillset. It could also align to the growth in LPOs and the use of lower cost legal talent that might not be part of your legal department or in the same country as you to increase efficiency and decrease cost.

It can also point to the increase in additional skillsets in the legal department, such as data privacy specialist, data engineers, technology experts, or security experts, who may all be working together to create solutions to balance risk and opportunity for organizations.

There can also be much more lateral applications – for example, the story about engaging local realtors to help educate residents is how this path can be applied.

"We can if we remove x to let us y"

A head of legal operations in a global bank was looking to introduce a rationalization of their extensive contracting function that was using a lot of resource and taking much more time than the business desired. Many of the contracts were formulaic but a thorough analysis also revealed that all contracts contained an NDA, including internal contracts. The head of legal operations realized that if they removed the need to sign an NDA for internal contracts – where it was not needed – that would speed up those contracts and allow him to more easily bring in technology solutions and self-service solutions for very standardized contracts.

A common issue for legal teams is getting stuck in a reactive mindset and behaviors. Being proactive can be a challenge because of this. For one fast-moving consumer goods brand, it was about working to remove the mindset their lawyers had about having to respond to every request and thereby seeing themselves as purely service-oriented. This took time and a range of tactics, including new processes and ways of working, but what was central was the chief legal officer and their chief of staff focusing on modelling this to the team to effectively say, "If we remove over-reactiveness, we can be more strategic business partners".

"We can if we access the knowledge or perspective of..."

This can be a transformative mindset for lawyers, who may feel divorced from the main purpose of the business.

Any business unit that isn't frontline customer-facing can lose sight of the perspective of the ultimate end user. This can be a common pitfall for in-house lawyers, especially in big organizations with more layers separating what the legal professionals do from the experience of the ultimate beneficiary of their product or services. Applying the Can if framework, the introduction of the knowledge and/or perspective of the end user can be transformative to how lawyers approach a task or a problem. It seems simple but is so often forgotten!

In one example from our training programs, an in-house lawyer shared how accessing the perspective of the end consumer as the ultimate beneficiary of a piece of internal comms was transformational in how they drafted their communications going forward. They said:

> *"I can communicate more clearly if I know my target audience. I had a situation where I was drafting a two-page letter that would be sent out by somebody who's not a lawyer. It made me think not only about who in the business units might be sending it, but also the intended recipient, who is one of our customers. So, I broke down many of the complexities. If I said*

something in one long wordy sentence, I broke it down into two or three shorter sentences. I think ultimately that the message was clearer. For me, remembering the target audience, especially when we're working with the business units, or we're doing something that will be interfacing with customers who don't have legal training, it's important to be able to explain things clearly and concisely and in terms that they'll understand."

"We can if we introduce a..."

One legal department we worked with introduced a highly innovative model for ensuring that its use of outside counsel was truly inclusive. Its CLO wanted this use to reflect greater equality. This initiative started before 2020 and the murder of George Floyd and the protests in its wake, but certainly gained greater interest from other legal departments after that time.

Many initiatives on increasing equity across the use of outside counsel have faltered partly because too much emphasis is placed on the outside counsel and their behaviors, rather than the inside counsel who hire them. What the CLO realized was that the mindsets and behaviors of their people had to change. They identified how to achieve that: "We Can if we introduce an incentive to achieving diversity goals".

All members of the legal team who instructed outside counsel had to demonstrate how they were increasing the use of diverse partners in majority law firms and the use of minority owned law firms.

"We can if we resource it by..."

For most legal departments, the issue of resourcing is constantly problematic. Even in the Exponential Age, it is likely to remain so. Aligned with the challenge to use technology and innovative solutions to meet these constraint challenges is the fact that many of these solutions cost significant amounts of money and have additional cost in terms of the time and personnel needed to implement them. This can produce a standoff for many legal teams – being told to become more efficient and streamlined via technology tools but not having the time or resource to invest in proper investigation and implementation.

The use of AI, which at the time of writing is the hot new buzzword in legal departments, is a good example of this. It can produce fantastic results if you can really understand what that will look like for your legal department and then be able to invest the resources needed in the change management piece with your people.

"We can if we want to go to jail"

In one course we were teaching, one of the participants, while generally engaged, liked to tell jokes and bring humor into a situation. When we introduced Can If, he declared that he already used this with clients, saying, "We can if we want to go to jail...". There was an interesting dichotomy here. The Can If statement was being used to block, rather than open, ideas – or was it? Was this actually an opportunity for us as a group to reframe that as a prompt?

When we asked for more details, the lawyer said it was generally done in a lighthearted way. The instances were never really ones where the possibility of jail time was a reality. What this use of Can If did was introduce some levity into the exchange. It also allowed everyone to create a bit of space and perspective on the problem.

We agreed that by deconstructing his use of Can If, he was actually creating a space to get both himself and his business stakeholders out of what might have been their default mindset and a position where either side might feel pushed into a reactive response. The in-house lawyer felt that it gave him common parlance, as well as some stress relief around a challenge.

When faced with an impossible deadline, for example, he could change his response. Instead of thinking, "This is awful. I can't believe that they tell me at the beginning of October about something we need to have done by 1 January", Can If brought a bit more structure around bringing the temperature down, figuring out what the schedule would have to look like, what things would have to move, and what things are realistic.

Disrupting the triggers

This points to an important factor in the consistent use of many of these tools – they disrupt our normal way of thinking. They also give us space if we are locked into a reactive mindset, which might cause us to panic and therefore give a response resulting from that panic. Maybe it's panic at not knowing the answer; maybe it's panic at facing a new problem; maybe it's panic at feeling a response must be immediate. Maybe it's all those things. If injecting humor takes the pressure off, that's useful because it's opening possibility and getting you away from the tunnel vision that can happen when you're in fight or flight mode and the initial reaction is just, "Oh my god, this is terrible. We can't get this done. It's impossible!"

When we are problem solving, anything that can cause us to take a pause and gain a bit of objectivity is welcome – even if it's a joke.

Of course, there are times when lawyers must say no. What Can If teaches us is that "no" shuts down one avenue, but we must look for the next avenue of possibility.

The impact of Can If

We have used Can If on many courses, and the impact has been myriad. Participants broaden their thinking and think more laterally about how to solve problems. This is a crucial part of creative thinking. As we have discussed, creativity is one of the core competencies of the Exponential Age mindset.

Thinking laterally makes us more open to ideas and solutions from beyond the normal scope of how we might solve problems – this is the key skill in Duality Master.

The mechanism of applying the Can If framework ensures a different perspective on the challenge. This is applying the competency of Zoom Master. The technique of changing perspective is a key factor in coaching to ensure people can start to think differently about a problem.

Lawyers do need to use their "no" words

A lawyer on one of our programs shared that she did not like that she consistently had to shut down new ideas because of the way that business stakeholders wanted to fund these via regulated costs. She explained:

> *"One of my least favorite parts of my job is that basically every other day, someone contacts me about either their pet project or something else that they have going on in an innovation-type space where they want to pay for whatever the initiative it is through regulated costs. I pretty much always say, 'No, you can't do that'. So instead, I've been putting on my creative hat. I've been trying to point them in different directions. They could go to other business units and tell them what they're trying to do and how it could fit in with something that I know is already going on within different business units across the company. I did wonder whether I was having too much fun as I had one VP tell me that sometimes the lawyer needs to use their 'no words'! But it's been successful, as far as giving different business units new ideas or different pathways that they can take to pursue their goals."*

This example shows how the link between mindset and language is so fundamental. Sometimes by changing the language we can also change the mindset and then the skillset. Just try saying, "We can if..." and see what it opens up.

References

1 Lian Parsons, *Harvard Business School Blog*: "How to Give Negative Feedback to Employees", 8 January 2024: https://professional.dce.harvard.edu/blog/how-to-give-negative-feedback-to-employees/#What-is-the-best-way-to-deliver-negative-feedback-in-a-performance-review

2 https://en.wikipedia.org/wiki/Linguistic_relativity

3 Adam Morgan and Mark Bardem, *A Beautiful Constraint* (Wiley, 2015) pp80-81.

4. *Ibid.*

Chapter 15: Lift Off – propelling legal leadership into the Exponential Age

Over the next three chapters we will describe four different programs where we applied the Exponential Age Mindset Attributes and the tools to work with real-life legal departments and wider businesses to show how these are applied in practice.

Lift Off was an immersive, year-long leadership development experience designed to transform legal professionals into visionary, enterprise-wide leaders equipped for the demands of the Exponential Age. Rooted in the core themes of creativity, curiosity, and visioning, the program equipped participants to steer legal departments through complexity, disruption, and opportunity by embracing strategic transformation, influence, and innovation. Mastery charts helped each participant assess their current level and stretch toward growth, supported by feedback loops and peer learning.

This was a 12-month program we ran in 2023 with two cohorts, which were then split into four sub-cohorts. One cohort comprised mid- to senior-level in-house lawyers who wanted to be more focused on strategy and operational effectiveness. The second cohort comprised legal operations professionals who wanted to become more strategically effective but also wanted to enhance leadership skills that would help them in increasing the operational efficacy of their legal departments.

The program comprised legal professionals from very different organizations with very different levels of maturity around operational efficiency. Some were incredibly advanced in some cases, with heads of legal operations who had literally pioneered the discipline of legal operations. In other organizations, the lawyer or legal operations professional was the first mover in this space. One thing that the participants had in common was that their general counsel recognized the need for strategy and operations to be considerations for the legal department of the future. What united them all was the desire to explore how legal leaders can act as catalysts for change rather than just custodians of risk.

The Lift Off program was the first program where we used the Exponential

Age mindset attributes. In fact, these were developed explicitly for this program. It was after using them in this program that we realized these had much broader applicability and could be used with a range of leaders across legal departments and other teams, as well as be effective with subject matter experts or even support staff.

When we developed the program, we started by talking to a range of thought leaders in legal operations – these formed our advisory board. A theme that linked all the feedback we got was that there was very little training and development that focused on the strategic soft skills or human-centered skills needed to really transform legal departments operationally and therefore strategically for the future.

Like most of our programs, this one culminated in a capstone project. In this case it focused on a proposed adoption of AI in the legal department. This was frankly the aspect of the program that really sparked the interest of most of the GCs we spoke to who sent people to this.

Program philosophy – from legal or operations expert to enterprise leader

Legal departments are increasingly expected to contribute not only legal expertise but also strategic insight, cross-functional leadership, and innovation. Lift Off recognized that traditional mindsets – rooted in process, predictability, and subject matter expertise – are no longer enough. The program invited participants to embrace an Exponential Age mindset, one that thrives on ambiguity, synthesizes complexity, and balances agility with strategic focus.

This was not always easy. Many of the participants were very focused on delivering outcomes. Being able to take a much more strategic point of view did not come naturally and had not often been a definition of "success" in their role. What has worked for the legal department of the Industrial Age mindset will not work for the legal department of the Exponential Age. We synthesized the Exponential Age mindsets from several sources:

- Our prior experience working with in-house teams.
- Prior experience coaching in-house lawyers, including general counsel.
- Extensive research conversations with thought leaders in legal operations and the future of law.
- Research more widely on the Exponential Age and the changes this is bringing to business and the world at large.

At the core of the program was the aim of developing three competencies that are going to be increasingly significant in the Exponential Age – curiosity, creativity, and visioning. We then introduced the nine key Exponential Age Mindset attributes that could help participants become more adept at applying the overarching competencies. Lift Off participants were asked to adopt and develop three of these over the course of the year through targeted projects, self-reflection, and application to real-world challenges.

As communication and influence was such a hallmark of this program, and runs through many of the attributes, we also introduced the practice of using metaphors as a throughline for each session. Participants had to try and use metaphors at least once in an interaction between each monthly cohort meeting.

Why metaphors? Metaphors were once described to us as the ultimate storytelling tool because they are so visual and work like a mini movie in the listener's mind. They take something that might be complex, abstract, or not fully fleshed out and help people find a hook or a way into it. Metaphors draw parallels between the abstract and the concrete, making complex ideas easier to grasp by relating them to something familiar. For example, comparing a complex problem to a jigsaw puzzle helps people understand the need to piece together different parts to find a solution.

Kick-off experience – ignition in New York City

The program began with an in-person kick-off in New York, setting the tone for the months ahead. The full-day workshop included sessions that combined strategic frameworks, storytelling, experiential learning, and case-based discussions. It introduced the participants to key concepts that would frame their journey through the program, all grounded in the notion of being match-ready for the Exponential Age.

The Exponential Age primer

Participants were introduced to the foundational concepts of the Exponential Age Mindset and were given their first view of the Exponential Age Mindset Attributes, business insights vs KPIs, the Four Zones of Curiosity, and the Exponential Age Mindset. They were asked to consider which three Attributes they were least adept at but could assist them in role, and to select these for the next cohort session.

Storytelling as influence

Participants were asked to craft and share personal leadership narratives using metaphor and storytelling techniques. The goal was to develop executive presence, influence skills, and authenticity – critical tools for leadership where you might not have a defined leadership title or where you might be trying to influence change with peers, as many of our participants were.

Legal department transformation through case study

The participants were asked to analyze the transformation journey of telecoms company BT's legal department as a real-world case study in change management, strategic alignment, and operational maturity. Participants assessed their own departments against the BT maturity model and began to identify the levers for transformation in their own contexts.

Unlocking strategic curiosity

Participants were then introduced to the Four Zones of Curiosity Framework (see chapter 13), to guide them in shifting from reactive problem-solving (Zone One) to proactive, future-oriented strategic questioning (Zones Three and Four). We asked them to use this framework to reflect on a current project they had and how they could move from answering today's questions to shaping tomorrow's possibilities.

Creativity as a core competency

We then gave the group a break from strategy-focused tasks to play a storytelling game where each person had to move the story on by adding three words to the narrative others had created to keep the story going. In this fast-paced, collaborative storytelling game, participants had to flex their creative thinking muscles. This playful yet purposeful session emphasized cognitive agility, improvisation, and the power of shared visioning – a counterpoint to the risk-averse tendencies often found in legal practice.

From KPIs to business insights

Participants were asked to create a small group presentation on themes gathered from the BT case study and to take a different set of KPIs and move these into business insights. This exercise brought together storytelling, data analysis, and strategic thinking to create enterprise-level strategic contributions. This was an abbreviated version of what they would be asked to work towards at the end of the program in their presentations to a public company board member or a Fortune 500 general counsel.

Year-long learning journey

The kickoff was only the beginning. Lift Off continued with a series of monthly sub-cohort meetings, self-guided work, and coaching exercises that deepened learning and built habits of leadership. Key deliverables across the year included:

- Individual strategic development plans informed by a 360° feedback exercise undertaken for most participants.
- Five business insights derived from their legal department data.
- One to two Generative AI use cases for each participant to shape legal technology strategy in their team. The most compelling of these would form the basis of their capstone presentation.

Sub-cohorts functioned as learning pods, encouraging collaboration, peer accountability, and knowledge sharing across industries and roles. Participants supported one another in applying their learnings back to their organizations – turning insights into action.

How this worked for legal operations

In the legal operations track, run with two cohorts of six, we followed a program that considered the varying level of experience that the group had in this space. Some were fairly experienced whilst others were in their first legal operations role. We used the group sessions as much as peer coaching sessions to share insights and experiences along with key concepts that underpinned each session.

We started each session by having participants individually share how the metaphor exercise had gone month and how they had applied one or more of their Exponential Age Mindset Attributes in their role.

In the first session, we looked at how to start an analysis for an AI innovation in participants' legal teams via a needs assessment. This was followed in session two by a focus on how to gather vision and strategic insights from these, using insights from Chris Fowler, who spearheaded the operational innovations in BT's legal department via a podcast I had recorded with him for the program. The key attributes Chris outlined to get to vision and strategy from his experiences at BT were curiosity, adaptability, communication, and effective stakeholder management and a culture that embraces fast failure – one that will identify and resolve failures quickly and cheaply by encouraging rapid prototyping, testing, and experimentation to learn from errors and iterate on ideas, rather than investing heavily in a potentially flawed concept for too long. This business concept, often found in technology and Silicon Valley, views failures as opportunities to learn, innovate, and pivot towards success, ultimately leading to better products and strategies. Very akin to the idea of Chaos Converter (see chapter five).

In session three, we went back to the drawing board and considered what aspects are key when creating a legal operations function. The key takeaways from the discussion were that legal operations professionals need to be strategic, adaptable, and inclusive. Building a legal operations function requires a comprehensive understanding of current operations and alignment with business strategy.

A strong narrative that demonstrates understanding and addresses the needs of the organization is essential for securing funding for legal operations initiatives. This last point aligned with the focus many of the cohort members had on the communication-related Exponential Age Mindset Attributes of Supreme Storyteller, Champion Chameleon, Bias Jiu Jitsu and Superlative Synthesizer.

Coaching insights

As the program progressed, it became apparent that some of our initial thoughts on what added most value needed to change. We had started with the idea that using the experiences of more seasoned operations professionals would be a core focus. Instead, we were seeing that a more coaching-focused discussion based on the participants' own experiences of applying their Exponential Age Mindset Attributes was more valuable. We continued to record podcasts with experienced practitioners to supplement the learnings in the cohort sessions, but did not make these the focus of the remaining sessions.

We pivoted to the coaching approach for the rest of the sessions, which ran from May through September. This allowed both of us as coaches and facilitators to lean into some of the most important Exponential Age Mindset attributes in our own engagement with our cohorts:

- *Zoom Master:* Being able to focus on both the bigger picture and the details of each cohort member's individual journey.
- *Agile Juggler:* Helping participants understand the balance between the core aspects of their day-to-day role and opportunities to become more creative and strategic within that.
- *Duality Master:* Being able to make connections between the different challenges and opportunities participants had.

We began to provide individual coaching sessions alongside group cohort sessions when participants requested additional support, to facilitate their development of the Exponential Age Mindset Attributes and assist them in preparing for the Capstone Project.

Capstone presentations – applying strategic vision

The program culminated in capstone presentations, tailored to each participant's track:

- Those on the Legal Operations Track (led by Catherine) presented to a Fortune 500 General Counsel (not their own), demonstrating GenAI use cases and how they can drive efficiency, cost savings, or strategic value.
- Those on the Think Like a GC Track (led by Lloyd) presented to a public company board member, showcasing how legal can drive enterprise-wide innovation and mitigate risk in complex, ambiguous environments.

These presentations synthesized participants' learnings in storytelling, strategic insight, and exponential thinking.

Topics that the cohorts explored in their final presentations included:

- Running a pilot to spearhead greater use of Microsoft's Co-Pilot within a legal team.
- A way to document the current state of workflow and process through the legal team to provide opportunities to optimize and find efficiency.
- The use of AI to streamline invoice review.
- A pilot for an AI tool to review contracts.
- A process and pilot for AI to be deployed through contract lifecycle management for contract review, resource collaboration and support, risk evaluations, and remediation analysis.
- Strategic AI governance to fast-track optimum AI use cases in the legal team.
- Using an existing AI chatbot in the company to allow business stakeholders to share their issue with the bot using plain language to either resolve the issue or be directed to the right legal team member for a solution.

Core competencies developed

Throughout Lift Off, participants worked on the areas that they had individually identified. For many of the legal operations-focused individuals that I coached, their major challenges centered around communication and influence and moving out of the operational realm into the strategic realm.

The Exponential Age Mindset Attributes manifested for the group in various ways.

A legal operations professional in an insurance company worked on her Zoom Master. Through consistent application of trying to take ideas to make the biggest possible impact in her organization beyond solving the specific issue, she was able to approach projects differently, focusing less on the detail and more on the bigger picture. Through consistent application of this attribute in role she reported that her perspective on projects was changing and that business stakeholders had commented on her more strategic mindset.

A contract manager at a technology company leaned into her Joyful Tightrope. When choosing this competency, she mentioned that she generally did not do well with uncertainty and would avoid it, waiting until she had complete certainty on an issue before mentioning it. Her team were now in flux, and she did not have certainty as to what their new roles and structure would be. Usually, she would not say anything until she had clarity from her leadership. However, given the work she had been undertaking on the Joyful Tightrope competency, she shared this uncertainty with her team. Rather than being upset, the team rallied around and embarked on a spontaneous brainstorming session about how the team could pivot depending on what leadership decided.

A legal operations manager at a financial services company focused on his Supreme Storyteller. This participant felt his effectiveness was being hampered by communication that was too factual and overdetailed. Yet he instinctively recoiled from the description of Supreme Storyteller. In discussion, we decided that this very recoiling was a powerful message and was one of the areas he should focus on. He started to do this by working on the metaphor homework we gave as part of the course and by trying to get more creative with his metaphors rather than defaulting to tried and tested business or legal ones. As his confidence increased, he was able to start using analogies and metaphors that he felt would resonate with his audience, thereby also leaning into Champion Chameleon. This focus on how he presented both in actual presentations and meetings also made him feel more confident about the very act of presenting.

Becoming sherpas for legal transformation

The Lift Off program transformed the legal professionals from advisors into strategic sherpas – leaders capable of guiding their departments, companies, and peers through exponential change. Participants left the program equipped not only with frameworks and skills but also with a mindset shift – from reactive problem-solver to proactive opportunity-creator. They were less afraid of taking a risk and better at leaning into discomfort to grow.

The result is a cohort of legal leaders prepared not just to navigate the future, but to help shape it. They were also sherpas in providing us with the first insights into how valuable the Exponential Age Mindset Attributes could be to help other teams develop.

Chapter 16:
Upskilling paraprofessionals for the Exponential Age – the Paraprofessional Leadership Development Academy

We designed the Paraprofessional Leadership Development Academy (PLDA) to cultivate strategic thinking, communication confidence, and enterprise-level awareness among legal professionals in the legal department of a US national retailer. Spanning nine months, the program guided participants through a series of structured learning experiences that steadily built their leadership capacity, culminating in a high-impact capstone presentation to senior legal leaders including the general counsel.

Program overview and impact

The PLDA was designed to empower paralegals within a global retailer's legal and compliance department by developing key competencies necessary for professional growth and enhanced collaboration with the broader business. This program blended strategic insights, process improvement, risk management, and communication skills to foster a proactive and innovative mindset. The program coincided with a team-wide initiative under the new head of legal operations to develop a center of excellence to create more effectiveness and efficiency in the legal department's legal professionals who were not lawyers.

Communication and presentation skills

There was significant improvement in communication and presentation skills amongst the cohort. When we started the program, most of the group felt they would never be able to present in front of the general counsel and the legal leadership. Most of the group felt extreme discomfort with the idea of presenting or speaking in public at all. Participants learned structured approaches to presentations, such as understanding audience needs, and using a roadmap.

This newfound confidence translated into impactful presentations that engaged audiences and led to positive recognition from peers and leadership.

The program also enhanced the communication and influencing skills of the cohort. Participants discovered the importance of structured thinking using strategic thinking techniques and the Can If problem-solving framework, which helped them communicate project stages and expectations more effectively. The participants also used the Exponential Age Mindset Attributes as throughlines for their own personal development throughout the program. These learnings helped participants better articulate ideas, engage colleagues, and lead discussions with clarity. This resulted in more structured, effective, and engaging communication within teams.

Strategic thinking and problem-solving

The PLDA also enhanced the participants' capabilities in strategic thinking and problem-solving. Participants learned to approach problems methodically rather than jumping straight into solutions. Examples included how they evaluated projects, shifting from immediate implementation to a more consultative approach that ensured alignment with stakeholders. This consultative approach drew upon empathy, a skill that is increasingly needed by everyone in legal departments, and is significant in this time of rapid change. Ensuring that the discipline of empathy and understanding is used when analyzing problems helped the groups to more effectively get to solutions.

Professional recognition and career growth

The program led to increased control and ownership of participants' careers versus a feeling that their career was happening *to* them. It also empowered the group via an improved ability to apply strategic thinking and to influence business outcomes.

Participants noted that the skills they focused on in the program would open doors to future opportunities, including leadership roles and expanded responsibilities. It led most of the group to consider the direction of their career. After the program, one participant enrolled in law school.

News about the program spread throughout the legal department and beyond, especially after the final capstone presentation. Program participants mentioned getting messages from people throughout the team from around the world who they might not normally interact with. Those based in headquarters reported being stopped in the corridors by curious colleagues!

Practical application to workplace challenges

The focus of the program – like that of all our offerings – was not about the Exponential Age tools and concepts in isolation or merely in theory, but how these could be applied iteratively to real-life work challenges. The learnings throughout the programs were applied to real work scenarios, and ultimately the capstone project focused on a live issue for the participants. These included issues such as improving billing processes and rolling out new protocols – issues that made an ongoing difference to them and their teams or even the entire legal department and – by extension – their business clients.

In summary, all these impacts led to:

- Greater professional recognition.
- Improved team dynamics and collaboration.
- Expanded career perspectives.
- Actionable innovation ideas to improve the legal department.

The genesis of the PLDA

The program started with a discussion with the general counsel and some of her direct reports. This led to an invitation to create a one-off workshop for paraprofessionals as part of their legal department annual meeting, with the potential for this to be a pilot for further training in the legal department.

Prior to undertaking this workshop, as is our practice, we undertook interviews with paraprofessionals in the group from which our participants would be drawn so that we could understand their specific needs and context and therefore design our workshop to be the most efficacious for them.

During these interviews, we discovered a real desire amongst many of the paraprofessionals to focus on refining the department's strategy and processes. There was an identification of silos as a pervasive issue impacting the effectiveness of the entire team.

The most significant issue for many of the paraprofessionals was how the advent of the center of excellence would affect what they did in the short-term, but also how, longer-term, the potential for increased use of technology might impact their roles. For many, it was unclear if this would be a positive or a negative change. However, the underlying message was that just doing the same thing and working in the same way as they had for years would no longer work.

This shift felt by these paraprofessionals is indicative of broader changes to the world of work, which are a result of the changes in professional life being brought about by the adoption of greater technology.

These changes can be defined as:

- Increased agility and the need for continuous learning.

- Reskilling of existing employees as a strategic imperative.
- The need for employees to feel part of these changes and to understand why promotion and development is changing.

A significant part of the large-scale changes taking place in the workplace due to AI and other new technologies means that human skills – and the continuous development of these – will be tantamount.

Another issue was an overwhelming feeling that learning and development opportunities had historically prioritized lawyers versus other legal professionals in the team. There was a feeling of neglect in the non-lawyer community (which is a common theme we have found when working with legal departments). It is interesting to us that some of the most innovative and forward-thinking general counsel in terms of talent development are starting to prioritize development for legal professionals more broadly – mainly due to a realization that it is these staff who will be crucial to technology implementation in the Exponential Age. Whilst many paraprofessionals we have worked with feel under threat, our message to them is that there are many ways in which their roles – particularly if approached with a continuous learning and agile mindset – will be less under threat than many lawyers who are subject matter experts.

The third issue was that of large-scale change in the world, in addition to changes in the legal team with the advent of their new general counsel and new head of legal operations. This was leaving some of the non-lawyers in the department feeling vulnerable and as if they had no agency. This is a common theme throughout this book and is one of the most important factors that legal leaders need to think about when introducing change, particularly the sort of large-scale changes likely to follow AI adoption. This department was very thoughtful about adopting change – but even when being mindful, employees will still feel vulnerable. That is simply part of human nature during times of large-scale changes.

Creating the Paraprofessional Leadership Development Academy

There was a gap between where paralegal and paraprofessional roles at this retailer currently were and where they needed to start to move towards. This meant our remit as coaches was designing a program that would do several things:

- Give the paraprofessionals a broader view of what their skillsets were now and how these could be applied outside of their normal remit.

- Introduce the paraprofessionals to new ways of thinking about their role and their career more strategically.
- Introduce the paraprofessionals to skillsets that might be new or less utilized within their roles and get them to use these in role throughout the program to build comfort with these.

Even more focus on "human" skills

While technical proficiency remains important, soft skills like communication, collaboration, problem-solving, and decision-making will become paramount for career advancement as AI handles data analysis and repetitive tasks.

Employees will need a basic understanding of how AI works and how to interpret data generated by AI systems to effectively utilize its insights and make informed decisions. This includes asking the right questions and knowing how to effectively formulate the right prompts for AI. But it is interpreting the stories that AI data tells us and being able to make the creative and imaginative leap to what possibilities that data opens. AI understanding and data literacy will be foundational in the new world of work, but where the most innovative leaps will be found is where AI and data literacy are combined with adept application of the core human-centric skills. It is this intersection that forms the basis of our programs.

Continuous learning and upskilling

The Exponential Age – including rapid developments in AI – necessitates a commitment to ongoing learning to stay relevant and acquire new skills as the workplace evolves. This will mean that learning is never done. Rather than seeing learning and development as something extra layered on to the core of our role, learning and development is now fundamental and ongoing to what our roles mean. The idea of being an expert will only ever be conditional because of the pace of change. This is not necessarily a new idea. The most effective professionals have always understood the importance of staying curious.

Personalized development plans

This will lead to learning that is much more personalized. Organizations will likely tailor training and development programs to individual strengths and career aspirations, leveraging AI tools to identify areas for improvement. We already see this in many of the programs we offer. In many of our programs there is a significant amount of personalization. This is where our duality as coach and teacher comes into play, and will, I believe, become a hallmark of all learning and development in the Exponential Age and a core aspect of successful leadership.

The Six Criteria for Success

As part of preparation for the program, we interviewed three former paralegals at another legal department client who had moved into bigger roles – in two cases, this was a lateral move outside of legal and into a non-legal role and gave the individuals a much more business focus. While there were differences in these stories, we could clearly see themes that had led to success for each of these individuals. They are ideas that hold true for success in all careers, whatever your level in a legal department (or even outside of one).

1. *Vision:* Seeing an opportunity. Specific vision of what they wanted and how it would benefit the organization.
2. *Increased risk tolerance:* Taking on a new responsibility/project in which success is not guaranteed.
3. *Intentionality:* Taking a specific action or series of actions to move towards a new goal or opportunity, for example making a specific request to a manager to take on a project.
4. *Embrace discomfort:* Being prepared to try new things and leaning into new skills or competencies that may seem difficult.
5. *Sustained action:* Being prepared to put the effort in to achieve growth. Leaning into new skills or taking on extra projects to gain experience.
6. *Being curious and agile:* Demonstrating this attribute throughout all steps in the process.

We quickly realized that the criteria we identified are actually central to successful development for anyone in the Exponential Age.

The paraprofessional program

Unlike some of our other programs designed for paralegals where participation was voluntary, this program was compulsory for paraprofessionals. The group we were working with numbered 25.

The paraprofessionals would end the program presenting to the general counsel and their leadership team in groups of four to five.

We wanted the program outcome to have some efficacy in their role, so each person would identify a process improvement idea and the steps to make this happen. This was undertaken in conjunction with application of the Can If problem-solving framework. Some of the original Can If statements went on to form the starting point for the final presentations.

Our programs to equip teams to succeed in the Exponential Age flow through a methodology of toolset-skillset-mindset. The PLDA was no different. The ultimate goal is a change of mindset. This is achieved through gradually doing new things in role – the skillsets. Doing these new things is made easier via application of the toolsets we introduce in the sessions, which give a structure and a roadmap to the application of the skillsets in role. Together, the application via skillset and toolset solidifies the mindset changes.

We undertook a further series of interviews with a selection of participants from the academy before embarking on the program so that we could ensure the ideas and tactics being used were most effective for this group.

The key themes identified through these interviews were:

- A desire to build on the work started in the previous workshop with the Exponential Age Mindset Attributes.
- A strong desire to concentrate on competencies they needed to expand their professional growth.
- Iterative application of skills in role between sessions.
- A strong desire to focus on communication and presentation skills – both informally in a meeting and a formal presentation.
- Recognition from all interviewees that being able to present effectively is a prerequisite for advancement and that not having this skill was holding many of them back.
- The presentation and communication focus also included being able to craft their message for different audiences – a clear confluence with our Champion Chameleon attribute.
- A strong desire to get to know others from throughout the legal department in similar roles and to connect with and learn from colleagues.
- Linked to this was a recognition that there was ineffective communication currently through the department and too many silos, which was hampering innovation.
- Trepidation but also excitement about the opportunity to present in front of the general counsel and her leadership. This was generally viewed as a stretch assignment that would reap rewards for the group.

The toolsets for the Paralegal Leadership Development Academy were:

- The Can If Framework.
- The Exponential Age Mindset Attributes.
- The Six Dimensions of Risk.
- Communication techniques.

The Paraprofessional Program was designed with a bold and inspiring purpose – to empower participants to take charge of their careers by developing their mindset, skillset, and toolset. From the very start, participants were encouraged to view their professional growth as a proactive journey – one that would stretch them beyond their comfort zones and prepare them to thrive in a rapidly transforming legal environment.

At the heart of the program was a challenge – each participant would collaborate with peers on a process improvement project for the legal department. This was not an academic exercise. The final deliverable would be presented directly to the general counsel and the leadership team, ensuring that the work had tangible impact.

Building the mindset for growth

The journey began with an exploration of the Exponential Age Mindset. Participants reflected on the reality of constant change – driven by innovations like Generative AI – and what it meant for their own roles. They learned that thriving in the Exponential Age requires a willingness to be uncomfortable, to see opportunity in chaos, and to develop a habit of connecting their skills to the broader organizational mission.

Through small group discussions, participants identified the mindset attributes they most needed to strengthen. Could they learn to zoom in and zoom out, balancing detail with big-picture thinking? Could they adapt their communication styles to connect with different stakeholders? These reflections helped each participant chart a path toward the skills of the future.

Can If thinking and curiosity

The program didn't stop at theory. It introduced practical tools to help participants make change happen. One of these was the Can If problem-solving framework, which reframes obstacles as opportunities: "We can achieve this goal, if we...". Working on their own team projects, participants identified the high-priority challenges in their work and applied Can If thinking to generate creative solutions.

At the same time, participants explored the Four Zones of Curiosity, a framework for understanding both the known and unknown needs of the general counsel and the business. This exercise expanded their ability to see around corners, anticipating emerging risks and opportunities. It also provided a structured way to think beyond their daily tasks and consider how their work drives business value.

Strategic insight and best practices

As the program progressed, participants were introduced to strategic thinking in the legal department. They examined best and worst practices – aligning legal work with business goals, using data to anticipate risks, and collaborating across functions. Real-world examples – such as improving M&A due diligence or automating contract management – brought these ideas to life. The goal was clear – to shift from reactive problem-solvers to proactive strategic partners.

Risk awareness and opportunity

The third phase of the program expanded participants' understanding of risk. Using the Six Dimensions of Risk framework (financial, reputational, legal, personal, political, and safety/security), participants analyzed their process improvement ideas through a broader lens. This exercise underscored a crucial insight – risk is not just something to mitigate; it can also be a driver of innovation and growth when approached strategically.

Communicating with impact

Recognizing that even the best ideas can fail without effective communication, the program devoted significant time to presentation and communication skills. Participants practiced delivering messages that were clear, emotionally resonant, and tailored to their audience. They learned to lead with the key takeaway, provide a clear roadmap, and build human connection with their listeners. Importantly, they rehearsed how to talk around their slides, engaging their audience rather than reading verbatim.

The bigger picture

The program culminated in a showcase of everything participants had learned. In groups, they presented their process improvement projects to the GC and leadership team, receiving feedback and refining their presentations for a second round. This iterative process allowed them to practice resilience, confidence, and adaptability – hallmarks of the Exponential Age Mindset.

By the end of the program, participants weren't just more skilled professionals; they were more intentional leaders of their own careers. They had learned to view themselves as agents of change, capable of influencing not only their own paths but also the future of the legal department.

Ultimately, the Paraprofessional Program wasn't just about legal processes or technical skills. It was about empowerment and transformation. Participants left with a heightened ability to anticipate change, to communicate with clarity and impact, and to turn risk into opportunity. They experienced firsthand that career growth is not accidental – it is intentional, strategic, and fueled by curiosity.

The sessions

Session 1: Introducing the concepts

The journey began with a foundation in strategic mindset and self-awareness. Participants were welcomed by leadership and grounded in the concept of strategic insights – the ability to integrate business knowledge, data, and intuition to drive proactive decision-making. This session introduced or re-introduced the Exponential Age Mindset Attributes, which some of the participants had first met during the previous half-day workshop. We also introduced the Can If framework for the first time, encouraging participants to explore their team's high-priority projects through a lens of inquiry, process improvement, and innovation.

The development focus and aims for this session were to start the group transitioning from reactive to proactive, strategic thinking. We began this via identifying opportunities for process improvements and to connect their personal roles and responsibilities to broader business priorities.

As mentioned earlier, a significant challenge in introducing change, particularly change around how people work, is making them feel included and making them feel that they have some control – that this is not just happening to them. Both the Exponential Age Mindset Attributes and the Can If problem-solving framework help participants feel that they can have an impact on changes and the challenges that they are facing. As we ask participants to identify an Exponential Age Mindset Attribute that will uniquely help them, they can find their own path to plug into change, rather than being told the best way to do this.

Participants explored their personal and professional "superpowers" as an introduction to the Exponential Age Mindset Attributes. The participants all identified one Exponential Age Attribute that would help them in their role and shared why this would be useful. To engender both support and accountability, we asked the group to share the attributes and their choice with their manager.

To give a feeling of control, we started by focusing the group on challenges and opportunities that were very real for them via the question: "What would make your role easier?".

The group got very energized around sharing issues that emerged for them and found significant aspects of commonality around processes that were increasing work and effort.

Whilst identification is the first step on the path to solving the problem, it can be easy to get lost in focusing on the negative and not thinking about the opportunity. In our coaching practice, both Lloyd and I learned the power of taking something negative and asking clients to find opportunities in challenge. We directed the questioning here in the same way. "What's the opportunity here?" "What could you do to make a difference with this?" We asked the group to apply the Can If problem-solving framework to these challenges.

Each participant left with an assignment – apply the Can If problem-solving framework to a real-life process improvement idea and reflect on it with their manager, seeding the groundwork for practical, applied leadership development.

Session 2: Strategic thinking

We started this session by demystifying the concept of strategy, breaking it down into its constituent stages of how you take an idea from its most narrow and specific to its broadest and most impactful. We then asked the participants to work in smaller groups and identify examples of best and worst ideas they had come across in their roles. We asked them to try to identify why some ideas had worked and others had not.

In the afternoon, we took this further by revisiting some of the challenges the group had identified in session one and applying a well-known strategic insight exercise to it – the Five Whys and the Big So What.

The Five Whys and The Big So What? (Root-cause analysis in legal ops)

The objective of this exercise was to encourage deeper thinking about legal inefficiencies and their business impact. We asked the group to pick a recurring pain point from their prior process improvement ideas that everyone in the group could relate to or recognize (e.g., "Why do we have so many contract delays?").

Then the group needed to ask "Why?" five times to drill into the root cause:

1. Why do contracts get delayed? ➡ Because legal reviews take too long.
2. Why do legal reviews take too long? ➡ Because we are constantly asking the business to explain clauses.
3. Why is there this need for back and forth? ➡ Because we don't have enough contract templates.
4. Why don't we have enough templates? ➡ Because we create them on an ad hoc basis.
5. Why do we create them on an ad hoc basis? ➡ Because no one has ever taken the time to review the process between legal and sales.

After identifying the root issue, the groups would ask, "So what? What does this mean for the business?"

This would then be the starting point for the group to discuss potential strategic fixes (e.g., building a contract playbook).

We asked the participants what was different about approaching a problem in this way. The majority found that this systematic drill-down into all the constituent parts of a problem, rather than trying to rush to a solution, gave a more nuanced understanding of the issues, which would then unlock more ideas around how the issue could be solved.

At the end of this session the participants were asked again to work on applying their Exponential Age Mindset Attributes in role.

Session 3: Six Dimensions of Risk and Six Dimensions of Opportunity

Session three focused on broadening the group's understanding of enterprise-level risk and improving their judgment and communication around risk-benefit trade-offs. It also helped to further increase their self-awareness of confidence and growth. Building on the foundation of strategic insight in session two, we focused on the groups finalizing the topic that they were going to present to the GC and her leadership team.

This session deepened participants' enterprise thinking by introducing the Six Dimensions of Business Risk (financial, reputational, legal, personal, political, and safety). As discussed previously, the Six Dimensions of Business Risk was developed via conversations with public company Board members on what they feel are the major areas of business risk that their companies need to consider. We frequently use this tool to bring legal department professionals to a broader perspective on risk beyond just legal risk. Using the Benefits/Risk Matrix we created for the participants based on The Six Dimensions of Business Risk and The Six Dimensions of Business Opportunity, they evaluated how their ideas could impact the organization and identified strategies to mitigate risk whilst also amplifying value.

The groups applied these concepts via a benefits and risk matrix to their presentation topics. This provided an additional check and balance on the validity of their ideas and began to align the groups around the most effective ways to present the ideas to their GC.

Session 4: Communication skills

The groups started this session with at least a basic framework of what they wanted to present. They then shared their process improvement ideas and received feedback from their peers. They were challenged to present their ideas twice – first for content, and then using structured presentation techniques (road-mapping, leading with the key point, or Bottom Line Up Front (BLUF).[1] After the first presentation for content only we noticed a certain amount of discomfort amongst many of the group. On the fly, we decided to confront this via the coaching exercise of "Naming it". We asked each person to share their biggest fear in presenting. As coaches and with feedback from their peers, we were able to start to demystify these fears. For many of the participants, the very act of naming their fear was cathartic.

Doing this meant that when the participants presented again using the communication techniques of road-mapping and BLUF, the structure that these communication techniques provided was more evident as they were less blinded by fears.

The development focus and aims for this session were to strengthen persuasive communication and increase presence and influence in presenting ideas, and to practice adaptive storytelling for stakeholder engagement.

Session 5: Presentation rehearsal

In the final session, the development focus was on bringing everything together and getting the group comfortable with communicating and presenting to a larger group.

Essentially, this was about demonstrating full-cycle leadership – insight, influence, and execution. They would be able to advocate for business-relevant ideas with clarity and impact and operate with increased self-efficacy and strategic visibility.

In the final stages of the program, participants practiced their capstone presentations, synthesizing months of learning into a single ten-minute narrative that gave each person in the group a chance to present and to showcase their learning in front of the GC and the legal leadership team. Each presentation was designed to demonstrate strategic insight, clear communication, risk assessment, and personal leadership growth.

The program culminated in a formal capstone presentation where each participant presented their process improvement proposal to senior legal leaders, including the GC, showcasing the leadership evolution they had undergone.

The presentations

Despite having run similar programs previously, we were concerned about this program as the participants were not volunteers – attendance had been mandatory. We offered extra rehearsal sessions but not every group took us up on this. Their rationale was that they were worried they "would rehearse too much" – not a sentiment either of us ever worry about! We entered the auditorium that morning with a bit of trepidation. Luckily our fears were unfounded. In the first session in January, many of the participants were unwilling to stand up and speak with a microphone. We now saw a group of near-consummate performers!

There were certain specific factors that helped this, such as the unwavering support of their leader and the strength of collaboration that the group found in each other. This collaboration had not previously been a hallmark of the legal department, with some participants revealing that despite more than ten years of working together they never interacted if their work did not naturally overlap.

This program really demonstrated the efficacy of the tools and the learning process we have developed, not only to improve specific skills but to create a mindset of continuous learning – a significant advantage for the Exponential Age.

Another benefit of the program was that every process improvement idea was very robust and likely to be adopted by the legal team. A key outcome was therefore not only professional development, but a grassroots innovation program to make the entire legal function more future-ready. In fact, right after the program, the general counsel called an impromptu meeting of her legal leadership team who had attended the presentations and assigned them each one of the projects to sponsor to ensure they were operationalized.

The learning journey – from discomfort to mastery

The program was underpinned by a powerful developmental model: the Seven Stages of Learning, from "There is new stuff" to "New stuff feels more comfortable".

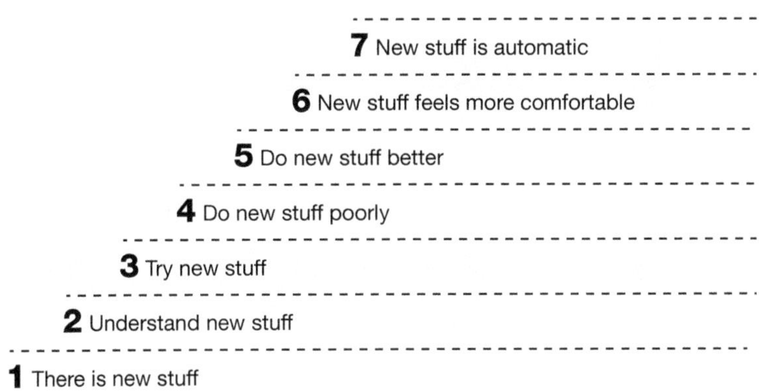

Figure 16: Seven Stages of Learning. Source: Chief Legal Executive LLC.

Each session intentionally moved participants from conceptual understanding to behavioral practice, then into confident application. The spark for change – *discomfort* – was embraced as a driver of growth. By the end, what began as unfamiliar concepts and tentative presentations had evolved into strategic confidence and enterprise fluency.

Our preference is usually to structure our programs around a capstone presentation. Some clients do push back on this, as do many participants. Our reasoning though is this – it pushes those who are not currently in the higher stages of executive leadership out of their comfort zone and provides a focus point for their development. It allows them to demonstrate to leadership and – even more importantly – to themselves, what they are capable of and how they can grow.

The feeling of discomfort is necessary for growth. The pace of change and growth that we will continue to experience in both our personal and professional lives during the Exponential Age means that embracing discomfort will be necessary – indeed, it will be the new normal. This is hard. As explored in chapter two, our brains are not wired for change – we prefer routine and comfort. But if we only settled into comfort and did not embrace change, we could not survive as a species. The pioneering PLDA group at this global retailer showed that via confronting their own discomfort they could change and make a strategic difference. A proud moment for us came when one of the cohorts who had seemed very uncomfortable with a lot of what we addressed came up to us at the end of the program and revealed that the skills she had learned not only helped her professionally but were actually life-changing.

This chapter is therefore dedicated to these paraprofessionals who faced the discomfort and opportunity of change in the Exponential Age head on!

Reference

1 With thanks to Ivan Fong, former GC at Medtronic, for this phrase.

Chapter 17: Beyond law – training leaders for the Exponential Age

Between 2024 and 2025, we partnered with a large US energy company to design two interconnected leadership programs. The first focused on emerging talent within its legal function, while the second extended to managers, supervisors, and individual contributors across diverse business support areas such as IT, facilities, compliance, claims, cyber and physical security, supply chain, and environmental services.

Both programs were built around equipping participants with the skills, mindsets, and tools needed to lead effectively in the fast-changing environment of the Exponential Age – an era characterized by complexity, speed, and disruption.

Outcomes and impact

Across both programs, several themes stood out:

- *Mindset shift.* Participants moved from a reactive posture to a proactive, solution-oriented approach – seeing themselves as catalysts for change rather than executors of tasks – a fundamental shift needed for human identity as the Exponential Age progresses.
- *Improved communication.* Lawyers and non-lawyers alike became more effective at framing complex ideas, tailoring their style to their audience, and using storytelling to increase engagement.
- *Nuanced view of risk.* Leaders began to balance legal, operational, and strategic considerations, seeing risk not just as something to be mitigated but as a source of opportunity.
- *Shared language.* The frameworks introduced created common ground across departments, breaking down silos and enabling more effective collaboration.

Participants' reflections captured the transformation:

"This course helped me move from saying 'We can't because...' to 'We can if...,' which completely changed how my team approached a critical project."

"I learned the value of storytelling – not just presenting facts but shaping a narrative that moves people to action."

"Looking at problems through multiple structured lenses pushed me out of my comfort zone and revealed possibilities I would have missed otherwise."

Program 1: Developing future-ready legal leaders

The first program, launched in 2024, was designed for lawyers across the legal department. It combined practical tools, mindset shifts, and real-world applications to prepare participants to move beyond traditional advisory roles and become strategic, opportunity-focused leaders.

Key elements included:

- *Crisis role-play.* Participants assumed the role of general counsel at a fictional energy company facing a large-scale cyber-attack, requiring rapid judgment calls in conditions of uncertainty.
- *Strategic project simulation.* A scenario based on an offshore wind project challenged participants to weigh financing, regulatory, and construction risks while considering long-term strategic opportunities.
- *Problem-solving frameworks.* Lawyers learned to reframe challenges from "We can't because" to "We can if...", building creativity within constraints.
- *Risk and opportunity thinking.* Introducing a model of Six Dimensions of Risk helped participants broaden their perspective beyond narrow legal considerations.
- *Communication mastery.* Skills such as Bottom Line Up Front (BLUF), storytelling, and the use of metaphors helped participants distill complexity and engage executives with clarity.

By the end of the program, participants reported significant improvements in problem-solving, communication, and cross-functional collaboration. Nearly 90 percent said it had changed how they advised business clients, moving them from reactive responders to proactive partners.

This program was a forward-looking, multi-session initiative designed to build future-ready legal leaders capable of driving innovation, influencing cross-functional collaboration, and thriving amid complexity. It spanned nearly a year and wove together critical leadership mindsets, practical tools, and real-world applications to embed transformation into daily legal practice. The legal leaders' program was based on the Exponential Age Mindset Attributes as well as the Can If problem-solving framework.

The key focus of the program was to equip lawyers to be more adept in leadership and to be able to make decisions more quickly and with more certainty, including when information was unavailable or there was time pressure. A fundamental aspect of the program was the notion of being opportunity focused.

Eighteen people took part in the program, all lawyers from across different areas of the legal department. Engagement varied. Some embraced the ideas within the program wholeheartedly and started applying these in their day-to-day role. Others were more skeptical and could not understand how this would enhance their effectiveness as in-house lawyers.

Program structure and progression

The program launched in April 2024 with an in-person kick-off focused on establishing foundational leadership concepts including self-awareness, communication presence, and creative problem-solving in the context of exponential change. From there, participants engaged in a sequence of virtual and in-person sessions that built their capabilities progressively.

In the first session, we introduced the overarching concept of the Exponential Age and explained why this needs leaders who can be more agile. To apply this, we created a role-play based on an energy company that has suffered a cyber-attack affecting its transmission services.

Most energy companies' businesses are dependent upon sophisticated information technology systems and network infrastructures, the failure of which could prevent them from accomplishing critical business functions. Because the companies' transmission facilities, pipelines, and other facilities are interconnected with those of third parties, the operation of their facilities and pipelines could be adversely affected by unexpected or uncontrollable events occurring on the systems of such third parties. This is the case in this hypothetical.

We asked participants to role-play being the general counsel of a fictional energy company called Sparx Energy.

Session 1: Role-play: Sparx Energy cyber-attack

The network running two of Sparx Enery Company's largest transmission facilities undergoes an outage late on a Sunday night. Sparx has thousands of calls from worried customers who have lost power. The customer service department is unable to cope with the surge in demand at a normally quiet time and customers have been waiting for well over an hour to speak to anyone but there is no concrete information about when things will get back to normal. Sparx has also been very slow on getting social media communications out. As a result, the company's share price drops when markets open on Monday.

The executive committee and the Board call an extraordinary meeting for Monday afternoon and want the GC to brief them. It emerges that the outage is due to a cyber-attack on the third-party provider of Sparx's network.

The role-play was formulated to set up six smaller scenarios in the GC's fact-finding mission, so that the participants were organized in groups and each had a different component to respond to. Everyone therefore had to respond separately. Each group had a faculty member who was a deputy GC in the legal department to present their response to. In each situation, there was a legal aspect but – more importantly – judgment calls to be made.

We further explored this in the next interactive exercise, where we introduced the Can If framework and explained how this facilitates creative problem solving.

Moving to (almost) real life

We took another scenario based in near-reality for the client company, focusing on its strategic aims to get to net zero. The key issue here is the balance of the advantages of alternative power sources with its challenges. Another is the consideration of the set-up costs involved.

Tackling the challenges with Can If

Again splitting the participants into four groups, we gave each group a different aspect of the challenge. We asked them to explore this using the Can If problem-solving framework and then come up with three Can If statements to move their component of the deal forward. The four different areas we focused on for problem solving were:

1. How can we minimize financing and construction risks for the company?
2. How can we keep the monopoly but give a finance partner a way to share in the revenue from alternative energy sources?
3. Costs and time may overrun; how can we make this attractive to a finance partner by adding in some safeguards or hedges to our structure?
4. Many construction partners in this space will not be US-based but European. This opens us up to supply chain issues and currency fluctuations. How can we build a structure with construction partners which might limit our exposure to these issues?

We also asked the group to apply the Can If framework at least twice in their role between session one and session two, focusing on how the application:

- Changed their perspective on the problem.
- Changed the outcome.
- Changed others' perception of them and/or the issue.

Session 2: Exponential Age Mindset Attributes

In the next session, we focused primarily on the Exponential Age Mindset Attributes and getting participants to build their own connection with these. Participants explored the concept of Exponential Age leadership, focusing on agility, self-awareness, and the ability to lead through ambiguity. They learned to recognize and begin applying attributes like Joyful Tightrope, Champion Chameleon, and Supreme Synthesizer in their daily work.

Leaning into the notion created by neuroscientist Dominique Ashby (see chapter one) of "happiness versus headache" in approaching change, we asked each participant to focus on a "superpower" they had at work and then find an Exponential Age Mindset Attribute that they felt corresponded to that. Leaning then into the headache, we asked each participant to pick three of the nine attributes that they felt they did not currently do or do well, but could be helpful in their role. We asked them to apply as many of the three as they could in their role between sessions, alongside continued application of the Can If problem-solving framework.

We also added a communication technique of stating a brief three- to four-point roadmap summary of content that would take their audience through the journey of the presentation: "First this, then this and finally this". This could be applied in a presentation or even a conversation.

Session 3: The Six Dimensions of Risk, BLUF, and metaphors

In the third session, we introduced the group to The Six Dimensions of Risk and added this to the Can If problem-solving method. We gave the group two interrogatories to come up with ideas for using the concepts of balancing the Six Dimensions of Risk – and not just legal risk. We also asked them to consider where there is opportunity in the risk. This session focused on teaching the group to think not just defensively, but entrepreneurially.

Between sessions three and four, the participants started to put their individual presentations together and were introduced to two more communication techniques – Bottom Line Up Front (BLUF) and metaphors.

BLUF leads with the point or the punchline of your presentation. This might seem counterintuitive, but this immediately clarifies *why* the audience should listen to you and what they will get from it. This is a vital skill when presenting to business executives.

We also introduced the idea of using a metaphor to ground their presentation. Metaphors, as we mentioned before, have been described by speech writers as a gift, because they conjure visuals and set the scene like a mini movie.

Final sessions and conclusion

In the fourth session, the group practiced their Can If presentations in preparation for the final session with their managers and executives the following month. By the conclusion of the program, participants had not only internalized practical skills but also experienced a meaningful shift in their leadership identities. They emerged as more agile, self-aware, and future-oriented legal executives – ready to lead through uncertainty, partner effectively across the enterprise, and champion innovation from within.

Impact and outcomes from the Next Generation Leadership Program

The Next Generation Leadership Program significantly enhanced participants' ability to integrate legal risk with business strategy, making them more effective partners to their executives.

In the survey we conducted at the end of the program, most participants (88 percent) reported that it had changed how they advise their business clients. By improving their communication, problem-solving, and stakeholder engagement skills, they had positioned themselves as critical contributors to both their department and the company's success. Continued reinforcement of these skills – creative problem-solving techniques, communication and presentation skills and storytelling and influencing techniques – will maximize the long-term impact of the program.

Participants' feedback highlighted how the methodologies introduced in the program, along with the requirement to continually apply these in role in between sessions, transformed their mindsets and skillsets in leadership.

Changing mindset and impact – participant feedback

The Can If framework

Many participants highlighted how this structured but agile approach to problem-solving helped them think more creatively while staying within business constraints. Participants also reported that the framework gave them a shared vocabulary to speak about creative problem solving throughout the legal team with other colleagues. Several participants reported improved relationships with business stakeholders, including in some cases where this led to more proactive collaboration on issues earlier on rather than the lawyers being stuck in reactive mode.

Communication and presentation skills

Participants reported being able to present legal and strategic insights to executives in a more engaging, tailored manner. They benefited from the structured feedback we gave them on their presentations in the rehearsal sessions and practice of the roadmap technique to outline the key points in their presentations. The introduction of the concepts of storytelling via using narratives and synthesized information to communicate complex ideas in a digestible format was also transformative for many of the cohort in how they engaged with business stakeholders and thought not only about what they say but how they say it.

Nuanced risk assessment

The use of The Six Dimensions of Business Risk in both the sessions and via application in role gave the group a more nuanced view of risk in its different manifestations and how risk and reward need to be balanced in business. Several of the group reported that understanding this framework enhanced their ability to balance legal considerations with business priorities, making them more effective advisors.

Self-reflection and feedback

Several participants reported actively reviewing their communication styles and seeking feedback to refine their skills in a way that they would not have done without participation in this program.

Impact on business partners and teams

Participants' improved skills also translated into tangible benefits for their teams and business stakeholders.

Increased stakeholder confidence

Enhanced communication skills led to greater trust in the lawyers as business enablers rather than blockers. Several participants reported enhanced relationships with business leaders, particularly because of their more creative problem solving empowered by the Can If problem-solving framework.

More strategic legal input

The participants on the Next Generation program were able to position themselves as proactive problem solvers, ensuring timely and relevant guidance that aligned with corporate goals. This was further enhanced via case studies and role-plays that asked the participants to assume the role of the business stakeholder so they could start to think with that mindset as well as the legal point of view.

Enhanced decision-making

By synthesizing and distilling complex legal and regulatory requirements, participants were able to help executives make more informed, strategic choices, and demonstrate that they were considering both how the business viewed issues and how the end consumers might view and understand issues.

Cross-functional influence

Participants noted that their ability to engage across departments (e.g., compliance, safety, and innovation) strengthened the company's overall operational stability. The program culminated in personal impact statements, which reflected deep individual transformation. Examples include a lawyer who embraced Joyful Tightrope to shift her mindset during a departmental change, creating a more resilient and positive team environment. Another lawyer found new rigor in applying familiar tools like Can If, recognizing that consistent practice elevates these frameworks from intellectual exercises to instinctive habits. His analogy of legal roles as "buoyant forces" in the company underscored the importance of influence and communication in high-stakes domains like compliance and safety. Another lawyer focused on communication excellence. She integrated Can If and Exponential Attributes of communication such as Supreme Storyteller and Champion Chameleon into her legal advisory work, enhancing her ability to advise leadership with greater clarity, confidence, and relevance.

Cultural and mindset shifts

A significant takeaway from the program was a shift in mindset towards more proactive leadership. Participants reported moving from a reactive legal function to a forward-thinking, solutions-oriented approach.

Empathy and adaptability

The concept of the Champion Chameleon from the Exponential Age Mindset Attributes resonated with several of the group, helping many of them tailor their communication styles to different audiences – a skill that many report they continue to deploy to this day.

Commitment to continuous learning

Many described their development as an ongoing process, with a focus on internalizing new skills until they become second nature.

In summary, the program helped to align these future leaders with more effective legal–business collaboration and improved their clarity in strategic discussions. These developments would align with a larger strategy implemented by the business leader of the whole division, who had also been chief legal officer, to stimulate an entrepreneurial mindset throughout the whole department.

Program 2: Developing an entrepreneurial mindset

Halfway through 2024, we were asked to consider how some of the methods and tools we used in the Next Generation program could be used to amplify two concepts that the leader of the division in which legal sits had used to inform his own leadership effectiveness. He hoped to cascade these ideas more widely as shared concepts through the teams he led to make them more innovative and future-ready across its business services division in 2025.

The goal was to nurture an "entrepreneurial mindset" within a large organization – encouraging individuals to act like owners, embrace experimentation, and seek opportunity in ambiguity. What was particularly interesting about this program was the way in which we were able to combine our frameworks and tools with what the company was already using to amplify the effect of both.

To make this practical, participants were introduced to a structured set of five lenses that the company's leaders had used informally for years to interrogate projects. This multidimensional approach – looking at challenges through perspectives such as resources, people, capability, technology, and transformation – helped teams uncover underutilized opportunities and reframe stuck conversations.

Core frameworks and competencies

The training emphasized several integrated frameworks. The concepts were:

- *Entrepreneurial mindset.* This mindset encouraged participants to act like owners – taking initiative, feeling ownership in their roles, embracing experimentation, and navigating ambiguity with confidence.
- *The five lenses of operation.* This was a structured set of five lenses that the leadership team had co-created to identify underutilized resources and unleash hidden value within teams and systems.
  These were:
  1. Resources – what we have.
  2. People – who we have and how engaged they are.
  3. Capability – the talent we have now and the talent we will need.
  4. Technology – digital tools.
  5. Transformation – how will this really move the needle?

Participants would learn to use these for both large-scale strategic initiatives and everyday improvements.

The Exponential Age tools we brought to the program were:

- *Can If.* Our creative problem-solving framework seamlessly complemented the central tenet of entrepreneurial mindset and was a great first step for many in operationalizing this.
- *Coaching leadership.* Through experiential triads (groups of three) and role-play, participants practiced bottom-lining, shifting perspectives, and asking powerful questions. The coaching style was positioned not only as a people skill, but a strategic leadership and influencing tool.
- *Exponential Age Attributes.* These attributes reframed traditional leadership norms. Participants learned to adapt their style for greater agility and impact, for example:
  - Joyful Tightrope – balancing change with acceptance, leading to greater enthusiasm for new frameworks such as the five levers.
  - Champion Chameleon – tailoring communication and influence to show colleagues the value of an entrepreneurial mindset and the impact of the tools such as Can If.

- Supreme Synthesizer – distilling complexity for clarity and impact in coaching team members to apply the tools in role.

The genesis of the Entrepreneurial Mindset and the Five Lenses

The executive we worked with is one of a select band of legal leaders who have moved beyond the role of GC or CLO to become a business leader. His mindset embodies the opportunity-focused and creative energy of the Can If problem-solving framework. In many cases, he became the executive of choice that the company's CEO would call on when others had stated that a project was "impossible".

Having progressed from GC to CLO and now a business leadership role, this executive realized early on in his tenure that his personal mindset was something that needed to cascade more broadly to make sure that the organization did not get left behind in the Exponential Age.

He recognized the need to cultivate a new kind of leadership – one that blends agility, creativity, and influence with practical problem-solving. The notion of entrepreneurial mindset and the Five Lenses were born from this insight. Entrepreneurial mindset is the goal and Five Lenses interrogates opportunities and challenges to get there.

This leader approached us to create a structured learning experience to help participants – particularly mid-level managers and individual contributors – shift from passive execution to proactive innovation.

At the heart of the whole endeavor is an entrepreneurial mindset, which is about being able to bring the spirit of being an entrepreneur to roles within a large corporation. This is this executive's MTP (massive transformative purpose), one of the aspects that defines an exponential organization (or in this case, division).

Entrepreneurs are less likely to admit defeat or fall into the place of "We can't because" simply because they are so personally invested in the success of their business. This is due to feeling a sense of ownership and purpose with what they do. Entrepreneurs will also be much more agile and able to change both strategy and operations when it is needed.

University of Virginia professor Saras Sarasvathy published research in 2008 based on looking at the specific ways that entrepreneurs solved business problems versus those who were in established roles.[1] She defined five principles:

1. Bird in Hand Principle – Start with the means available.
2. Affordable Loss Principle – Set affordable loss; don't focus on expected profits.

3. Lemonade Principle – Look to leverage surprises, even unwelcome ones.
4. Crazy-Quilt Principle – Form partnerships with willing stakeholders.
5. Pilot in the Plane Principle – Control the controllable.

The defining idea behind these is looking at what is possible and having the resilience to adapt. It's a theme that also defines many of the Exponential Age Mindset Attributes such as Joyful Tightrope (embracing uncertainty), Chaos Converter (seeing the opportunities in chaos), and Agile Juggler (balancing consistency with agility). It is also the theme that defines the entrepreneurial mindset of feeling you own your role – the ability to find opportunity in ambiguity, navigate complexity, and catalyze change from any seat in the organization.

The five lenses – resources, people, capability, technology, and transformation

These are five levers through which entrepreneurial thinking can drive practical, business-relevant change. These levers were distilled from the ways in which the leader and his executive team approached projects. The team realized that they often interrogated challenges via these five dimensions to figure out the best ways to approach them. Not all the levers were always relevant, but often considering the issue via all five would show which made the most sense to use. Sometimes this approach would force individuals to think differently about a project by considering it through a lens that they might not have done previously.

On the program, one of the managers in IT shared that in working with a new vendor, the usual approach would be to consider the choice via the perspectives of resource and technology. However, when the team also applied the other perspectives, this produced some interesting insights:

- Employee engagement – which solution would be most effective to scale adoption and use of?
- Talent – which solutions might be the most effective use of existing talent and provide the best talent development opportunities?
- Transformation – which solution would aid the goals the department had for transformation?

With both the concepts of the entrepreneurial mindset and the Five Levers, an additional goal was to create a shared language amongst the different teams in the division – many of which had vastly different remits and might not normally collaborate. The shared concepts would help with taking the first steps to much greater collaboration. This would be underlined in the training, which was undertaken in cross-functional groups.

We would create a program that provided a grounding for managers and supervisors, as well as a selection of individual contributors, to find ways to connect to these concepts and become comfortable applying them in their day-to-day roles. The managers and supervisors went through a five-session program with three in-person and two virtual sessions, whilst individual contributors went through a three-session program with two in-person.

We decided that we needed to do four things within this program:

1) Get participants familiar with the key concepts of entrepreneurial mindset and the Five Levers, primarily through showing how these could be applied in practice. We also needed to ensure there was agility in the definitions and examples so they would work and be relatable to as wide a group of people as possible.
2) Introduce participants to other tools that could help with their individual connection to the entrepreneurial mindset and Five Levers and how to apply these. Specifically, the Exponential Age Mindset Attributes and Can If.
3) Get participants to use these in a safe environment in the workshops and then apply them in their own ways in between workshops via the tasks we would set them.
4) Give participants tools to influence and coach others to help in promoting the ideas and to get others to recognize and try them.

Session 1: Foundations of the entrepreneurial mindset

The journey began with a grounding in the concepts of the entrepreneurial mindset and the Five Levers. We also started to introduce the Exponential Age Mindset Attributes as ways to connect individuals to changing their mindsets and behavior amid volatility and complexity. To connect the groups to this, we invited participants to explore their personal "superpowers" at work. This is a common way we get participants to connect with the mindsets via sharing non-technical skills, which help them in role as a bridge to introduce the Exponential Age Mindset Attributes and how they can function as additional "superpowers".

We then connected these to the Exponential Age Mindset Attributes and asked them to identify areas where they needed to stretch – such as being a

Zoom Master or Chaos Converter. We asked participants to describe how they would apply their chosen stretch attribute in their role and how this might align with using the Five Levers. Some ideas included utilizing Supreme Storyteller skills to help bring the entrepreneurial mindset to life more with their teams. Another was living in the realm of uncertainty more with Joyful Tightrope by using the Five Levers as a wildcard of problem solving in meetings. In one of the first sessions, we had a cuboid stress toy with the Five Levers printed on five of the six sides, and one manager proposed having his team throw that like a die and see what the lever on top unlocked (or didn't!) for them about the issue being discussed.

In this session, we also introduced Can If as a tool specifically designed to operationalize the entrepreneurial mindset and show ways within their roles that individuals could start to feel ownership. To try this out in the training, we created some hypotheticals based on strategic dilemmas for the company. We specifically tried to align individuals with areas they would be less familiar with to disrupt their thinking and to encourage work in cross-functional groups. Through the Can If framework, they practiced creative problem-solving by asking, "What *can* we do *if* we reframe the constraints?". Participants were invited to see their roles differently – not just as executors of tasks, but as *owners* of change.

The day closed with a reflective homework assignment – apply these ideas in real-world conversations with managers and bring back insights to build on in the next session. For some, focusing on the skills embodied by the entrepreneurial mindset was able to create a unique in-road or connection to their own opportunities and challenges within their role and highlight opportunities to connect to the entrepreneurial mindset and apply the levers.

Session 2: Influence, communication, and collaboration

Building on these foundations, the second session helped participants sharpen the interpersonal tools essential to entrepreneurial impact. The focus was on influencing versus persuasion – learning to go beyond logical arguments and instead tailor communication to how people actually think, feel, and decide.

The standout learning moment came through the "Know Your Audience" exercise, where participants mapped communication styles – Sensing, Intuition, Thinking, and Feeling – and practiced adapting their messaging accordingly. In a subsequent scenario exercise, they explored how to explain the concepts to skeptical or overwhelmed stakeholders, helping solidify their understanding of the concept and build confidence.

Survey data from this session was striking – 91 percent found the application of the tools in their roles useful or very useful, and 81 percent felt confident or very confident in applying what they learned about influence and communication. Participant feedback underscored the impact of learning how to adapt, influence, and listen with strategic intent.

For many participants, this linked back to their chosen Exponential Age Mindset Attribute of the communication-linked attributes of Supreme Storyteller, Champion Chameleon, Bias Jiu Jitsu and Superlative Synthesizer.

Session 3: Coaching and collaboration for innovation

The third session marked a shift from understanding frameworks to enabling others through a coaching style of leadership. Participants explored core coaching tools – Powerful Questions, Bottom Lining, and Changing Perspective – through role-play and triad (groups of three) coaching scenarios.

Initially, we had just thought about using coaching with the managers and supervisors, but the power of this session persuaded us it would be useful to apply more broadly to the individual contributors as well. What this session did was really prove the maxim that the best way to learn something is to teach it yourself. Whilst trying to coach a colleague through scenarios of lack of understanding or resistance to the concepts and toolsets, many in the program had their own lightbulb moment in their own understanding of and personal relationship to the concepts.

These scenarios mirrored real-life workplace mindsets – colleagues who felt disempowered, dismissive of new initiatives, or simply too overloaded to engage, and whose mindsets could be summed up as:

- "I can't be an entrepreneurial leader as I am not empowered to make decisions. How is this relevant to me and what I do?"
- "This is just another management fad; it will go away. There is no point in me spending time on applying the Five Levers or developing an entrepreneurial mindset as it will change in six months."
- "I already have too much to do. I cannot cope with adding something else onto what I do."

These were all based on real-life challenges we had heard during the training sessions, so they resonated with the participants. The participants practiced using coaching techniques to help shift these narratives – moving from resistance to possibility.

The session also revisited the Five Levers framework through a hands-on activity. In small groups, participants selected real workplace challenges and applied the Five Levers lens to generate actionable Can If statements. The goal – make transformation tangible, not theoretical.

One participant noted, "We can improve response times if we train two people on the reporting dashboard instead of waiting for IT". This kind of thinking – practical, empowered, and proactive – epitomized the entrepreneurial mindset the program aimed to instill.

We finished this session by asking both sets of participants in the manager/supervisor and individual contributor streams to "bottom line" what they took away from the entrepreneurial mindset for them personally. By phrasing this in their own words they were able to cement their individual connection to the ideas and make them easy to reconnect with throughout their role.

Bringing it all together

As the program moved toward its culminating sessions for managers and supervisors, and at the end of the program for individual contributors, participants were tasked with drafting impact statements – personal reflections that articulate what they've learned, how they've applied it, and the ripple effect it's had on their teams and culture.

Different aspects of the program resonated with different participants – from entrepreneurial mindset as an overarching mindset, to the Five Levers as a new way to interrogate projects, to Can If as a way of thinking creatively, to communication and influencing to affect change, to coaching to better collaborate and shift mindsets.

The ultimate goal of this journey to an entrepreneurial mindset was not just individual development, but organizational transformation from within. Through influence, coaching, and creative thinking, participants were now equipped to become catalysts for change – right from where they stand.

Impact on participants

Participants' reflections highlighted a range of personal and professional shifts. Many reported a deeper appreciation for the importance of soft skills – particularly the ability to inspire, connect, and motivate others. They emphasized that true effectiveness as a catalyst within the organization came not only from technical expertise but also from the capacity to leverage individual strengths to foster collaboration, communication, and innovation.

Several participants described how applying the leadership attributes introduced in the program helped them reframe their roles. For example, those who embraced the idea of becoming a "storyteller" noted how crafting compelling narratives allowed them to move colleagues both emotionally and intellectually, making it more likely that new ideas would be embraced across the organization.

A recurring theme was the shift from a reactive stance to a proactive one. Participants explained that they had learned to approach new projects or business requests by asking questions first, exploring needs more deeply, and applying structured lenses to uncover efficient solutions. This approach encouraged them to move beyond their comfort zones, speak up more readily, and think creatively about challenges.

Others focused on how the frameworks introduced during the program fostered ownership and accountability. By interrogating the underlying reasons behind initiatives – asking "Why are we doing this?" – they found greater buy-in from stakeholders. This emphasis on broad engagement aligned with existing organizational leadership competencies such as driving engagement, customer focus, and action orientation, giving participants a clear way to connect the program's tools to performance expectations.

Finally, participants valued the opportunity to practice creative problem-solving through the Can If approach. Many described this as a pivotal shift in mindset, helping them move from "We can't because" to "We can if...". By reframing constraints, they found ways to propose scalable solutions rather than settling for temporary workarounds. This transition from reactive fixes to more strategic, long-term solutions was seen as one of the most practical and impactful outcomes of the program.

Conclusion

These leadership programs provided a powerful platform for cultural change within the organization. By developing both future-ready legal leaders and entrepreneurial, opportunity-focused contributors across the business, the company was better equipped to navigate complexity, influence strategically, and drive transformation from within.

The journey is ongoing, but the shift in mindset – from reactive problem-solving to proactive opportunity creation – is already reshaping how leaders and teams collaborate to meet the challenges of the future and will be fundamental as we get further into the Exponential Age.

Reference

1 Saras D, Sarasvathy, *Effectuation: Elements of Entrepreneurial Expertise* (Edward Elgar Publishing, 2008)

Chapter 18:
Leading humanly in the Exponential Age

The Exponential Age is not simply a technological revolution – it is a human one. Beneath the noise of digital transformation, artificial intelligence, and accelerating change lies a quieter, more profound challenge – how do we remain human, creative, and connected when the pace of progress threatens to overwhelm our capacity to adapt?

Throughout this book, we have explored the frameworks, mindsets, and leadership attributes that allow professionals – especially those in the legal and business worlds – to meet that challenge. What we have found is that thriving in this era is not about mastering more information or tools. It is about learning to think, decide, and lead differently. It is about cultivating the human skills that technology cannot replicate – curiosity, creativity, empathy, and courage.

From expertise to influence

For generations, professional success, particularly in law, has been built on expertise – what we know, how accurately we apply it, and how effectively we mitigate risk. In the Exponential Age, however, knowledge is no longer the currency it once was. Machines can access, sort, and synthesize data far faster than any human. What differentiates us now is not *what* we know, but *how* we use what we know.

The leaders who will thrive are those who can connect insights across disciplines, communicate with clarity and empathy, and influence others through trust and storytelling. They will be those who can stand at the intersection of the technical and the human and act as translators between the two. This is what we mean by being a "Zoom Master" – knowing when to move between detail and the big picture, between control and creativity, between certainty and exploration.

Discomfort as the doorway to growth

The Exponential Age requires us to befriend discomfort. As Dominique Ashby's[1] neuroscience insights remind us, the brain's instinct is to resist uncertainty. Yet every breakthrough in this book – from Joyful Tightrope to Chaos Converter – depends on leaning into that very uncertainty with curiosity and even joy.

Lawyers and leaders who succeed in this new landscape are those who see ambiguity not as a void, but as a space of possibility. They experiment, they iterate, and they allow for imperfection. They recognize that learning is no longer a phase that ends with qualification or promotion – it is a constant state of being. The most powerful realization of all is that the discomfort of not knowing can be the birthplace of innovation.

Reframing risk and redefining value

One of the most significant mindset shifts of this era is the redefinition of risk. In a profession long trained to avoid it, the Exponential Age asks us instead to *understand* it – and to see within it the seeds of opportunity.

The Six Dimensions of Business Risk and the Six Dimensions of Business Opportunity frameworks were designed to help legal professionals and business leaders make that shift. When risk is seen as multidimensional and interconnected – strategic, reputational, operational, financial, ethical, and human – it ceases to be merely something to minimize. It becomes a map for innovation.

This reframing transforms the role of the lawyer from gatekeeper to guide, from advisor to strategic co-creator. In this new paradigm, value is not defined by how well we prevent problems, but by how courageously we help others move forward despite them.

The human advantage

Artificial intelligence is already redefining the boundaries of what work can be automated. But what cannot be replaced is the human capacity to connect meaning to action. The attributes that will distinguish the most effective leaders – Supreme Storyteller, Champion Chameleon, Superlative Synthesizer – are all grounded in empathy, communication, and emotional intelligence.

Neuroscience supports this – joy and creativity are not luxuries in uncertain times, but survival mechanisms. Joy creates psychological safety, enabling the brain to think expansively. Creativity sustains our sense of agency when the external world feels uncontrollable. Together, they form the emotional infrastructure of resilience.

When AI automates the routine, our humanness – our insight, intuition, and imagination – becomes our ultimate differentiator.

From tools to transformation

The toolset frameworks explored in this book – Can If, the Four Zones of Curiosity, the Six Dimensions of Risk and Opportunity – are not meant to be checklists or corporate jargon. They are invitations. Each one offers a different way of asking better questions, thinking more broadly, and connecting more deeply.

Used together, they form a living system:

- Curiosity opens perspective.
- Perspective enables creativity.
- Creativity turns risk into opportunity.
- Opportunity inspires influence.
- Influence builds impact.

This cycle of growth is the foundation of Exponential Age leadership. It is not static, but dynamic; not prescriptive, but adaptive. It allows each leader, team, and organization to evolve at the speed of change without losing their humanity in the process.

A call to lead differently

To lead in the Exponential Age is to stand at the edge of the known and help others find their footing there. It is to balance structure with spontaneity, expertise with empathy, progress with purpose. It is to be, in essence, a *sherpa of transformation* – someone who helps others ascend while carrying the tools to make the climb possible.

The invitation for every reader is to choose their own path of mastery:

- To be the Zoom Master who can shift seamlessly between vision and detail.
- To walk the Joyful Tightrope with courage amid uncertainty.
- To become the Chaos Converter who finds opportunity in upheaval.
- To embody the Supreme Storyteller who turns data into meaning.
- And to live as a Duality Master, embracing contradiction as creative energy.

The future is human

As we have seen in every coaching session and leadership program we've led, transformation begins not with systems or software, but with people – individuals who dare to think differently, to collaborate courageously, and to find joy in the uncertain.

The Exponential Age will continue to accelerate, and the world will grow ever more complex. But in that complexity lies immense possibility. If we stay curious, connected, and creative, we will not just survive this age – we will thrive in it.

The final task for all of us is simple, though not easy – to remember that in an era defined by machines that can think, the greatest revolution will still be the messy, unpredictable beauty of human creativity.

Reference

1 For information on Dominique Ashby and her work see www.neuro@work.com

About Globe Law and Business

Globe Law and Business was established in 2005. From the very beginning, we set out to create legal books that are sufficiently high level to be of real use to the experienced professional, yet still accessible and easy to navigate. Most of our authors are drawn from Magic Circle and other top commercial firms, both in the United Kingdom and internationally. Our titles are carefully produced, with the utmost attention paid to editorial, design and production processes. We hope this results in high-quality publications that are easy to read and a pleasure to own.

In 2021, we were very pleased to announce the start of a new chapter for Globe Law and Business following the acquisition of law books under the imprint Ark Publishing. Our law firm management list is now significantly expanded with many well-known and loved Ark Publishing titles.

We are also pleased to announce the launch of our online content platform, Globe Law Online, which allows for easy access across firms. Details of all titles included can be found at www.globelawonline.com. Email glo@globelawandbusiness.com for further details and to arrange a free trial for you or your firm.

We'd very much like to hear from you with your thoughts and ideas for improving what we offer. Please do feel free to email me on sian@globelawandbusiness.com. Happy reading and thank you for your time.

Sian O'Neill
Managing director
Globe Law and Business
www.globelawandbusiness.com

www.ingramcontent.com/pod-product-compliance
Ingram Content Group UK Ltd.
Pitfield, Milton Keynes, MK11 3LW, UK
UKHW052056260226
468444UK00013B/42

9 781837 230976